Civil Liberties
and
American Democracy

Civil Liberties
and
American Democracy

John Brigham

*University of Massachusetts,
Amherst*

A division of Congressional Quarterly Inc.
1414 22nd Street, N.W., Washington, D.C. 20037

Library of Congress Cataloging in Publication Data

Brigham, John, 1945-
    Civil liberties and American democracy.

    Bibliography: p.
    Includes index.
    1. Civil rights—United States. 2. United States—Constitutional law. I. Title.
KF4749.B73   1984   342.73′085   84-1869
ISBN 0-87187-303-6   347.30285

To Mom and Dad

Table of Contents

Preface

This book is organized around ideas, not outcomes or decisions. It tries to get beneath the surface events to the meanings, standards, and conceptual parameters that comprise the tradition of civil liberties. Such an approach is not without precedent in constitutional scholarship. But this presentation systematically distinguishes between the politics of rights and the ideological arena in which they take place. The politics of constitutional rights are a function of the events, the participants, and the pressures that come together at a particular time. The rights themselves can be understood only by transcending the politics and gaining insight into the ideological framework within which the politics take place.

The result is a framework based on a conceptual rather than the more traditional doctrinal or historical perspective. The frame is tied to doctrine through judicial opinions, where the lines of reason are employed to substantiate positions. Whether they are appealing to narrowly constituted professional groups, or to a wider audience, opinions manipulate doctrinal material according to recognizable patterns. These patterns are the key to understanding constitutional rights. For the most part, the patterns will be familiar. They include standards such as "clear and present danger," ideas such as fundamental fairness, and conceptual parameters such as suspect classifications. On the occasions where the interpretation may be unfamiliar, there are explanations and examples.

Chapter 1, on "Rights," develops the implications of the phenomena on which the particular constitutional protections are built. The substantive investigation begins in Chapter 2, with the first right in the tradition, "Freedom of Expression." The criminal protections are combined with important civil guarantees in Chapter 3, which is on "Due Process." Perhaps the least well defined of the constitutional rights are those associated with "Liberty" in the Fourteenth Amendment. These receive separate treatment in Chapter 4 because they cover such a wide range of concerns. A chapter on "Property" is offered in this study even though conventional wisdom has been that property protections are not part of constitutional rights. Chapter 5 suggests that this view is mistaken. "Equality," discussed in Chapter 6, has become the most contested and perhaps the most important constitutional guarantee, and it provides a critical link between bourgeois rights and democratic prospects. This relationship between rights and democracy is explored further in Chapter 7, the final chapter.

John Brigham

Acknowledgments

In this book the approach to the Constitution has been drawn from a number of sources, and many people have contributed to its present expression. This project has gone on for some time, and even before it was formally undertaken I came under the influence of some very special men and women. This list is partial; limited out of deference to the reader.

Vera Smith assisted over the years in preparation of the many versions of the text. At various points in writing this book, I enjoyed the use of the Hampshire County Law Library in Northampton, directed by Barbara Fell-Johnson. Research assistance at different stages was provided by Nina Tousignant, Kathleen Engel, Patricia Rucidlo, Barbara Baker, Meredith Michaels, Pam MacKay, and Diane Burns. The project received support from the University of Massachusetts, Amherst, and the Women and Social Change Project at Smith College.

Colleagues in the Legal Studies Department at the University of Massachusetts began a tradition of critical inquiry about law on our campus and have been examples to me in my work. My extended family is a law and society group that includes Sheldon Goldman, Susan Silbey, Austin Sarat, Sally Merry, Barbara Yngvesson, Adelaide Villmoare, and Ron Pipkin.

I thank Joanne Daniels, director of CQ Press, who told me to stop everything and write this book. It was a tall order, but in the end I came very close to doing nothing else. I am also grateful to Sandy Lifland for her editorial assistance and to Janet Hoffman, the project manager.

Other contributors have been the teachers and colleagues from whom I have drawn heavily: Ken Dolbeare, Stuart Scheingold, Martin Shapiro, and John Gunnell. One teacher has been special, C. Herman Pritchett. His work is a challenging example and his support generous. A very special colleague is also my wife, Christine Harrington. I am fortunate in a marriage so complete.

Finally, where the activities of daily living touch accomplishment, my son Peter comes in. He has a sense of fairness that makes him a pleasure to live with. At one time, we were both writing about the Constitution. I liked that, probably more than he did.

John Brigham

Rights | 1

Throughout American history, the meaning of the Constitution has emerged from disputes over rights. When William Marbury appealed to the Chief Justice of the United States in 1803 for a job that he had been promised, he thought the promise gave him a right. When Linda Brown's parents objected to the segregated schools in Topeka, Kansas, in the early 1950s, they did so on the basis of a constitutional right. Not too long ago, a pusher named "Bandit" was convicted on the basis of evidence found in the trunk of his car. He thought he had a right to a new trial. The Chief Justice, in the first case, acknowledged that Marbury had a right to the job he was promised, although he never actually got the job. When Linda Brown's claim was upheld, there was pressure to change the schools. The pressure is still on, and it is fueled by the right Linda Brown won. The courts decided that Bandit had gotten all of his rights, so he stayed in jail. Each of these struggles relied on existing ideas about constitutional rights, and each added some ideas of their own.

This chapter offers a look at legal rights as a perspective for understanding constitutional rights. This perspective should facilitate access to these important resources. The chapter has four parts. The first introduces the concept of rights, indicating their conceptual significance and ultimately suggesting that it is on this basis that they should be understood as a political resource. The next section sketches the history of rights in America, with attention to constitutional law and the Bill of Rights. This leads into a discussion of the context of rights, that is, the social and political institutions through which rights emerge and in which they can be observed. Finally, we turn to the ideology of rights and consider the superiority of the ideological view and interpretation that has been used as a framework throughout the book. The ideological view demonstrates how important language and ideas are to interpreting the Constitution and offers greater insight than more formal or political approaches to rights.

The Concept: Rights Defined _____

In order to understand the common denominator of this book, one has to comprehend what rights are. The fuller that comprehension is, the greater will be the mastery of the individual concepts and traditions that make up civil liberties. We begin here with attention to the evolution of the idea itself, the notion that there are rights. This is followed by a more philosophical inquiry into the nature of these social phenomena—the sorts of things we take rights to be. Then we look at the characteristic forms of rights. This book only discusses some of the forms, but we indicate what the others are to show what the whole field looks like. Finally, we indicate that it is valuable to be able to understand what rights are because they are political resources; that is, they can be used and they carry some weight.

Evolution of the Concept

It has become quite common to speak of individual rights and even to distinguish them from the rights of a community (Abraham, 1982). But this is a modern practice. It appears that the concept of a right was nonexistent in Aristotle's day (Pennock, 1981). At that time, there was a great deal of attention to ideas of justice and right conduct, what we now call "natural" law. This was the way earlier people treated "the legal precepts that governed kings, counsellors, and courts" (Pennock, 1981:13). The idea of a "right" emerged from this foundation. The antecedents of constitutional law include the idea that law is discovered. They appeal to custom as a source of judgment and to the juxtaposition of positive or man-made laws against the law of nature (Corwin, 1928:59). The Roman achievement was administration through set rules and regulations, so that the governance of strangers was possible (Wolin, 1960:27). In the Roman Empire, political problems that had been obscured by the homogeneity of the Greek polis were handled through universals developed from a range of cultural traditions; these universals amounted to a sort of "common law" for the Roman Empire, which helped to promote a common citizenship (Barker, 1930:23). The codification of this tradition ultimately became a source of "Higher Law" in the Middle Ages, when it was appealed to against the "sinfulness" of mankind and when it served as a limitation on rulers. Unlike the Greek concept of justice, which conferred its chief benefits by "entering into the more deliberate acts of human authority," Higher Law in the Middle Ages operated by checking and limiting authority "from without" (Corwin, 1928:38). The texts of the Roman law, the scriptures, and the ecclesiastical tradition placed law above politics. What the medievalists lacked in the secular realm, however, was an institutional base.

Originally represented simply by custom, the legal notion of right action, or a reasonable decision, came to be characterized as the "right reason" of those men learned in the law. The Inns of the Court in medieval England had provided an opportunity for men of position to acquire a profession, and to develop a socially desirable form of expertness independent of popular custom. Although the ways of thinking about things developed at this time claimed a universal validity, they also depended on a separation, a professional mystery described as the "science of bench and bar" (Corwin, 1928:37). It has been as a mystery that law found its institutional base in judicial authority.

According to Edward Corwin, the legacy of John Locke for America was the creation of rights. The legacy amounted to a transformation of the professional mysteries of lawyers and judges, in particular the legal form, into the basis for government, as well as into a unit of political exchange that is comparable to money in the economic sphere. It is through this conception that the right reason of lawyers became the basis for relating the individual to the state. Emerging from past conflict or the threat of conflict, a right provides the agent who holds it with a warrant for taking or refusing to take an action. Thus, liberalism, in the "classic Lockeian sense" (Hartz, 1955), depends on legal forms.

Through rights, law became associated with individualism and distinguished from communitarian or collective interests based on fixed relationships, like an accident of birth. With rights, the language of social relations was grounded in a formal autonomy of individuals and an official respect for members of the community in their citizenship. People could speak of what they took to be "right" as guaranteed by the government. That guarantee began to determine what was right. The legal culture in America places the official right of the government apart from the customary right of religion or expertise. Exactly how far apart and what the relationship is between the culture and legal right is interesting but difficult to establish (and it is not the subject of this investigation).

The Practice of Rights

Constitutional rights are most completely and usefully understood as practices (Flathman, 1976)—those ways of understanding by which we get around in the legal world. Rights, as practices, are not *just* ideas. They are relevant to politics and social life because people believe them, use them, and act on them. But rights depend on knowledge, and although they may not be widely known, they must be knowable.

Rights exist along with other social practices, such as politics in general and the economic relations of a people. Consequently, fulfillment of biological needs are required at some level for the enjoyment of rights to be possible. In liberal societies, rights exist in conjunction with legal, administrative, and electoral processes. Rights also must have substance; the practice of rights is an abstraction from specific rights to have or do something. For instance, we have property rights in things like land, houses, or promised benefits.

Rights also reveal the world. When we say "I own that house" or "I have a right to a hearing," we are saying something about how we view the world. Often a claim about a part of the world—the legal part—is not so much different from describing the color of a house or the testimony in a hearing we might have attended. Rights are more than matters of opinion. As such, the interpretation of rights is based on social research.

Rights, and claims for rights, do not blend well with generosity, gratitude, loyalty, and friendship. Rights are possessive assertions, and they appeal to the state for protection. They function very differently from voluntary attributes such as generosity or friendship. Like any aspect of our culture, of course, rights cannot be totally isolated from these other concepts, but the relationship is not harmonious. Rights are contentious. Rights claims are even more incongruous with relationships like sisterhood or feelings like love. Relationships based on a bond like sisterhood affect us more deeply than rights, and of course they do not need to be enforced by government.

Historically and epistemologically, the social world precedes the individual, and society is the source for the meaning and significance of rights. In America, however, rights appear to come first because of a picture of the "autonomous individual" associated with liberalism. The picture has shaped legal practice in the United States. But despite the emphasis on the individual and individual rights, rights are social phenomena; they involve interactions among people and cannot have any meaning simply in terms of individuals. Society remains the basis for rights. Rights work to the extent that individuals are expected to satisfy their interests and desires within stipulated limits guaranteed by the state. The state is presumed to be autonomous—a neutral referee and servant of the community. Founded on this basis, American government is built on practices that dissolved natural law into the natural rights of "life, liberty, and estate."

Forms of Rights

An influential analysis of rights was developed by Wesley Hohfeld, an American law professor writing in the early part of the twentieth century (1919). He looked at the mass of professional activity involving rights and tried to make sense of it. The result was a catalogue of rights that has become something of a standard. It is not absolutely clear what he intended, but there are indications that Hohfeld's effort was prompted by his desire for better use of legal forms. His description became a standard for proper use, a sort of grammar or guide for how to do things right. Like all grammars, however, the Hohfeldian scheme drew from actual practices. This formulation, somewhat modified and more concerned with practices, serves as an introduction to the subject of constitutional rights. It sets out four main kinds or forms of rights: powers, claims, immunities, and liberties.

Powers are available to people by virtue of specific authority or provisions of law. In the Hohfeldian formulation, specific grants of consent are not required, although in more general terms powers in a constitutional democracy depend on popular consent or at least acquiescence. People with power derived from the Constitution are usually in positions defined by law. The government has the power to prosecute people it believes have committed crimes, and police searches stem from a similar power. Many of the guarantees that the Constitution holds out to individuals stand against these powers. Although many constitutional guarantees are a barrier to individual acts of government, constitutional rights, such as due process of law and equal protection of the law, are generally guaranteed by the power of the government.

What have been called "rights in the strict sense," or *claims,* are referred to in law as the expectations between individuals and of individuals contracting with the government. In this sense, claims exist where some person or institution has a definite duty to the holder of the right. In the case of government officials, for instance, considerations of public trust and responsibility exist when such persons claim power over others or the right to legislate in certain areas. Similarly, welfare recipients or the holders of other entitlements provided for by statutes—statutory entitlements—have claims to certain benefits if they meet the eligibility criteria. Like all of these kinds of rights, claims are popularly referred to as "rights."

The rights explored in this volume are all associated with the Constitution. Powers provide a background for understanding constitutional rights. Claims have recently become important in the constitutional setting. The rights conventionally associated with civil liberties, however, are called *immunities* and *liberties.* An immunity is an exception to a power. Most of the constitutional protections that delineate the criminal process (discussed in Chapter 3) are immunities. The Fourth Amendment protections against unreasonable searches and seizures are good examples of rights as immunities. The government's power to police and to protect is conditioned or limited by public immunity from unreasonable searches and seizures. As instances where a general liability does not hold, immunities are a special, specifically delineated form of liberty. Liberties themselves are rights held against authorities. They limit interference with a variety of activities deemed worthy of special protection. The government's duty not to interfere with the exercise of free speech comes, not from the freedom to speak, but from the right or liberty not to be interfered with in the conduct of that activity.

Whatever their specific form, rights exist as practices characteristic of the American political experience. Like elections, in which the struggles are over votes, contests over rights such as equal protection of the laws or freedom of expression are part of American politics. Knowledge of rights is a key to the American experience that can be brought to bear in politically significant ways. Because they are social practices, rights in general, particularly the claims, immunities, and liberties that are the focus of this book, are the socially recognizable forms in which individuals can stand against the government.

Rights as a Political Resource

Because rights contain beliefs about how things should be done, they are a political resource (Scheingold, 1974). This idea can be traced to a time when critics of the Supreme Court pointed to the political nature of the Court during the struggles over New Deal legislation. At that time, law was not just out there, it took a political stand. Later, this insight, termed "legal realism" in the law schools and "judicial behavioralism" in social science departments, was expanded to incorporate a political view of the courts and their processes (Shapiro, 1964). During this period, people lost track of the distinctively legal nature of the process. This conceptualization of the legal order as just a political arena, however, would have to be changed in order to place ideas about rights at its core instead. When this was done, the belief in rights by the practitioners of law and the institutions charged with their preservation would make their rights potential resources (Scheingold, 1974). By appealing to rights or calling the attention of those responsible for them to possible transgressions, rights would empower those who could invoke them.

Stuart Scheingold has provided a reconsideration of what he calls "the myth of rights" (Scheingold, 1974:83). He has described rights as a belief system to which one could appeal for redress. The significance of rights lay less in the political power behind them, and much more in their congruence with beliefs about social justice or right conduct. There is still a connection between rights as a resource and the power to go to court, but in The Politics of Rights (1974), Scheingold identified a source of power that could be extended beyond the courtroom by an appeal to rights. The struggles over civil liberties, as described in the chapters that follow, exemplify both the litigious and the more broadly political character of rights as resources.

The shift toward greater appreciation of law as a resource was aided in the civil liberties area by the mobilization of masses of people around legal rights that they hoped to expand and incorporate into law. The insight here too was first as a politics in the legal sphere, in which the contests were over rights and the outcomes were new laws (Casper, 1972). As the struggles were treated with greater sensitivity, however, the interconnection between political struggle and conceptual development could not be ignored. Some of the most impressive developments were in the work of journalists whose stories of litigation strategies were held together by the emergence of new concepts of rights. Thus, in *Simple Justice* (Kluger, 1976), the legal fight to eliminate segregation in the South was presented as a gradual reconstruction of the right to equality in the Constitution. This fight continued until the Supreme Court was willing to say that segregated educational facilities were not compatible with the concept of equality.

The area of civil liberties has thus been a sphere in which politics and ideas are intertwined. The first group claim to constitutional liberty was made by the abolitionists in the early part of the nineteenth century (Roche, 1961b:67-68). It was their contribution, most notably the Fourteenth Amendment, which became the foundation for the later expansion of constitutional rights and liberties. The next creative development was focused on the protections of property. The craftsmanship of various legal scholars and Supreme Court justices in the late nineteenth century exemplified this development (Beth, 1971). With the shift of judicial attention to political rights after President Roosevelt had remade the Supreme Court by appointing three new justices, the politics of rights in the civil liberties arena was underway. It was facilitated by groups such as the American Civil Liberties Union (ACLU) and the National Association for the Advancement of Colored People's (NAACP) Legal Defense Fund. The result was transformation of the Bill of Rights from a document with limited application to the national government to one for all Americans.

Litigation is thus a subset of the political culture which relates to the means for resolving or subverting conflicts. While litigation, like political action generally, is theoretically open to all, participation in litigation is restricted by knowledge and resources. Lawyers and judges control who gets to use the courts to resolve a dispute, and they thus monopolize access to rights. Most people are excluded from the exercise of meaningful power in this arena. This is true even at the constitutional level. Knowledge of the Constitution, which should be widespread, has become a tightly controlled political resource. The people from whom the Constitution gets its authority, nonprofessional people, must employ others to advise them on the use of their rights. Use of the resource has come to require familiarity with legal practices and judicial opinions on the Constitution. Because the knowledge of rights is not widespread, becoming familiar with this resource is itself a political activity that enables individuals to attain their own goals. The purpose of the present work is to increase the general capacity for constitutional interpretation by introducing people without legal training to the practice of fundamental rights.

The History of Rights: The Constitutional Basis

To know the history of constitutional rights and the process by which it unfolds is to be in a position to take control of it. These rights are products of struggle. They protect the citizen from state power by defining the limits of that power and by setting minimum standards of treatment for all. The Constitution itself set up some relationships. The "founding" of the American Republic established constitutional authority and gives constitutional rights meaning today. Judicial review was a subsequent development, and the model for civil liberties—the Bill of Rights—was added later. Struggle over those rights at the federal level fleshed out their basic meaning. With some new developments, the doctrines were extended to the states in the twentieth century. This heritage of substantive growth and dissemination is the basis for the ideology of civil liberties.

Constitutional Law

Two hundred years ago, a revolt in western Massachusetts led by Daniel Shays, a farmer who had participated in the American Revolution, took on monumental proportions. The authorities in Massachusetts had a great deal of difficulty putting down this uprising in which 2,000 men seized an armory and closed down the courts for a time. This revolt was one of the circumstances that led to the constitutional convention in Philadelphia, which would draft the proposal for national union. This convention produced the Constitution as the basis for a new political order, with principles and arrangements drafted at least in part as a response to Shays' Rebellion.

The Founding. The men who wrote the American Constitution made a major contribution to the "science" of politics. They were well versed in the elements of politics from their study of the past and their arguments over the challenges that faced them in 1787. Their contribution was a careful construction of the institutions of government so that they would endure and provide some degree of stability for the new nation. The Constitution was formulated to provide a written source that would authorize the government to constrain action. The idea of providing a written basis for the political order stemmed from colonial experience with "trading company charters, proprietary grants or royal charters" (Hurst, 1960:200-201), which relied on written contracts. The idea of a document as the basis for the new government was also associated with the emerging capitalist economy, since capitalism required rational structures of law and administration (Weber, 1968).

Establishing political order in eighteenth century America required transforming an association into a nation. For Thomas Paine, the contribution of the American Constitution was "to liberty, what a grammar is to language." Paine wanted people to see the Constitution, not as an act of a government, but rather as the action of a people constituting a government. Americans spoke of a new conception of a "conscious formulation by a people of its fundamental law," but they included in the conception the idea that constitutions had "to be deduced from a nation's actual institutions and their development" (McIlwain, 1940:3). Fundamental law would come to be treated as having both natural and deliberate qualities. This is the dual capacity that eventually accorded the justices of the Supreme Court, as legal experts, a special place in setting the boundaries of politics.

The importance of the Constitution made it both a limitation and a source of political power. The shift of authority from the Senate—where it had resided from Rome to the modern West—to the judiciary, was a function of associating "the founding" with a document. The document as a symbol of stability and common agreement established the special role of the judiciary. Judical supremacy has depended on the Constitution being seen as a Higher Law, with the Supreme Court claiming responsibility for interpreting its meaning. The key to the practice of interpretation, establishing the document's transcendent qualities, was this claim of special competence. Thus, it was the fact that the fundamental principles of government were set out in a legal document that gave form to the politics of fundamental rights in America.

For Alexander Hamilton, judges could handle power beyond popular control because their very independence would make them different. He described "the complete independence of the courts" as "essential to a limited Constitution," which by its nature contains exceptions to legislative authority. In *Federalist #78*, Hamilton argued that, "Limitations of this kind can be preserved in practice no other way than through the medium of courts of justice. . . ." In subsequent papers, Hamilton reviewed the tasks set down for the Court and revealed his conception of the judiciary. In *Federalist #81*, he said that the Constitution was the source of judicial power. The Courts, he argued, were not to be regarded as superior because they could declare the acts of another branch of government void. Since the Constitution was the fundamental law, acts contrary to it were not valid. The courts did not simply substitute their view for that of the legislatures, according to Hamilton, rather they relied on their learning to understand things beyond the capacity of people operating in the political realm. Hamilton saw a voluminous code of laws as binding the judges. He wrote, "There can be but few men in the society who will have sufficient skill in the laws to qualify them for the station of judge."

Judicial Review. Judicial power in American democracy depended on an authoritative referent to which the claims of expertise could be attached. The Magna Carta, both in the English experience and as elaborated by Coke in the Virginia Charter of 1606, provided a model. This became the basis for royal charters in America. The significance of the charter had grown in England as the classes it served widened and as it became identified with the common law. Although Lord Coke might have been stretching the historical record a bit when he declared in 1628 that "Magna Carta is such a fellow, that he will have no 'Sovereign,' " this view of the charter model became "a potent weapon. . . ." (Roche, 1961a:4). The document had been incorporated into the legal tradition and afforded an institutional setting for constitutional politics. Montesquieu's discussion in the *Spirit of the Laws* was reflected in American confidence that institutions would provide the basis for a stable government (Arendt, 1963:186-187).

William Blackstone portrayed expertness as essential to the activity of judging and he said that judges were to have acquired a mode of thinking that would make them repositories of the law (Blackstone, 1859:67). He also provided the substance of what they were to think in his *Commentaries on the Laws of England*. The work, which collected years of judicial decisions and offered the knowledge needed by a gentleman, acquired its own Higher Law status. Through identification with English custom, and as one of the few available sources of law when it was published in America in 1771, the *Commentaries* contributed to the supremacy of law over politics.

One of the paradoxes in the development of judicial power is that the Constitution has been transformed from a basis for popular government into a sacred text for a legal elite. The Court, even after the founding, was not the institution it is today. During their first three years on the bench, the justices had no cases, and they were decidedly outside of what little limelight there was in the new national government. In the initial plan for the nation's capital, for instance, the Supreme Court was relegated to a subordinate place. Neither on a hill nor surrounded by a mall, the Court had to share quarters with other institutions for the first 150 years of its life.

The original practice of sharing the power of interpretation among political leaders (Ellis, 1971:66) was a basis for the struggle between President Thomas Jefferson and Chief Justice John Marshall. Marshall's position was in the tradition of Blackstone and Hamilton. The Chief Justice took the first steps to link the Constitution to judicial review, which would amount to the power to nullify a statute or administrative action. The steps came in *Marbury* v. *Madison* (1803) in a power struggle between the newly elected Jeffersonian Republicans and the outgoing Federalists over appointment of William Marbury as a federal magistrate.

The reading of judicial prerogatives by Marshall in *Marbury* v. *Madison* as a foundation for judicial review was, at the time, a standoff in the political struggle for interpretive authority. John Marshall asserted his power as a judge to say what the Constitution meant and to determine when Congress had legislated beyond its power. He prevented his decision from being overturned or ignored by holding that Congress had no power to provide for an appeal to the Supreme Court in Marbury's case. Thus, the Court declined to order Madison to make the appointments. The weakness of the judicial claim at that time is suggested by the strategic retreat taken by the justices. It led to a political standoff between Marshall, the judge, and Jefferson, the president. In itself, however, the fact of a standoff was something of an accomplishment against the tradition of political supremacy as represented by Jefferson.

Marshall had given Hamilton's suggestions for an expanded judicial role practical significance. The basis of his position was the Blackstonian concept that "The government of the United States has been emphatically termed a government of laws, and not of men." Thus, law would serve as the means to link interpretive action to the Court. Since the president gained his power as an officer of the law, he would be answerable to the laws for his conduct. Marshall presented his separation of powers argument in terms of differing capacities, saying, "It is emphatically the province and duty of the judicial department to say what the law is. Those who apply the rule to particular cases, must of necessity expound and interpret that rule." Thus, the institutional standing of the Court was derived from its availability for settling disputes on the basis of a body of law not generally accessible.

Conventional analysis of *Marbury* v. *Madison* emphasized the ease of this transition from the fact of a written Constitution to the claim of expertise by pointing out that Marshall's argument proceeds "on the basis of a single textual reliance; namely the fact itself of a written Constitution" (Bickel, 1962:4). To achieve the institutional significance it now has, however, judicial review required intentional political action to transform the idea into political practice. Marshall's reasoning was not very strong, but his was a political rather than a conceptual innovation. Preventing the decision from being overturned immediately was the Chief Justice's coup. He placed the Court in the mainstream of American politics, so that it could develop along with the other branches of government. The move from legislative supremacy, however, was not complete with Marshall's assertion in *Marbury* v. *Madison* that the power existed.

Fifty-four years after Marshall's claim, there was a second assertion of judicial review over Congress. This was in the *Dred Scott* case (1857). Even then, Chief Justice Roger Brooke Taney's reading of the document with a proslavery emphasis turned out to be antithetical to the direction in which the country was moving, and it did little to enhance the status of the justices. The Civil War sought to establish that the Constitution did not mean what Taney said it meant, and further diminished the stature of the Court. Not until after the Civil War, did the Supreme Court begin to reassert its power. Its initial efforts were uncertain, but the tide of institutional power gathered strength. Thus, in contrast with the prior century, from 1865 to 1970, the Supreme Court held that 84 acts of Congress were unconstitutional, either in part or in their entirety (Pritchett, 1977:128). Here, the Court had the apparatus of an emerging professional bar for support.

The second half of the twentieth century saw continued shifts and competing claims in clashes such as that over impoundment and President Richard Nixon's litigation of "executive privilege." In *United States* v. *Nixon* (1974), the conflict over presidential prerogatives under the Constitution arose with reference to a severely weakened presidency. The capitulation of the president strengthened the image of the Court. The challenge the Court posed to Nixon sounded familiar, "... but if the courts are the ultimate interpreters of the Constitution and can restrain Congress to operate within constitutional bonds, they certainly should not be empowered any less to measure Presidential claims of constitutional powers" (Jaworski, 1974). It was Marshall's rhetoric employed in a new age.

Judicial review, the authority of the Supreme Court to determine the meaning of a written Constitution had thus been "placed" in the document (Bickel, 1962:1). Justice Learned Hand asserted that judicial review, although necessary, is an "interpolation" and not explicitly in the document (Wechsler, 1959). And William O. Douglas claimed that "once there is a written Constitution it is but a short step to the assertion of the power of judicial review..." (Paulson, 1959:65). But the idea of a Higher Law provides the interpretive scheme for the politics of rights. The Supreme Court exercises power over the other branches of government, which it has built out of the authority given it and the mythology surrounding the Constitution. While the Court's contribution is the basis for the exposition of constitutional rights in subsequent chapters, the Court's claims to special competence and considerable exclusivity in the arena of interpretation arise out of the historical context.

Rights and Liberties

A constitution is not just a description of how the government works. At least since the American contribution to this form of government, constitutions have stipulated the government's obligations to the citizen which enable the government to claim authority over the population. Thus, the government is dependent on its promises and obligations to the citizen, their rights and liberties. This reciprocal relationship between liberties and institutions can be traced to the ratification of the Constitution, and the decision to include the Bill of Rights as part of the fundamental law.

The Bill of Rights. Through a network of powers and rights, institutions were created in 1787 at the Constitutional Convention in order to "form a more perfect Union." Unlike state constitutions of the period, however, the Constitution drawn up in Philadelphia contained no *bill of rights*. The Federalist's argument was that they had created a new government of delegated power. They held that the government would not claim to exercise power beyond that explicitly granted in the document. Slavery was another reason those who wrote the Constitution had limited enthusiasm for a bill of rights. Such bills conventionally began with images of human equality and dignity, and the compromises that had taken place in Philadelphia denied that equality to black Americans.

Yet, following the fertile summer of 1787, the doctrines of civil liberties became a cause for those who were suspicious of the new Constitution. Thus, in their votes for ratification of the Constitution, the state conventions, beginning with Pennsylvania, made provisions for a bill of rights to be drawn up and added to the Constitution. Well before the power of the courts would turn the Constitution into a professional mystery, the Anti-Federalists gained some concessions that became the Bill of Rights. This collection of ten guarantees, many of which address problems stemming from the period of revolution, such as the right to bear arms, became the basis for fundamental rights in America.

The suggestions from Virginia became the major factor in shaping these additions to the original document. Thomas Jefferson, among others, demanded a bill of rights, and James Madison was the instrumental force on the scene to draft it. Their concerns were with freedom of religion and the press, protection against standing armies, restraint against monopolies, habeas corpus, and trial by jury. Madison was the key, both during the period of ratification and in the first Congress that drafted the Bill of Rights.

Limitations in the Constitution channel human action in order to build a particular kind of institutional structure. There are both implicit and explicit limits. The most important are part of the Bill of Rights and the Civil War amendments. Much of the relationship between the new government and the states was implied in the Constitution. It was by implication that Indians, slaves, women, and the foreign-born were prevented from full participation in the new policy. The explicit limits in the body of the Constitution appeared, in many cases, to be the protections that balanced the newly created power. Some of these limits carved out powers from the states, such as those having to do with foreign treaties, coining money, and obligations of contract. Others directly addressed congressional power, such as those involving export duties, direct taxes, titles of nobility and habeas corpus, bills of attainder (or legislative punishment without trial), and ex post facto laws (legislation that makes a crime out of something that already happened).

The fundamental rights that we refer to as civil liberties are the explicit limits on government power that were added to the Constitution by the Bill of Rights and subsequent amendments. They are largely restraints on Congress, but they amount to a sphere of individual action that is beyond the purview of the government. They are as specific as the right to bear arms and as general as the promise of equal protection of the laws. They vary in the amount of attention they receive, from the often-litigated promise of freedom of expression to the rarely considered protection against quartering of troops. Their conceptual coherence provides the structure for this book.

Civil liberties can be approached through conceptual categories. The first *freedoms* of expression and religion are characterized by tolerance, a value grounded in social diversity and serving as a safety valve for the expression of dissent. The twin functions of respect for the individual and an open forum for gaining access to the truth are associated with *due process*. This applies to the criminal as well as the civil processes, whenever people are in jeopardy. *Property* is the concept we associate with historical protection of settled expectations, not just in land or personal effects, but in promises that come from the state. *Liberty* in the constitutional context has been treated as a lesser right because it has no clear doctrinal foundation, yet it is part of the heritage of republican government that there are spheres where the state cannot intrude. *Equality* has a limited doctrinal foundation, but it has developed dramatically as the state has taken on increasing responsibility for the maintenance of public welfare.

Incorporation. Although originally meant for the national government, by midway through the twentieth century, federal constitutional rights had been effectively applied to the relationship between citizens and government at every level. By this time, the protection of the Bill of Rights had joined protection for equality and property, which had already been applied to the states through the Fourteenth Amendment. The process which is generally identified with this development is called *incorporation*. It is a recent and dramatic part of the transformation of constitutional rights. It is hard now to imagine that in this century the First Amendment guarantee of freedom of expression was not a right that applied to state governments. The states did have their own constitutions and generally their own bills of rights with various guarantees similar to the First Amendment freedoms and many of the others. Yet, the federal standard, which began to develop as recently as 1910, was not applied to the states for nearly two more decades. Other federal interpretations of the rights in the Constitution came much later.

Incorporation of the Bill of Rights is a measure of national power. It occurred as the locus of power changed from the states to the federal government. The process really began after the Civil War with the guarantees of equal protection and due process generally. The latter was often used to protect property. This and the later incorporation was an assertion of federal supremacy. Anticipated by Justice John Marshall Harlan at the turn of the century, further incorporation relied on the Civil War amendments—particularly the Fourteenth—and the guarantee of a national union that these amendments held out. Nationalization of constitutional rights parallels the establishment of the legal foundations of corporate power. At issue was more than a concern for free expression after World War I or a desire to extend the due process protections in the criminal process. Incorporation meant the ascendancy of the federal judiciary. The process was a manifestation of the rise of judicial review, for after the initial legislation that followed the Civil War, incorporation was brought about by judicial interpretation.

The process of incorporation was uneven, and this unevenness suggests the relative significance of the various rights and liberties we take to be fundamental. Equality under the Fourteenth Amendment was the first right to be made applicable to the states. This was done in 1896, in *Plessy* v. *Ferguson*, where a black man had challenged the imposition

15

of segregation in the South. His claim was unsuccessful, but the Supreme Court did consider the meaning of equality in the Constitution as it applied to state legislation. The decision was followed in the next year by protection of property. Under various constitutional doctrines, property dominated constitutional interpretation until well past the turn of the century. Finally, it is the subsequent application of the Bill of Rights to the states that is conventionally associated with incorporation. The process began in earnest in 1925 with freedom of expression. This was followed by incorporation of freedom of the press, the general right to a fair trial, and the limited right to counsel in the 1930s.

It is worth mentioning here the decision by Justice Benjamin Cardozo, in *Palko* v. *Connecticut* (1937). This decision was a bench mark in the process of incorporation, and it set the terms by which the debate would be carried out. After this decision, there was little doubt about the general supremacy of federal constitutional rights. All that remained was determination of whether incorporation applied in specific contexts. The standard announced in *Palko* was that rights would be applicable to the states—that is, the states would be responsible for upholding constitutional standards, where the rights were the very essence of a "scheme of ordered liberty." The change has been so dramatic that the protection from double jeopardy, which was the right at issue in this case, and which was not incorporated under the standard announced in *Palko* at that time, is now hard to imagine as anything but essential to a "scheme of ordered liberty."

Gradual expansion of constitutional protections to the states continued under the *Palko* doctrine for 25 years, until in the 1960s it was transformed into a nearly wholesale application of the criminal procedure protections to cases tried in state courts, with the expectation that fundamental rights are for everyone (Sandoz, 1978). The process exemplifies the post-1937 shift in the Supreme Court's attention from constitutional protection of property to protection of political freedoms. The shift followed *Palko* and was given its most powerful interpretive reading in *United States* v. *Carolene Products Company* (1938). Here, the author of the opinion, Justice Harlan Fiske Stone inserted a footnote to explain his views about the propriety of turning away from judicial intervention in public regulation of business and toward judicial supervision of the more narrowly defined political and legal process. The footnote is the interpretive source for what has come to be known in constitutional discourse as "the double standard."

The Double Standard. The double standard is an institutional practice that distinguishes the economy from politics for the purpose of attention by the Supreme Court. By using two standards for review, the justices have given "certain fundamental freedoms" closer judicial scrutiny than others. The distinction has been described in a variety of ways by commentators. As Henry Abraham writes, ". . . what the post-1937 judiciary did was to assume as constitutional all legislation in the proprietarian sector . . . but to view with a suspicious eye legislative and executive experimentation with other basic human freedoms" (Abraham, 1982:13). The standard has operated as an aspect of constitutional adjudication, although with somewhat diminishing significance over the years. It is triggered when the Court reviews a statute passed by Congress or a state legislature in the area demarcated, roughly, as "the economy." According to the practice, the justices have merely asked of that statute that there be a reasonable basis for it.

One consequence of the double standard is that property has all but been read out of the field of civil liberties. The present treatment puts it back in because of recent developments and because the distinction, although employed by the justices, has always been problematic (McCloskey, 1962:54). Justice Potter Stewart called the dichotomy between personal liberties and property rights "a false one" (*Lynch* v. *Household Finance Corporation*, 1972). Thus, it is necessary to treat property as a civil liberty due to the fundamental interdependence between the rights to liberty, equality, and property.

The Context:
Social and Political Institutions

In order to understand legal rights, it is necessary to know what can be done with them and how they work. In the case of constitutional rights, this is accomplished by looking at the culture, the structures, and the primary institution associated with these rights—the Supreme Court. The rich commentary on constitutional rights delivered by the Supreme Court is an important source for understanding the Constitution. It provides a history of the issues that have been raised and how they have been treated. Since that commentary caps the mass of legal activity, this chapter traces its roots in legal culture—from social life to the law office—through its distinctive structures to its expression in opinions of the appellate courts. Special focus throughout this book will be on the legal community and those who fashion the ideas that are its tools. Subsequent chapters will indicate ways in which a convergence of the legal culture and the larger culture creates particular rights.

Legal Culture and Lawyers

Since America was founded by an agreement, a contractual arrangement, in the form of the Constitution, the legal culture has been important in American social and political life as a way of interpreting what the Constitution means. Although the Declaration of Independence symbolically heralds the national beginnings, the Constitution "constitutes" the nation itself. This quality is reflected in the ongoing acculturation of waves of new citizens as they learn the rules of the game as a test for citizenship.

The nature of the Constitution cannot be understood except in terms of the legal culture more generally; for now, two hundred years from the founding, the fundamental law has a continuing significance in that it serves as a basis for all subsequent laws that are enacted. These new laws are influenced by constitutional requirements. The current character of law and legal ordering generally go hand in hand with a professional understanding of fundamental law.

One measure of the legal culture in the United States is the number of lawyers in this country as compared to others. In the early 1980s, there were approximately 600,000 lawyers in the United States. The number increased from 22,000 in 1850 to 114,000 in 1900, more than keeping pace with general population growth (Bonsignore, 1979:192). The result is nearly 1 lawyer for every 390 people in the country. There is no other country in the world that relies as heavily as the United States on this sort of professional group, which claims to have a special capacity to understand the rules and traditions by which the country functions. Japan, for instance, has 1 lawyer for around 10,000 people. Western European countries fall somewhere in between Japan and the United States.

Alexis de Tocqueville is often reported to have said that lawyers are America's aristocracy. He meant that they held a place comparable to that of the ruling elites in Europe. Writing in the middle of the nineteenth century, he noted that there were few disputes that did not end up in court. This estimation was not very accurate at the time, and it is still technically wrong since few disputes actually go before a judge. But the implication has become quite appropriate in the present setting. The influence of law and lawyers has grown quite large. The influence is not as great as the legal profession seems to think and would sometimes want us to believe, but the legal profession does dominate politics. That is obvious. It is far less easy to see the reach of legal culture into the processes of social life generally.

In other countries, disputes and conflict simply do not mature in the same way. While comparisons emphasize the different ways of doing things, they only begin to suggest the need to understand more fully the nature of these characteristics. America has been uniquely oriented to the resolution of disputes by mechanisms relying on the authority of government. Sometimes these are formal, as in the case of the trial or appeal. More often they are informal and take place in conjunction with governmental authority. Institutions like courts and administrative agencies play an important role in supporting the professional authority of lawyers in their task of resolving disputes. The tradition has been to take disputes to lawyers and to see them in terms of the law. A challenge for understanding this process is gaining an understanding of the impact and significance of the structures and contexts of the law.

One approach is to view the ordinary processes as existing in the "shadow of the law." The idea is that law sets the frame within which struggles are carried out in the United States. This conception of shadow or frame, developed with reference to plea bargaining in the present volume (see Chapter 3), suggests that the process of informal negotiation is influenced at least to some extent by the formal requirements of the criminal justice system. This characteristic of the legal culture can also be extrapolated to include the myriad transactions of business, those of the civil law, and even the supposed informal processes of mediation and arbitration (Harrington, 1980). Recent work in the tradition of law and society has attempted to explore the extent to which the legal culture influences the rest of society. An insightful formulation focuses on the "transformation of a dispute" with attention to the way the dispute is defined by participants (Mather and Yngvesson, 1980-1981). Even when a dispute does not get into the professional legal sphere, the categories of fundamental rights and constitutional law, such as the category of equality (see Chapter 6), will influence political issues ranging as widely as racial injustice and feminist politics.

Whatever the precise level of interaction, however, it is clear that legal activity is significant to social and political processes. It is believed to be so significant that the expansion of legal services has been a central theme in the movement for social justice. This is not simply because more lawyers promise a greater share of the pie, but because lawyers and legal skills are understood to be an important part of the pie itself. In the area of the law under consideration here—constitutional rights and civil liberties—group activity, such as that by the NAACP Legal Defense Fund and the American Civil Liberties Union, has brought to the forefront the legal needs of those without the ability to pay.

Comparison of different societies in terms of the level of legal activity and discussion of the legal system's influence on other social and political processes suggests an evaluation of litigation's effect on societies' health. Unlike some professional activities, medicine for example, legal activity may be something we could do without (or at least do with less of). The comparison is not as one sided as it once seemed, however, since we have learned that more surgeons mean more surgery, not necessarily better health. While it is easy to criticize unnecessary surgery, the criticism of excess law is much harder since it is an element of the practice of law to generate more activity. Law must be evaluated in terms of the social life it supports, and legal or professional forms should be compared with more democratic or popular forms. The amount and quality of legal activity, its nature, and its effect must be assessed by democratic standards. It is not satisfactory to throw up one's hands. In some cases, the structures created are rather wholesome, while in others they are not. Information is necessary to be able to evaluate the system. That means, initially, information about the nature of law, its structures, and its processes. It also means gaining a deeper understanding of professional legal activity in order to make knowledge of the law more generally available, and thus more democratic.

Although the Constitution is the ultimate legal frame, its influence is generally felt through intervening processes, conventions, and structures. Because the legal culture in America has become a professional one, these intervening structures have acquired great significance for constitutional interpretation. Yet, it must also be acknowledged that from the beginning, from the environment out of which the Constitution sprang, legal culture in America has been a culture of apparatuses, a context for getting things done, an arena of authoritative action. From the culture generally and its orientation toward law, we turn to some specific characteristics.

Structures and Courts

There are any number of ways to describe the structures of the law. One could look through the eyes of the participants—plaintiffs whose problems make the work of the legal system—or through the eyes of practitioners—lawyers or judges. One could also look at the most obvious physical manifestations—the courthouses and the prisons—and get some sense of the legal system. In the section that follows, the choice has been to focus on the structural elements necessary to understand the operations of rights in America. We start with the most general logical relations, and then move to some institutional distinctions bearing on kinds of sanctions, where the dispute is brought, and the sort of law that is employed.

Dispute Processes. The peculiarities in the American system of courts and law can be traced to the job these institutions have in handling disputes and resolving conflict. Disputes are such a common characteristic of social life that they offer a perspective on courts and a chance to generalize about how and why the courts work as they do. When two persons come into a conflict, a common response is to call upon a third for assistance, thereby revealing "the logic of the triad" (Shapiro, 1981). This logic accounts for the challenge to any institution attempting to resolve two-party conflicts.

The challenge is that a new conflict may emerge between the losing party and the institution settling a dispute after a decision has been announced. The very decision it is called upon to make is thus a threat to the effectiveness of a court because it produces an "unstable" and potentially explosive situation involving the institution and the losing party.

Much of what courts do can be understood as attempts to prevent their claim to neutral third party status from breaking down. There are circumstances where, in order to avoid this institutional failure, the two parties make a prior agreement to respect the third party decision, regardless of who wins or loses. Limited democracies like the United States do not have to depend on these prior agreements or specific acts of consent. Courts in such systems rely on the authority of the institution to back up their decision. Many of the most important institutional practices are aimed at enhancing this authority. For instance, in courts where a number of judges join in the decision, agreement on the bench is an important element for increasing the authority of the institution. The effort to achieve such agreement is one of the more obvious examples of institutional practices aimed at enhancing a court's capacity to deal with a dispute.

Martin Shapiro's description of courts provides a link between dispute processes generally and institutional structures (Shapiro, 1981). Building from a widespread phenomena—the triadic structure of dispute resolution—Shapiro has described court-like institutions in terms of the way they respond to conflict and maintain authority over a dispute. His contribution to our understanding of courts incorporates institutional structure and law into the process of dispute resolution. This is a step beyond mere identification of a basic form that can be found in most societies. It is a basis for pulling together a number of facets of the legal system. Disputes take place in a context, and the context is so general and so familiar that it is often taken as a given. Yet, these givens are the structures that make both disputes and their resolution what they are in a society. By affecting the opportunities for justice, they condition the access to justice. In the following discussion, these structures are presented as the institutional structures bearing on constitutional rights.

Institutional Structures. The process of disputing brings one into contact with the institutions responsible for maintaining social order and charged with handling disputes. American institutional structures originated in England, but they evolved according to the American experience. In the United States, we distinguish among disputes on the basis of the penalty imposed, and according to whether civil or criminal law applies. From this, a distinct institutional structure has developed, where the penalty is a criminal sanction. We distinguish by jurisdiction, between state and federal courts, with the latter being the more recent and the former the more removed from the Constitution. There is also a difference between the court structure at the initial hearing, and subsequently a difference between trial and appellate courts. From the appellate courts, we get judicial commentary on the law. Finally, there is a distinction between the law that comes from judges, the law passed by legislatures, and the law established in the Constitution. These are the court structures in the United States, and they have influenced the development of constitutional rights.

The distinction between criminal law and civil law begins with the basis and meaning of the penalties provided by each (Goldman, 1982). Civil penalties do not include incarceration and the moral sanction that goes with it. Civil disputes involve a conflict of interests, with a finding for one party or the other on the basis of right or the stronger claim, but not on the basis of guilt or innocence. In criminal law, social morality is involved. The finding is of "guilt," with its connotations of evil or wrongdoing, or "innocence" with its contrary implications of blameless-ness and purity. Criminal penalties imply transgressions for which the guilty party is expected to feel responsible. In civil actions, legal responsibility is much less likely to imply evil conduct. Civil law is, however, the "larger" body of law, in that it constitutes the more ordinary processes of social life, the law of family, business, and property, for instance (Goldman, 1982). Consequently, in the civil context, the parties are individuals or private groups. They have their own lawyers. Nobody is paid by the government to protect the social interests. In the criminal context, however, one party is an individual, but the other is always the state. The rights that are the focus in this book involve both criminal and civil matters. A unique aspect of the Constitution is that its guarantees are the ones from which the others derive their authority, and these guarantees cut across other institutional structures.

At another level of abstraction, or at least at the next level in the legal process, there is a distinction between trial and appellate courts. A trial court is a court where one starts in the process. It is where matters of "fact" are determined, sometimes with the help of a jury. The contribution to the reading of the law is minimal here. But at the next level, the appellate courts, what the justices or judges have to say about the meaning of the law will be recorded and have a continuing influence beyond the particular case. A dispute that gets to the appellate level can have great significance for the development of legal doctrine. It is here that the commentary on legal traditions goes forward to set the context for subsequent disputes. (See Howard, 1981.)

In America, there are different places you may (or may not) go for a legal forum. The most dramatic distinction is between the various state systems and the federal system. This has become perhaps the best-described instance of structural conditions in the American dispute settlement process (Black, 1969). These different forums have different judges, different processes, and different law. Each has some affect on a dispute. Most law is state law, both criminal and civil. We tend to think of the federal government as bigger and more important than state government, but actually it is not nearly the size, nor does it have the collective importance, of the fifty state systems. In both civil and criminal situations, the states provide the law of social life, of business, and of politics. Federal law has been added to the law that existed in the colonies. Although federal law has grown substantially, it is still highly specialized. Where it governs a situation, however, it has come to have supremacy. Constitutional law is a branch of federal law, and because of the Fourteenth Amendment, the rights and liberties that the Constitution guarantees now apply to all relevant contexts in all the states. This is a unique aspect of the constitutional sphere; although it is "federal," it is law for the states as well.

There are also different sources of law. Generally, these are distinguished in terms of common or judge-made law, statute law made by legislatures, and constitutional law—ostensibly made by the people, but which has come to be dominated by the appellate courts. Common law is the oldest form and was originally derived from the norms of the community and announced by judges. It is becoming less "common" as the society becomes more professionalized. Law made by legislative bodies is newer. Legislatures simply used to appropriate money. Only in the last 200 years have they become major sources of law. Finally, constitutional law is the fundamental law, the law that delineates the basic rights and principles by which people are governed. Although at the national level, justices seem to be the source of constitutional law, their decisions are actually interpretations of the Constitution. Constitutional law gains its status as an expression of popular will. While the ideology of popular sovereignty as a basis for the authority to govern still exists, it is necessary to come to terms with the impact of judicial interpretation.

In constitutional law, appellate courts have been very influential. As the United States developed, legislative bodies and the citizenry became increasingly deferential to the higher courts on issues of constitutional interpretation. The deference resulted from the importance attached to the claim of judicial review, the special capacity to tell what the law means. The claim is part of an old tradition that goes back to the seventeenth century. At that time, the English jurists claimed that the sovereign did not have the ultimate capacity to say what the law was because he was not trained in its mysteries. In the United States, this assertion has been linked with separation of powers, resulting in a special claim to expertise based on competence in an assigned task.

The form of this claim differs, depending on whether the issue is constitutional law or statutory interpretation. In the case of the Supreme Court, for instance, its authority to interpret the meaning of statutes passed by legislative bodies depends entirely on its being the court of last resort. That position is also a factor when the Court interprets the Constitution. But for their constitutional authority, the justices of the Court rely more heavily on a claim of expertise. In order to evaluate this claim, we now turn to the tradition of constitutional interpretation.

Constitutional Interpretation and the Supreme Court

To understand what constitutional law has become and the major contemporary source of this law, it is necessary to be familiar with the Supreme Court. Anthony Lewis, one of the journalists who has helped to fashion our view of the institution, called the Supreme Court "a different kind of court" (1964). The simplicity of the observation should not mask its insight. The institution was the only court established in the Constitution, and it is thus sometimes called an "Article III" court. This in itself is unique and a great deal follows from this fact, but the Constitution says very little about this institution. The document does not even say how many justices it should have or what sort of preparation they should have. Consequently, although the number of justices has changed nearly half a dozen times, the institution persists. It is indeed a different kind of court for many reasons, but it is a court nonetheless. The discussion of interpretation that follows is based on this interaction between being a court and being unique.

The Supreme Court is an appellate court, like many others. But it is alone at the top of the judicial process in the United States. It has authority, not only over the federal courts, but also over the state courts. It is rare in this regard, and it is the institution that anchors the federal system. The Supreme Court is the final appeal for the enormous number of cases generated in the United States. A rough estimation of the number of these cases would be around ten million per year. Of these, approximately three hundred thousand are appealed to the higher courts in the states and in the federal system. About five thousand of these eventually reach the Supreme Court. But the justices actually choose less than two hundred of these cases to consider in depth and comment on extensively.

The Supreme Court stands alone at the top of a legalistic polity. This position at the top of the legal system in America makes it different from the other courts in the judicial system. It has often been remarked, in a clever jest, that the Supreme Court is infallible only because it is final, that is, because it has the last word. It did not get to have the last word because it was infallible, however, but, with that final say in legal matters the Court has come to be viewed as special.

Because the Supreme Court is the last official word on the Constitution, short of constitutional change through amendment, it deserves careful attention. It is equally important to realize, however, that the Supreme Court addresses relatively few cases. This leaves a variety of other less visible sources of constitutional law, or at least constitutional interpretation. The pipeline of cases coming up the appellate ladder is so narrow at its oracular confluence that some issues are never addressed by the Supreme Court. This results in authoritative decisions from lower courts as a result of negotiation and consent, as often as from a formal decision. Such decisions will be woven into the material that follows.

The Supreme Court can also be distinguished from other courts by some of its functions. Most courts are primarily engaged in the resolution of conflict, but the Supreme Court is known to make policy or general rules while it handles its cases. In this sense, constitutional interpretation is the product of choices that have given the original document meaning. The justices transform the law while applying it. In practice, the real-life drama is far removed from the workings of the appellate process, and it often seems that the individual cannot help but be ignored. Yet, it is from these individual disputes that the law is fashioned, and the institution therefore maintains its authority by settling disputes. Wherever choices indicate a decision of a governing institution, however, they constitute public policy and for all the texture of the dramas that are carried to the Supreme Court the result is an abstraction: law.

As part of two legal systems, the federal and the state, the Supreme Court is *the* court of last resort. As is the case with all federal courts, the justices are appointed by the president, paid out of the national treasury, and they serve for good behavior, which in practice has meant for life. In this system, these are standard practices. But there is a special quality to Supreme Court appointment due to the fact that the Court is sitting at the peak of legal power. Such an appointment does not go to the timid, and the pursuit of the position belies the tradition of passivity often associated with the judicial process and especially judicial selection. The process is political and a nominee's political party activity influences the appointment decision. In the case of the Supreme Court, there is just (a little) more concern about the quality of the nominee than there might be for a lower court justice. Life tenure in the national limelight heightens that concern; like other institutional parameters, it sets the stage within which the justices operate. Moreover, many a justice has sought to stay on past the tenure of some hated president. Justice William Douglas hung on longer than any justice in history, in part to avoid allowing President Gerald Ford to nominate his successor. A retirement from this institution has thus become a policy decision of some significance, not to be taken lightly.

The Supreme Court has appellate jurisdiction over disputes about law or facts. Congress sets the basic regulations and makes changes in the Court's jurisdiction when it chooses to do so. Although direct limitation of the Court in substantive areas is difficult to accomplish, it is often tried. In the early 1980s, there were as many as 30 bills pending in each legislative session to limit the Court's authority. Although up until the 1920s the justices had little discretion in the cases they took, since then, they have been able to choose from among the 5,000 cases that are appealed annually. This gives the Supreme Court the opportunity to influence its calendar and to take a more active role in setting the agenda before it than is usually thought to be the case with courts. In addition, statements in judicial opinions and occasional public statements by the justices stimulate appeals by indicating judicial predispositions. For example, the exclusionary rule, which prohibits the use of illegally obtained evidence, is a case in point. This rule has been subject to criticism by members of the Supreme Court since the 1970s, and challenges to the rule have been looked on favorably although it has not been eliminated.

Some social scientists and legal historians have turned away from the Supreme Court's pronouncements on the Constitution, characterizing these holdings as atypical and unrepresentative of legal activity. Due at least in part to this criticism of excessive attention to appellate courts, there has been more attention to the law in action in recent years, to the political behavior of judges, to intermediate courts and local trial courts, and to the impact of judicial decisions in the community. What began as a healthy realism became excessive and led to the belief that there was little reason to study high courts at all. For example, Morton Horwitz considered constitutional law to be "episodic" and "buttressed by a rhetorical tradition that is often an unreliable guide to . . . legal change in America" (Horwitz, 1977:xii). The tradition of commentary on the Constitution is, however, an excellent guide to national ideology. Although they are not representative of the mass of legal or even judicial activity, Supreme Court opinions are authoritative attempts to relate legal concepts to changing social and political conditions. The resulting commentary accommodates contemporary issues and values with tradition. By telling us how the government thinks about itself, the opinions of the Supreme Court constitute a running commentary on fundamental political concepts. From this body of discourse, the student can observe change and/or continuity and examine the judicial contribution to the structure of American politics.

The Ideology: Conventions of Rights and Law

Ideology is a body of conventional understandings that determine what is possible in politics. In discussing rights, what they are, the basis for constitutional rights, and the context in which they operate, we have been working in the realm of ideology. Having explored the terrain, we now step back a pace and try to describe what it amounts to. The effort here is to present a rationale for an ideological approach to constitutional rights and to indicate with some degree of specificity what that approach would involve. It is not enough just to say that rights are ideas that matter and that in the constitutional setting they have a degree of coherence that acts as a constraint on human action. An investigation claiming this sort of contribution must be justified and presented with reference to how the Constitution has been studied in the past.

The Constitution contains conventions spelling out the individual rights safeguarded as fundamental. As part of this ideological heritage, these rights help define a sphere of government action. Rights of this sort cannot exist without the state apparatus. While they are constituted by the state, their existence is evidence of a concern about the exercise of state power. To set this investigation up with reference to conventional understanding, we will look at "constitutional rights," a category of fundamental guarantees which includes civil liberties. The following investigation develops the tradition of constitutional interpretation within which even the most creative justices have operated.

Three Views of Interpretation

There are a number of approaches to the interpretation of constitutional rights. These approaches will be explained in order to set this investigation off against past conventions. They are: "formal jurisprudence," or the mechanical view, of our forebears; "political jurisprudence," popular today and associated with "realism" and behavioralism; and "ideological jurisprudence," which is elaborated in the chapters that follow. The ideological treatment accords more respect for the formal view than do realists who focus on politics. And although our discussion is critical of excessive focus on the political dimensions of constitutional interpretation, the transformative insight of political jurisprudence is acknowledged. The ideological view thus takes from both of its predecessors and is offered as an improvement on conventional understanding of rights. The aim is an account that incorporates both the forms of law and political practice.

Formal Jurisprudence. Part of the American tradition is that we aspire to be "a government of laws and not of men" (we know, of course, that the Founders meant a government of *men* and not of women, but the idea does not change). The idea was that law held sway over human desires and that in government the range of action was constrained by official guidelines, principles, and policies. Law was said to be above man, whether he be citizen, politician, or judge. Law could come from God, in the form of tablets brought down from the mountain, or from an agreement (like the Constitution) that a people would be governed in a certain way. Whatever its source, according to the formal view, law controlled people, rather than the other way around. Thus, when a judge made a decision, the claim was that it came from somewhere else, a higher plane from which even judges were guided.

This view has been called *mechanical* because it depicts law as functioning like a machine. The view was, according to the legal philosopher John Austin, a "childish fiction employed by our judges, that judiciary or common law is not made by them, but is a miraculous something made by nobody, existing ... from eternity, and merely deduced from time to time by the judges" (Austin, 1861:634). Austin attributed this "fiction" to William Blackstone. It was through Blackstone's *Commentaries* that American judges learned of this position and rode it to the pinnacle of political power. The myth was transformed into the basis for judicial supremacy in the late nineteenth and early twentieth centuries.

In ridiculing this conception of an eternally cast and judicially discovered law as a "sort of judicial slot machine" (Pound: 1921:170-171), more recent scholars created a picture of the justices as just having to flick a switch, pull a crank, or press a button. In fact, Justice Owen Roberts, who sat on the United States Supreme Court in the late 1930s, described the process he went through in deciding a case as "laying the constitution down by a statute and observing whether the latter squared with the former." Remarkable as this seems, the justice appears to have been serious.

Although old-fashioned-sounding to sophisticates like the people who study law and politics today, the formal view has had intelligent adherents from John Marshall and Joseph Story to Hugo Black. Today, however, it is mostly associated with grade school civics lessons and simple-minded judges. A remnant is the official version of the theory, the doctrine of *stare decisis,* which means that the decision should be left standing. This doctrine holds that once a rule of law has been handed down, that rule becomes a *precedent,* or governing principle, for all future cases. This is not far from Justice Roberts's position, although it sounds more like an instruction in how to act like a judge than a description of the world.

Political Jurisprudence. The dominant view for understanding how law functions these days is political. The convention is to talk as if the judge can do almost whatever he wants. With regard to the Supreme Court, for instance, we often hear that the justices decide as they wish and use the opinion to rationalize their decision. On the surface, this is what *The Brethren* (Woodward and Armstrong, 1979) taught, that judging is political and that opinions are rationalizations. The political interpretation has become so widespread today that it seems right. It is always hard to keep from automatically equating the day's dominant view with the one that is most appropriate or most accurate, but a little history helps in avoiding this pitfall.

The political view achieved prominence in the 1930s. This was when the skepticism of the social sciences came creeping into the studies and classrooms of "humanistic" disciplines like law. Professors found it hard to justify developing theories of law without going out into the world to see what was really happening. It was also a time when academics were unhappy with what the justices on the Supreme Court were saying about some of the academically inspired experiments for running the country. The professors found a lot of judges who did not follow precedent; some of the justices appeared not even to know what it was. In deciding cases, they voted the way they felt, rather than according to how earlier judges had ruled. The resulting response to the formal view came to be called "realism" in the law schools and "judicial behavioralism" in the universities.

Realism and behavioralism were linked by their common emphasis on men, and not on law. Realists were law professors who said things like "the law is what the judges say it is." Felix Frankfurter, a Harvard law professor before he became a Supreme Court justice, once said, "People have been taught to believe that when the Supreme Court speaks, it is not they who speak but the Constitution, whereas, of course, in so many vital cases, it is they [the justices] who speak, and *not* the Constitution" (Freedman, 1967:383). Behaviorialists had a similar perspective but, for the most part, they came from political science departments. Having turned from the study of judicial opinions to how the justices voted on issues, they emphasized judicial attitudes and investigated whether judges were liberal or conservative. Their view was dismissed by many old-fashioned types as too attentive to influences on the justices, such as what the justices had eaten for breakfast. (Consequently, the theory is sometimes called "dietary jurisprudence." Lawyers, having acquired this view in law school, gleefully claim that it is confirmed by clients who hope the judge has "had a good breakfast" before the sentence is handed down.)

Although more recent, the political view is sometimes as naive as the older, formal view. Its message, that judges have wide discretion, is not so wrong itself, but its reception has diverted attention almost completely away from legal considerations. The treatment given to the Supreme Court in *The Brethren* is an example of the political way of looking at things. Here the focus is on individuals, their goals, their limitations, and their frailties. The puzzle is that this observation was treated as a revelation, an unveiling of some new insight about how the Supreme Court operated and warmly received with a sort of cynical anticipation. Yet, a similar story revealing the political nature of the United States Congress would have gotten little attention. This is due to the cultural expectation that there is something more to judging and reading the law than wheeling and dealing in the world of politics. We expect something more, and yet we often describe politics as the reality. The truth is that both law and politics are involved.

Ideological Jurisprudence. Despite the present authority of the political view, politics is not the only reality. Law is not just a tool; it constrains and influences action, including politics. Law does not simply justify judicial authority, it is the basis for that authority. The law and the expectations it generates give people recourse from a poor decision, as well as a basis for evaluating judicial action. An independent legal doctrine guarantees that the judiciary is accountable to the public.

Much of the intellectual excitement in jurisprudence is a function of trying to incorporate the truth of both the formal and the political view. The consequence is a greater insight than either are capable of providing. Constitutional politics, like politics everywhere, takes place in a world understood through language, symbols, and conventions. In this case, the conventions are acquired as we learn the Constitution. They constitute an ideology that is separate from ordinary life. Concepts such as free speech, due process, and equal protection have technical meanings that must be understood in order to participate fully in constitutional politics.

The ideological interpretation of judicial decisions is neither a matter of rules nor of behavioral responses whereby the justices would be characterized as either reacting to stimuli or rationalizing their interests. According to the ideological view, ideas and language are essential to interpreting the Constitution. There are specific ways of proceeding in litigation. These are the possibilities and they determine the range of judicial action and give that action its meaning (Brigham, 1978). Thus, law influences justices, not through rules, but through the ideas in its language. People, especially appellate judges, do not have to obey some body of constitutional rules. To operate in the legal sphere they have to make sense. Conventions, like the one that holds that only defendants can appeal, are beyond the control of individual justices. When a case comes to the Supreme Court, it is seen in terms of concepts like "due process," "certiorari," and other unique forms of expression. If the language that makes up the case were taken away, the *legal* dispute would disappear. The language constitutes the case the justices will consider.

Legal language is an influence that pushes legal action toward uniformity (Schwartz, 1969a:490). In the ideological or ideational sphere of constitutional discourse, action is a function of professional practices because other lawyers who speak to the courts and the lawyers who are the judges of the courts have developed a special way of speaking about constitutional rights. Claims before the Supreme Court thus rely on language games steeped in professional experience (O'Neill, 1981). At the margins, this can be a creative activity where the actors have an influence on what others will deem intelligible.

Students of constitutional law have not usually referred to their subject as ideological. The approach is likely to be unfamiliar. For those who are unfamiliar with the study of ideology, this section of the chapter will set out the relevant considerations. Readers familiar with ideology may need to distinguish the following presentation from liberal and Marxist conceptions of ideology. Marxism refers to ideology as ideas that are imagined and false, the realm above the material and social conditions. According to the Marxist view, ideology is the set of beliefs of the dominant classes and a false picture of the world. In liberalism, on the other hand, ideology is considered aspiration or mythology. It is in opposition to "reality," and the gap between aspiration and practice is often subject to investigation. This book adheres to neither of these views of ideology.

Organized around the idea of ideology as social practice, and with attention to "artificial reason"—a traditional way of distinguishing the subject matter in the legal realm—and the process of "making sense" within a unique tradition, the ideological view of law is developed below through discussing "the discourses of the law." This is not a "trashing" of ideology. It is, rather, an investigation of conventions that operate at this level. The terminology used here, and the nature of the investigation, is meant to establish a position from which one may observe legal activity. Here in the domain of constitutional law, the effort is to understand the tradition rather than introduce something new.

The Discourse of the Law

The basis for an investigation of rights is the professional use of legal language. Use of concepts such as due process, equal protection, and free speech reveal the conventional practices. The justices of the Supreme Court hear, speak, write, and think rights. In order for an appeal to be heard, it must contain reasonable claims and be capable of a sensible response (Murphy, 1964:160-161). For reason to function, in law or anywhere else, there must be ideas available, "laid down in advance of action" (Read, 1938:51) by habitual interpretation. Edward S. Corwin, a government professor at Princeton, in describing judicial discretion, characterized the structure and limits on the justices' action, and hence the nature of the tradition, as "jural freedom ... which the Court has built up for itself piece by piece by its own past practices and precedents. ..." (Corwin, 1934:182). This tradition is what I call *constitutional language*.

Artificial Reason. In the early years of this century, Edward S. Corwin described the authority of American judges as grounded in a legal tradition that claimed to be superior to ordinary thought due to its special forms, its "artificial reason." He developed the idea in order to explain the extraordinary institutional position, for a democracy, that the Supreme Court had achieved. The issue forms a section of this introductory chapter because the claim to mastery over a technical and, by ordinary standards, artificial form of discourse still gives the legal process and particularly the appellate courts, their special place in constitutional interpretation.

The reason in law is a function of its conceptual tradition. Attention to concepts focuses on the propensity to distinguish in any realm of discourse; to "break up all the ordered surfaces and all the planes with which we are accustomed to tame the wild profusion of existing things" (Foucault, 1973). To demonstrate this distinguishing property, Michel Foucault, a philosopher concerned with these matters, chose a passage that describes a Chinese capacity to distinguish "animals" as falling into a number of categories that would be strange to most Americans.

> ... a) belonging to the Emperor, b) embalmed, c) tame, d) sucking pigs, e) sirens, f) fabulous, g) stray dogs, h) included in the present classification, i) frenzied, j) innumerable, k) drawn with a very fine camel hair brush, l) et cetera, m) having just broken the water pitcher, n) that come from a long way off look like flies.

Given the limitations of our own system, we know we could not talk like *that*. But, a comparable categorical litany can be found in constitutional law. When John Marshall used "commerce" in a discussion of the Constitution, he started a tradition of relying on ordinary discourse. The formulation he gave became a part of the Constitution and a basis for continual development. A claim based on the concept of "commerce" that did not make sense in terms of this tradition might be heard as something else, but it would not be heard by the Court as a "commerce" claim. Intelligible use of traditional concepts involves an intuitive recognition of their qualities or what is essential to them.

Rights cannot be understood only in terms of what falls within or without the conceptual sphere. Their meaning also depends on contexts and relationships. For Felix Frankfurter, ". . . words may acquire scope and function from the history of events which they summarize. . . . They bear the meaning of their habitat. . ." (Frankfurter, 1947:213-237). Rights are connected to the entire body of discourse that makes up a sphere like civil liberties or constitutional law. This structural dimension, as well as the conceptual dimension, makes legal discourse analogous to language. The structure or grammar of linguistic activities tells us what these activities are, that is, how they fit into their part of our life (Brigham, 1978:57). In the Constitution, "Senator" is defined in the document with reference to "Congress." The statement that "Congress . . . shall consist of a Senate and a House of Representatives" relies on relations between concepts rather than a single concept. These structures are evident in the way different concepts are joined, the contexts, and limits on substitution (Brigham, 1978:62-70). "Equal protection prohibits unreasonable searches," for instance, does not make sense because the concepts are not used appropriately.

Charles Black, of Yale Law School, took note, some time ago, of the structural factors that existed beyond (or beneath) precedent (Black, 1969:35). The decision in *Barron* v. *Baltimore* (1833), he pointed out, rests on a relationship between the federal government and the states, rather than on any provision in the Constitution. Similarly, the structure of American federalism precludes some forms of review by the Supreme Court. "Independent state grounds" take a case beyond the purview of the High Court when combined with constitutional protections such as those preventing the government from putting a person "in jeopardy of life or limb" more than once.

People v. *Anderson* (1972), decided by the California Supreme Court, voided the California death penalty on the basis of the California constitutional provision against "cruel *or* unusual" punishment. The ruling could not be taken to the Supreme Court of the United States because the California justices had overturned a penalty as inconsistent with California law. Structural limits precluded an interpretation of the federal Constitution that would have compelled California to keep the death penalty. (See Friedelbaum, 1982.)

These structural elements of legal practice are often taken for granted, yet they are more significant than precedent. Other structures include: (1) the adversary process and characteristics of litigation, such as conflicting claims at the appellate level, (2) the hierarchy of law, including constitutional, statutory, and common law, (3) the distinction between facts and law that establishes a relationship between courts, (4) the nation, the states, and the structure of sovereignty, and (5) the power of the judiciary to review political action. Understanding these structures is a prerequisite for understanding civil liberties.

Thus, artificial reason simply amounts to the sense of the law, what those who know the tradition take to be true. This is the stuff of the practice of rights. The ideology of civil liberties can be seen as artificial reason to the extent that a body of doctrine exists that serves to limit the range of action by people operating in its sphere. It is reason to those whose world is constituted by it, and artificial only to the extent that it is a professional language that has become divorced from ordinary experience. For those who understand the world in this way, it acts as a constraint. Those who use the law must make sense in terms of the tradition. The implications of this tradition and the way in which it limits action is the subject of the next section.

Making Sense. The range of possibilities in an ideological sphere like law has been described as "the framework within which political thought and action proceed" (Shapiro, 1968:39-44). The disarmingly simple truth is that in order to be raised or addressed, as a constitutional right, an issue must make sense in this context. Constitutional sense, or something like it, was neglected for a long time by scholars (Pritchett, 1967). Legal scholars were relatively unsophisticated in their treatment of how legal doctrine actually functions until recently. One early perspective on judicial interpretation that was sensitive to ideology, however, can be found in Edward Levi's "reasoning by example" (1949). Later, Julius Stone described the skills of the lawyer and the judge in terms of the rhetorical tradition (1968). From this tradition came a call for attention to the way law "constitutes" the world in which the politics of rights is played out (Brigham, 1978; Klare, 1979). Finally, and quite provocatively, Philip Bobbitt, a law professor, has given us an image of "the force field of constitutional law," in his *Constitutional Fate* (1982), an important contemporary examination of constitutional interpretation.

The tradition that determines what makes constitutional sense is evident in the appellate process. It plays a role in conference, in oral argument, and in opinions. In the fall of 1983, a group of citizens from

Morton Grove, Illinois, tried to appeal the town's ban on private handgun possession to the Supreme Court. They argued that the Second Amendment guarantee of the right "to keep and bear arms" rendered the ban invalid. One might guess that the claim would make some sense, and on the surface, it does. But the federal appeals court turned it down, and none of the justices of the Supreme Court expressed interest in hearing the appeal. There are other factors involved in the decision, but an important one is a long tradition of avoiding the Second Amendment. Conversely, in 1925, the Court said that the First Amendment might apply to the states, even though it is explicitly addressed to acts of Congress.

Sense in the Constitution is not static. It evolves. Thus, if a speaker had been jailed by a state in 1870, it would have made no sense for him to say his First Amendment rights had been violated. But a speaker jailed in 1926 would have made a lot of sense if he had said the same thing. If I say right now that I have a consitutional right to vacation in the sun, that makes no sense. But fifty years from now that same claim may make sense. For, in the meantime, Congress may enact a statute guaranteeing annual vacations for all Americans, and I may be able to claim that the employees that the boss likes are getting the vacations in the summer, and I am getting what is left over. Maybe some other things would have to change, too, but what seems to be inevitable at a particular time (or even outrageous) will change as the concept of what makes sense changes.

Although anyone can know an ordinary English version of such concepts as "state action" or "equal protection," it would be impossible to use these concepts intelligibly in the federal courts without knowing the constitutional tradition. Knowing the meaning of concepts depends on knowing their use. The clues to use associated with precedent are simply part of the process of formulating an intelligible statement. A favorite example of this is that the due process protections of the Fourteenth Amendment are limited to cases of "state action." This concept comes from the tradition for interpreting the Constitution, and it will not be readily apparent to people who are unfamiliar with constitutional rights. These rights can only be applied when government interests are part of the conflict, that is, when it is under state authority that some violation of the Constitution is claimed. For example, in *Burton* v. *Wilmington Parking Authority* (1961), a state-owned parking garage leased space for a restaurant to a private corporation that discriminated in its operations. In order for the "equal protection" guarantees to be applicable in this case, the government had to be involved in some way with the discrimination. In the parking authority case, the court decided that the government was involved. The requirement for such involvement was the basis for an important equal protection case eleven years later (*Moose Lodge No. 107* v. *Irvis*, 1972). It continues to be relevant in equal opportunity suits where the government can intervene if a corporation or school is receiving federal funds. Thus, Americans have a constitutional claim that they have been discriminated against only if the government is in some way involved. In order to use constitutional rights, one must learn such things.

A characteristic of this ideological sphere is that a claim may be legally wrong and still make sense. This is difficult to see because the legal community suppresses nonsense, as would be expected. Claims presented to the justices will have been filtered through a many-layered screen of lawyers and courts, thereby assuring consistency with the tradition. Yet, there are still some examples of claims that are legally wrong but that make sense. *In forma pauperis* petitions, which allow prisoners to file petitions with the Supreme Court through a less formal process, are examples of these kinds of claims because they have avoided any legal filtering. Evaluation of these claims is cursory, and it is not accidental that Justice William O. Douglas characterized most prisoner petitions as "surpassing credulity" (Lewis, 1964:34).

In *Gideon* v. *Wainwright* (1963), a Supreme Court case that led to an important due process holding, the petitioner had been convicted of a petty crime. His claim that he had a right to a lawyer at his trial was technically wrong. It had not been accepted by the Supreme Court, nor would it have been recognized as law by the legal community. His description of the right *as one he had* was therefore incorrect. Yet, his claim fit into a doctrinal tradition suggested by past opinions on due process rights. In terms of that tradition, the claim made sense, and it was accepted by the Supreme Court on appeal. Knowing the tradition is essential for constructing a sensible claim, but it is not sufficient for a decision in one's favor from a court, nor does such a claim need to have been accepted by a court for it to be sensible.

The key to understanding any ideology is to be able to see what is taken as given. The world of legal ideology requires that one learn how to transcend the usual preoccupation with the disposition of a case. This requires a focus on what has been called a tradition of intelligible discourse (Flathman, 1976; Brigham, 1978). In approaching the issue of making sense, the challenge is to comprehend the implications and elements of a sphere of discourse. This requires identifying its limits and the capacity for growth that might legitimately be considered *making sense*. The focus itself requires a diversion of attention away from some of the things that have traditionally seemed most relevant in the study of law, like the disposition of cases.

Given the framework of sensible communication, both parties in a case before the Supreme Court can usually bring to bear some constitutional sense on their side (Brigham, 1983). Thus, there are intelligible claims and at least a modicum of sense on either side in a controversy that has reached the highest appellate level. The outcome is not determined by this sense, and an investigation of who wins and who loses reveals relatively little about the nature of sense or legal ideology. There is a relationship here between ideas and outcomes, but the ideological impact is a prior one and it falls on whether or not an issue is contested. It is, however, reasonable to expect to find some indication of the import of constitutional possibilities in the division of opinion on the Court. In 1982-1983, for instance, 39 percent of the term's decisions were unanimous and 21 percent were decided by a bare majority of 5 to 4. At some level, unanimous opinions must reflect more assurance about what the Constitution requires than where the justices are deeply divided as to a decision. Where it is relevant, the treatment that follows refers to whether a decision is unanimous or divided. The study of ideology is such, however, that knowledge of what constitutes the constitutional sphere and what does not is limited and imprecise. Division of opinion, like the outcome, is influenced by political considerations as well as ideology, and although it is clear that this takes place within an ideological framework, it is not always clear what the relative significance is. Consequently, how a case is decided offers far less assistance in understanding legal possibilities than is conventionally realized.

The constitutional tradition does not exist in a vacuum. It is part of a social and economic order. Constitutional liberties are characterized by evolution and transformation as social and economic conditions change. Those who would give new meaning to the Constitution must extrapolate from convention, from the range of possibilities that reveal what is constitutional. But the interests themselves are not "outside," acting on the Constitution. They are partly constituted by its scheme. Though rooted in the rise of the middle classes in the late eighteenth century, constitutional rights have helped define American society. The respect for human life and personality that is central to constitutional democracy interacts with the social conditions. At times, the result is protection for a new dependency on the state. In other situations, it is simply giving a constitutional sense to new economic rights. The future of such rights will be clearer to those who understand the process by which we have received the existing guarantees of the Constitution. This is a topic to which we return in the final chapter. Now we turn to a discussion of freedom of expression, to see how constitutional interpretation has been applied to this right, and to show what the practical impact of this interpretation is.

Freedom | 2

The Aquarian Foundation of Seattle, Washington, was called before the Supreme Court in 1983 to defend a court order it had won against the *Seattle Times* and the Walla Walla *Union Bulletin*. The justices agreed to decide on the constitutionality of a protective order issued by a trial judge in Washington State forbidding the newspapers, which were defendants in a libel suit, from publishing any information obtained in the course of the trial for libel (*Seattle Times* v. *Rhinehart*, 1983). The paper contends that the order is a "prior restraint." The Foundation and its leader, Keith Milton Rhinehart, sought compensation for critical commentary by the newspaper, which had referred to the group as a "bizarre Seattle cult." * The dispute involved constitutional freedom. The significance of these ideas is their influence on how issues must be framed to be "constitutional." This chapter is about that frame.

The First Amendment is a multifaced guarantee with a number of specific rights delineating constitutional freedom. It reads:

> Congress shall make no law respecting an establishment of religion, or prohibiting the free exercise thereof; or abridging the freedom of speech, or of the press; or of the right of the people peaceably to assemble, and to petition the Government for a redress of grievances.

Active debate and judicial commentary has given meaning to these words. Although its roots lie in struggles over religion, modern First Amendment developments have been most dynamic in the area of secular, political expression. In only half of a century, protection for expressing controversial opinions has expanded to levels of toleration barely imaginable two or three generations back. This development has influenced the scope and treatment of all the First Amendment free-

---

* Rhinehart had also petitioned to the Supreme Court against the part of the protective order requiring that its records be turned over to the newspapers. The Foundation contended that the order to produce its records, even with protection, was a violation of its rights as a church. The Supreme Court passed over this claim.

doms. How the change took place, and its ongoing significance, is the focus of this chapter.

The chapter begins with the historical background for free expression and then describes the changes in interpretation of this right and the structural dimensions that set the boundaries for contemporary claims. Perception of danger to legitimate interests has governed development of the modern right to free speech and assembly and has led to characterization of some expression as being unprotected by the Constitution. Discussion of developments in this area precedes discussion of the special case of freedom of the press, which has been influenced by the beliefs and professional organization of journalists. The chapter concludes with a short summary of the constitutional issues surrounding religious freedom, placing particular emphasis on how this right is constrained by the way the guarantees were originally stated in the First Amendment.

Freedom of Expression

Mark Twain joked about protections for expression when he called free speech and free press two of the three great blessings enjoyed by the American people. The third, he observed, was "the good sense not to use either" (Murphy, 1972:15). Americans have actually tested the right of free expression on many occasions, and in the process they have defined its meaning. The history of this right is one of the expressive actions testing the limits set by government.

Some forms of expression have always been subject to limitation. In American constitutional practice, "freedom of speech" has never meant the freedom to say anything you want at any time and place without regard for whether saying it will hurt other people. The constitutional right is based on distinctions between speech that poses a threat to legitimate interests and speech that does not. Some, however, impute to the right a "purity" that precludes critical attention to the substance of expression. The myth has been that all expression is protected. The values embedded in the constitutional right are ignored in this "pure" view of free expression (Wolff, 1969). Freedom of expression is more appropriately viewed as a function of the practices that define the limits of toleration.

Constitutional freedom of expression has been among the most dramatic rights in its evolution and the most completely defined. In its history, the concept has shifted from the intolerant "tolerance" of the Puritans, to forbidding anyone to prevent expression before it takes place, to a focus on whether a person could be punished for what he has already said. It has led today to a conception that denies the capacity to set limits on speech and suggests the irrelevance of community standards in this area. I call this presently dominant conception "pure tolerance" and consider its implications in this chapter.

A Right Emerges

Freedom of expression in America has its roots in seventeenth century England. The period's great plea for toleration, John Milton's *Areopagetica*, came near the end of a generation of violent religious conflict. It was a speech in support of unlicensed printing. In 1644, Milton argued before Parliament that he "Who kills a man kills a reasonable creature . . . but he who destroys a good book, kills reason itself" (Milton, 1644/1927:5). For many, however, toleration in England was not enough. Their religious sects were citadels of intolerance raging against the corruption around them. They sought a purity in North America, and for a while, they found it in their outposts of civilization in the Western Hemisphere. But, by the second generation, factions began to emerge in America. The result was a colonial creation, an indigenous version of tolerance. It appeared in Roger Williams's *Bloody Tenet of Persecution* (1644), published the same year as Milton's piece. Williams, like Milton, was a righteous partisan. Having escaped the persecutions of the Massachusetts Bay Colony, he held that men could not be so confident of the truth as to have a right to impose it on others *by civil authority* (Miller, 1953:256). "There is a civil sword," he said, "called the sword of civil justice, which . . . cannot extend to spiritual and soul causes, spiritual and soul punishment, which belongs to that spiritual sword with two edges . . . the Word of God" (Miller, 1953:133). While the civil sword was used by others for less significant matters, Williams wielded the word of God in the cause of righteousness.

The Federal Period. Legal views in the period prior to independence depended heavily on the common law. The source was William Blackstone's *Commentaries*. In 1758, this work defined freedom of expression as prohibiting the laying of any "previous restraints upon publication." This meant the printer could not be jailed before he could start the presses. Thus the right allowed all views to be presented to the public, although it did not protect against subsequent punishment if the expression turned out to be improper, mischievous, or otherwise illegal (for the printer could be jailed or fined for what he had printed). Free speech, conceived in this way, became an issue in the ratification process, and many states sought to include it in the Constitution. It was one of the limits that defined the scope of the new government; debate about expression, however, assumed a public right to judge and to punish the content of expression.

In the nation's infancy, the perception was that constitutional freedom of expression only meant not preventing prior restraint of expression; it had no bearing on subsequent punishment for that expression. Thomas Jefferson's criticism of the Sedition Acts of 1798 focused on state and federal prerogatives, not on the punishment itself. He would have left with the states the power to punish sedition. In 1801, he wrote:

> . . . we have nothing to fear from the demoralizing reasonings of some, if others are free to demonstrate their errors. And especially when the law stands ready to punish the first criminal *act* produced by the false reasoning (letter to Elijah Boardman).

James Madison disagreed. He thought it unjust and paradoxical to be "free" to say something for which one could be punished. With this reading, Madison anticipated the shift in constitutional doctrine that would occur within one hundred years.

The Nineteenth Century. As a largely homogeneous community, the United States in the nineteenth century rarely put tolerance to the test. A few instances of critical discourse revealed a grudging willingness to tolerate some diversity. Paul Murphy (1972) has suggested that freedom of expression was taken for granted during the century of continental expansion. Where curtailment of civil liberties did occur, such as in the South after the Civil War, the situational limits were part of the right and not "a massive precedent from which the government would expand its power to cover the behavior of all citizens" (Murphy, 1979:34-35). In addition, since the constitutional right applied only to federal legislation, the possibility of clashes over local restrictions did not exist (Murphy, 1972:14).

The entrepreneurial spirit and confidence in the economic marketplace that characterized late nineteenth century American thought also influenced the conception of free expression. The most important example of this thinking came from England in John Stuart Mill's *On Liberty*, published in 1859. Mill articulated the hope that truth would surface in open debate. His was a model of free exchange and his doctrines emphasized the "struggle between Liberty and Authority." This gave individual rights a central place (Mill, 1859/1975:3), and in the United States, it helped to transform the protections in the Bill of Rights into a manifesto for individualism. Propositions such as Mill's idea that the sole end for which "mankind are warranted . . . in interfering with the liberty of action of any of their number, is self-protection" (Mill, 1859/1975:10) expanded the bounds of protected expression and associated the right with limited government. This theory was popular where confidence in the market was the prevailing ideology. Its form paralleled the American Bill of Rights. For Mill, the first freedom was "liberty of thought and feeling: absolute freedom of opinion and sentiment on all subjects" (Mill, 1859/1975:13). Skepticism about ultimate truths showed itself in Mill's concern that the opinion which is suppressed may be true and that the only way we can be confident about our opinions is by encouraging open debate. Mill's concluding remark, in his treatment of thought and discussion, is that ". . . the free expression of all opinions should be permitted, on condition that the manner be temperate . . ." (Mill, 1859/1975:51). This was very similar to the interpretation of the First Amendment that emerged in the United States fifty years later.

The Modern Period. Although this theory appeared in the nineteenth century, it did not come to prominence as a basis for the right to free expression in the twentieth century until there had been a transformation in American society. Those transformations appear to have been necessary in order for the change to happen. Political violence, from the Haymarket riot of 1886 to the assassination of President McKinley in 1901, exemplified the serious discord at the turn of the century in America. The influx of new people and ideas before World War I ended the relative cultural homogeneity that had been characteristic of the new societies in the Western Hemisphere. The middle classes and those who represented them at the center of power associated free expression with radical groups such as the International Workers of the World (IWW) and the Free Speech League. The popular view was that ". . . in utilizing libertarian principles . . . these people were attempting to camouflage disruptive action" (Murphy, 1979:35). In fact, pushing those very principles was an acknowledged strategy of these groups. What has not readily been apparent was the extent to which nativist movements attacked the radicals and their demand for free expression.

The repression against anti-war and anti-draft activity during World War I may have created a receptivity, if not a longing, for an expanded freedom of expression. Following the war, a consensus began to develop in the legal community concerning the value of toleration. Pluralism in social and political life led to legal tolerance of expression as a new way of containing centrifugal social forces. The standard, articulated by Justice Oliver Wendell Holmes, Jr., reflects the capacity of the legal community to change the basis for constitutional protection. The result was using the First Amendment as an alternative to using force against dissent. The new standard for expression would soften and rationalize the legal limits on "free" expression, and would mature into the dominant constitutional practice in this area.

Movement away from a tradition that prohibited prior restraints on publication but allowed subsequent punishment came early in the twentieth century. When the First Amendment was introduced in a 1907 Colorado case, Justice John Marshall Harlan argued that its protection should not be limited to prior restraint, but should apply to punishment as well. His opinion was a dissent from the majority in *Patterson* v. *Colorado* (1907), a case involving publication of articles and a cartoon critical of the Colorado Supreme Court. The majority opinion by Justice Holmes upheld conviction for contempt because the First Amendment did not apply to the states. Its purpose, he added, was simply "to prevent all such previous restraints upon publications as had been practiced by other governments." Justice Holmes, along with his brethren, did not believe that the First Amendment was meant to prevent subsequent punishment. For Holmes, the meaning of free speech was influenced by the tradition of punishment for libel and slander and other common law doctrines. Holmes amplified this view in the following way: "The preliminary freedom extends as well to the false as to the true; the subsequent punishment may extend as well to the true as to the false" (*Patterson*, 1907:462). Holmes traced his early views to Blackstone, the common law, and the tradition of prosecution for attempted crime whether or not it succeeded (1881: 54-55). Speech that could be proscribed—in *Patterson*, it was contemptuous speech—could be considered criminal action.

In the summer of 1918, Holmes began an exchange with Judge Learned Hand who, because of his influence on doctrinal developments, would be referred to as the "tenth justice." Hand argued that "opinions are at best provisional hypotheses" and thus should not be subject to punishment. Holmes replied that free speech is not different than freedom "from vaccination"—that is, it is subject to reasonable limitations. But Holmes's position had already begun to weaken. In subsequent cases, Holmes defined a new relationship between the power of government and the right to speak. The shift, initially a means of legitimizing government repression, expanded the realm of protected discourse. Doctrinal struggles were waged for the next 30 years over the status, meaning, and implications of the new freedom.

Tests and Standards

The expansion of the right by Justice Holmes enlargd the sphere of free expression by extending its boundary "out" from prior restraint and associating this boundary with dangers and threats to legitimate interests. This was a significant expansion, but there were real limits that remained. These limits, as they are related to the well-being of the state, concern various dangers, the press, and unprotected speech (for example, obscenity). These have been handled through tests that define free expression and determine the standards for prosecution. The historical movement from the clear and present danger doctrine deals first with variants on that test, including bad tendency, imminence of danger, and the "evil discounted by its improbability." These tests vie for interpretive authority, while a general pattern of balanced interests emerges. This becomes the foundation for a more aggressive interpretation of a pure tolerance that moves from the Court to the population generally as the framework for understanding First Amendment rights. The tests are structural elements, and they reveal the values behind this right and their place in a democratic community. The result is a setting in which the interests of the government became associated with limits, while the meaning of the First Amendment was associated with the absence of limits.

Clear and Present Danger. In 1919, in *Schenck v. United States*, the Supreme Court ruled on the extent of congressional power to proscribe speech or advocacy. The case involved members of the Socialist party who had clashed with federal authorities responsible for conducting a draft during World War I. The Socialists had circulated a document alleged to be "intended to cause insubordination and obstruction of the draft" to men called and accepted for military service. A federal prosecution was brought against the Socialists under the Espionage Act of 1917.

Justice Oliver Wendell Holmes, Jr., announced the opinion in the case. Included in that opinion was Holmes's formula, which set the parameters for suppresssion of speech under the Constitution with a vivid metaphor: "The most stringent protection of free speech would not protect a man in falsely shouting fire in a theatre and causing a panic." This picture has defined the relationship between the government and expression by setting the context within which adjudication takes place. As the doctrine emerged in *Schenck:*

> The question in every case is whether the words used are used in such circumstances and are of such a nature as to create a clear and present danger that they will bring about the substantial evils that Congress has a right to prevent.

The boundary for free speech had been expounded, and the courts were given a vision of how to patrol it. A threat to the community or its interests was thus a basis for limiting speech.

Pressure on the Supreme Court to protect expression grew as external threats diminished. In the issue of *The New Republic* dated November 16, 1918, Zechariah Chafee, a law professor, proposed an expanded protection for speech, and the next year, as a result of the article, he was able to present his position directly to Holmes in a private meeting arranged for the express purpose of such an exchange (Ragan,

1971). The view appeared in the dissent by Justices Holmes and Brandeis in *Abrams* v. *United States* (1919), a case that arose under the Sedition Act of 1918. Here the justices took the extent of the threat to national security as a matter for factual determination at trial. In assessing the threat, Holmes and Brandeis looked to the proximity of the danger to legitimate interests and introduced a new realism into adjudication. This was an early step in a continuing process of shift and definition centering around the doctrine of clear and present danger. The leaflets in the *Abrams* case were not found to be a danger to the war effort. The context became the relevant consideration, and the right began to be conditioned by perception of the threat. Similarly, *Frohwerk* v. *United States* (1919) and *Debs* v. *United States* (1919), which were both also decided in the same period and which involved the Espionage Act of 1917, were influenced by the belligerent context in which they arose.

It is possible to distinguish the development of a right from the outcomes of cases when describing doctrinal evolution. The defendants in *Schenck* went to jail, as did those in *Frohwerk*, *Abrams*, and *Debs*. In fact, throughout the first years of the new era (1919-1927), all those whose claims contributed to an expanded right failed to avoid punishment. In *Gitlow* v. *New York* (1925), the defendant was convicted under a criminal anarchy statute for publishing a newspaper, *The Revolutionary Age*. Holmes and Brandeis would have freed Gitlow because they saw no immediate danger. The majority, however, judged the danger sufficient for conviction because they looked to a "tendency" that the newspaper would foment revolution; and consequently, *Gitlow* is associated with the "bad tendency" test. In all these cases, the perceived propensity toward revolution influenced the justices' treatment of the threat, but there was also disagreement on the Court about the measure of proof the Constitution required. In *Whitney* v. *California* (1927), where Charlotte Whitney, a member of the Communist Labor party of California, appealed her conviction to the Supreme Court, Brandeis held that the danger of violence or illegal action should be a matter considered at the trial, but Miss Whitney's conviction was upheld. The same day, in *Fiske* v. *Kansas* (1927), the Court announced that it would uphold a First Amendment claim for the first time. Fiske, an organizer for the Industrial Workers of the World (IWW), was convicted under a Kansas law for soliciting new members and advocating syndicalism. The justices found reliance on statements in the IWW constitution (which urged a struggle between workers and employers) to be insufficient evidence of a danger. Although there were no ringing calls for tolerance, the Supreme Court, for the first time, made freedom of speech really mean something.

The implications of the Holmes-Brandeis formulation are puzzling.

The new doctrine broadened protection, yet it also constrained expression. A boundary was established that shifted from previous restraint to an approach with greater room for expression. The distinction between protected and unprotected speech set the parameters for the constitutional right and remains the key principle in this area of law.

Balancing Tests. The ideological approach has emphasized the similarity among free speech adjudication of subversion cases since World War I. In proceeding this way, tests such as "bad tendency" or "sliding scale" (Funston, 1978:179) are treated as having so much in common with "clear and present danger" as to be minimally distinguishable. The difference between these cases is not a matter of constitutional ideology. Rather it is a difference in the politics of the time and the perceptions of the participants. In these instances, the justices are participants, and they share the popular phobias.

The balance struck between expression and legitimate public concerns by the clear and present danger test was upset by the 1950s hysteria about a red menace. When the conviction of Eugene Dennis and other leaders of the American Communist party was upheld by Judge Learned Hand on the Second Circuit Court of Appeals, the judge referred to "abundant evidence to show that [the defendants] were all engaged in an extensive and concerted action to teach . . . the doctrines of Marxism-Leninism" (*Dennis* v. *United States*, 1951:206). The case set the pattern for treatment of dangerous speech in the post-World War II period. In the Supreme Court, the doctrine presented by Chief Justice Fred Vinson reflected the thinking of Judge Hand. Hand's contribution was a "discounting formula" to elaborate the clear and present danger standard. The emphasis was on the "evil, discounted by its improbability." The result was a version of the clear and present danger test, which was similar in structure to earlier formulations, but weakened in practice by the prevailing paranoia about communism.

After the hysteria had subsided, in *Yates* v. *United States* (1957), the clear and present danger doctrine showed compelling authority. In *Yates*, the Court reversed the convictions of fourteen Communist party officials for conspiring to overthrow the government in violation of the Smith Act. In this case, the justices looked for more than just an abstract doctrine of violent revolution and required the teaching of "concrete action" to justify conviction.

Another decade passed before constitutional tolerance reached full strength in *Brandenburg* v. *Ohio* (1969). The case stemmed from a situation in which a leader of the Ku Klux Klan (KKK) had declared at a rally that ". . . if our President, our Congress, our Supreme Court, continues to suppress the white, Caucasian race, it's possible that there might have to be some vengeance taken." He was convicted for what he said and the

47

highest court of Ohio upheld the conviction, but the American Civil Liberties Union (ACLU) took up the case, and their defense of the KKK epitomized the commitment to a right of free expression without regard to the substance involved. The decision was overturned by the Supreme Court in a short opinion holding to a standard of "incitement to imminent lawless action." The justices made it clear that mere advocacy of violence was not enough to sustain a conviction. Concurrences by Justices Black and Douglas lamented "manipulation" of the clear and present danger doctrine. The result was less a doctrinal shift than a move away from the paranoia of the previous decade and a confident expression that the nation could survive without substantive limits on discourse. For the most part, this confidence withstood the divisiveness that characterized debate over the Vietnam War during the 1960s. The most celebrated case, *United States* v. *Spock* (1969), discussed in the section on subversion, was dismissed at the Court of Appeals level and never got to the Supreme Court.

The historical legacy has broader significance. The confidence in the search for truth that characterized the early right to freedom of expression was becoming associated with ambivalence about any substantive evaluation of speech. This model created from the tradition of constitutional interpretation influenced public perception that the First Amendment prevented critical evaluation of speech. This model is referred to here as "pure tolerance," and upon close examination, its relationship to what has taken place under the Constitution is problematic.

Absolute and Pure Tolerance. Interpretation of clear and present danger has been a pragmatic application of the metaphorical guide concerning "shouting fire in a theatre and causing a panic." Expression needing protection inevitably threatens something, and attention to the threat has always been conditioned by how real it seems. In most free-speech contexts, there is some countervailing value that sets the stage for interpretation. These include concerns about subversive activity, a vigorous press, and a decent society. The interpretation itself has taken different forms within the general framework. The strongest tradition, that is, the one most favorable to expression, has looked for real threats; a weaker stance balances the interests at issue. In each instance, the line is drawn with reference to a structure that juxtaposes other governmental interests against the interest in free and unfettered expression.

An exception to the pragmatic tradition, however, is an "absolutist" or literal interpretation. Although it has seldom commanded a majority of the Court, it reflects the concern for purity. Grounded in the work of Alexander Meikeljohn, who was a major contributor to ideas about free speech between the world wars, its influence on the Court came from the stance of Hugo Black and, to a lesser extent, William O. Douglas. According to Meikeljohn, "the First Amendment to the Constitution, as we all know, forbids the federal Congress to make any law which shall abridge the freedom of speech." He argues that we cannot help but be startled by the absoluteness of the amendment because "That prohibition holds good in war as in peace, in danger as in security . . . the words meant literally what they say" (Meikeljohn, 1948:17). The ACLU believes in this interpretation of free expression and their reading has dominated interpretation in this realm (Emerson, 1970).

This position is associated with toleration and has been explored in Robert Paul Wolff's volume *A Critique of Pure Tolerance* (1968). In his essay, Wolff writes that the virtue of tolerance is an aspect of pluralist democracy. He argues that while traditional liberalism focuses on the relation between the individual and the state, pluralism reflects the reality of corporations, unions, and interest groups which have become ". . . necessary evils in a heterodox society" (see Murphy, 1979). This system integrates the interests in society and plays down their differences. A pure tolerance perspective without any admixture of interests, comes to characterize the modern form of social cohesion. The concept gets its strength from a refusal to make distinctions over the value of speech, as was evident in the ACLU position that Nazis marching in Skokie, Illinois, a predominantly Jewish community, must be protected so that Communists can march where they might otherwise be prohibited. Pure concepts, which are rooted in the politics of interest aggregation, ultimately become ends in themselves. They represent aspirations standing above policy choices, principles from which the polity as a whole can benefit.

The myth of purity developed while distinctions were being made in practice. Alexander Meikeljohn considered issues such as libel, slander, incitement, sedition, and treason as potentially outside the protections of the First Amendment. The position is evident in Justice Black's holding that his absolute position would ". . . not invalidate laws resting upon the premise that where speech is an integral part of an unlawful conduct . . . the speech can be used to illustrate, emphasize and establish the unlawful conduct" (*Konigsberg* v. *State Bar of California*, 1957). Black, like Douglas, did not view allegedly obscene films as he believed that they were protected speech, but he allowed prosecution of libel. Moreover, his speech/action distinction often made him less generous than some of his colleagues were as far as demonstrations were concerned (see *Adderly* v. *Florida*, 1967).

Protection for trade in ideas is strongest where they don't matter, and the pure tolerance basis for protection diminishes the significance of ideas. This is the criticism of the pure tolerance position on free speech, as made by Herbert Marcuse in the essay "Repressive Tolerance (1968)." Marcuse claimed that the objective of tolerance could not be fulfilled under a pure concept in a society with unequal power relations because for pure tolerance to work there has to be a foundation of social equality. The refusal to take sides, he argues, mainly serves to protect the machinery of discrimination since it seems to neutralize opposition and "flatten" discourse. To paraphrase author Philip Roth (1983), who compared countries that do not have this kind of freedom with the United States, it seemed to him that in those countries, "nothing goes and everything matters" while in the United States "everything goes and nothing matters."

A freedom that fosters social agnosticism is at odds with democracy and social cohesion. The school library censorship cases provide an example of this sort of consequence. When books are challenged by outraged parents because they are "un-Christian, anti-Semitic, or racist" (*Board of Education* v. *Pico*, 1982), the response has become a neutral or "pure" freedom to read, rather than a substantive defense of the materials or a discussion of their educational significance. This response may reveal a kind of drift or lack of values, rather than the higher value of tolerance it is sometimes presented as.

In the end, expression has always been subordinate to the interests of society and the state. Even in the most liberal settings, there have been limits to expression in order to preserve the social order. Recognition of this fact of social life is part of the practice of American constitutional politics. Paradoxically, such recognition has been inhibited by contemporary First Amendment scholars, who make up a rather ahistorical and generally intolerant group when it comes to opposing interpretations of what the First Amendment has meant. They believe that the absence of limits on expression is the only thing that it is permissible to be confident about, maybe the only legitimate object of intolerance. The result of this position has been that much political debate has lost its cutting edge. Recognition of the political and social reality of freedom of expression may give expression back its cutting edge and, ultimately, increase its capacity to produce meaningful political and social change.

Limits on Speech and Assembly

Constitutional interpretation starts with cases, and there cannot be a freedom of expression case unless somebody is concerned enough about an activity to proscribe or prosecute those who engage in it. Thus, there has to be speech or assembly, and official action to stop it. The noise has to be too loud or the content too offensive, the movies too risqué or the pamphlets too shocking. People have to be unhappy and/or the government has to be engaged in order for a claim to arise. In this section, we will consider a number of "dangers" that governments in some form or other have sought to repress. They are threats to the government itself, as well as dangerous situations and instances that present a threat because of the institutional setting. We include here issues of subversion and advocacy of revolutionary action, conflicts over public assembly, and concerns that take their meaning from places or contexts where special requirements for conduct are presumed, like outside hospitals or inside prisons.

There have always been efforts to expand the range of freedom of expression as a response to legal limits. The idea that some expression is dangerous replaced the doctrine of no prior restraint, which had been the norm for a long time. The modern idea of speech and assembly that presents dangers is the basis for the new limits on expression. Justice Holmes captured a quality of political authority in his proposition that some threats to some governmental interests need not be tolerated. For Alexander Meikeljohn, "Self government is nonsense unless the self which governs is able and determined to make its will effective." The key to understanding the rights associated with expression therefore lies not in the dynamic of freedom, but in the nature of the limits that delineate freedom in practice. We begin with the most significant of those limits: limits against subversion.

Subversion

Societies exist where there is some agreement on fundamental issues. Any group of people living together must maintain a degree of consensus in order to survive. Although survival might seem assured where dissent is most restricted, liberal societies nonetheless place great weight on the value of open discussion and public discourse because debate and open disagreement are said to be healthy, serving as safety valves. Despite this tradition, there is solid opinion to the effect that government can restrict expression where the existence of the institutions themselves are threatened (Emerson 1970:Ch. 3). Whatever its pretense, it is hard to imagine a government acting in any other way. First Amendment tradition follows these lines: interpretation of the Constitution has been sensitive to diverse opinion tempered by the extent to which it poses a threat.

During the first period in the development of modern free speech doctrine, danger to some legitimate interest became the basis for constitutional prosecution of speech. The interests were internal and external security, and the fears were of subversion. The result was legislation like the Espionage Act of 1917 and the Sedition Act of 1918, which were both aimed at radicals and political activists outside the mainstream. Prosecutions from *Schenck* v. *United States* (1919) to *Whitney* v. *California* (1927) led to constitutional standards for repression and protection from subversion. Although this period followed the disruptions of World War I, immigration, and the social unrest of the early twentieth century, there was still pressure for a pluralist practice, as well as the necessary breathing space for the doctrine to develop.

When Charles Evans Hughes was appointed Chief Justice in 1930, modern practice entered a new phase that lasted until World War II. The most important case during these years may well be *De Jonge* v. *Oregon* (1937). The speaker in *De Jonge* was convicted under the Oregon Criminal Syndicalism law for presiding at a meeting of the Communist party because "the CP" was viewed as advocating political violence and revolution. In 1937, the Court was willing to overturn De Jonge's conviction since the meeting at which he appeared was peaceful. According to Chief Justice Hughes, laws must deal with particular abuses because of "the need to preserve inviolate the Constitutional rights of free speech..." (*De Jonge*, 1937:364-365). Hughes did not explicitly invoke clear and present danger, but he extended protection to speech that did not involve "incitement" to violence.

The first peacetime sedition law passed since the Alien and Sedition Acts of 1798 was the Alien Registration Act of 1940, known as the "Smith Act." This legislation was a source of federal prosecutions for the next 20 years and set the pattern for the constitutional practice that developed. Section 2 of the act, dealing with advocacy, conspiracy, and membership, aroused the most controversy. These provisions made it illegal for any person to advocate the overthrow of the government by force, hold membership in any group dedicated to such purposes, and print or disseminate written matter advocating such overthrow. As Emerson noted, however, "whatever problems of internal security may have been in 1940, they did not arise from any public advocacy that the government be overthrown by force or violence" (Emerson, 1970:111). This was an earlier practice no longer in vogue. The act was invoked twice during World War II against Socialists (*Dunne* v. *U.S.*, 1943) and against pro-Nazis, but it did not get a hearing in the Supreme Court until the *Dennis* case in 1951.

The *Dennis* case shows how a focus on constitutional politics may distract from an investigation into the ideological authority of the Constitution. The political fact is that the conviction of Dennis was upheld; the ideological fact is the frame for evaluating government efforts to protect against subversion. In *Dennis*, the Court is said to have "bridged the gap" between the clear and present danger standard and the fact that there was not demonstrable danger (Grossman and Wells, 1980:1226). It was a balancing act. The justices were inclined to uphold the convictions of Communists during the Cold War. But to focus on outcomes and judicial motivation is to turn away from the expectations carried in the Constitution. The outcome, or the choice by a justice of the argument on one side or the other, is not determined by the Constitution, not in the case at hand. In the symbolic environment of the Constitution, there is a different frame and a language of rights that produces cases like *Dennis*. In this case, the governing principle was the standard that evaluated the right of expression in terms of the danger it posed. The Constitution is responsible for the case being considered, not the outcome in a particular instance; the right to free expression helps explain why the government must tolerate some challenge to its existence.

Loyalty oaths and employment in sensitive jobs were two of the subversion-related areas governed by the right to free expression in the Vietnam era. During this period and under the authority of the justices of the Warren Court, some of the internal security legislation of the Cold War was declared unconstitutional. For example, loyalty oaths were declared unconstitutional in *Keyishian* v. *Board of Regents* (1967) when they were no longer considered useful. And in *United States* v. *Robel* (1967), the justices turned to the freedom of association guaranteed by the First Amendment to protect the right of a member of the Communist party to work in a defense plant. This may have been the height of actual sensitivity to free expression. Subsequent references to the limitations on the "war power" discussed in this opinion have more often come in dissent (*Rostker* v. *Goldberg*, 1981). While it may have surprised ordinary observers, the Warren Court's concern in the area of subversive activities was in the grand tradition of the modern right to free expression.

Few of the celebrated draft cases of the 1960s reached the Supreme Court, but the doctrinal stance was evident in the lower courts. Wartime dissent is sometimes thought to involve external rather than internal security. It reached a particularly high level over Vietnam, and the "danger" it posed was a matter of contention at the time. In *United States* v. *Spock*, five leading opponents of the Vietnam War, including pediatrician Benjamin Spock, were indicted for conspiracy to "counsel, aid and abet . . . Selective Service registrants to evade the draft" (*Spock*, 1969:192). The convictions of these anti-war activists were dismissed by the Court of Appeals for insufficient evidence of intent to participate in an illegal conspiracy. The government did not appeal to the Supreme Court, fearing, perhaps, the embarrassment of an adverse ruling at that level.

Threats to Public Order

The American Nazi party and other groups outside the mainstream continue to make some of the most dramatic "contributions" to the right to assemble. In 1978 and 1979, the American Nazis planned to march through Skokie, Illinois, a predominantly Jewish suburb of Chicago, where 7,000 of the residents had been confined in Nazi concentration camps during World War II. The march involved not only an affront to the residents, but the threat of violent retaliation. The situation became a rallying point for the American Civil Liberties Union in their campaign to foster pure tolerance. The conflict was described by David Goldberger who represented the Nazis for the ACLU:

> The case began when the nazis [sic] scattered requests to several Chicago suburbs seeking permits to hold a rally in their towns.... Many of the towns that received the nazis' request just ignored it. Skokie did not. Skokie responded by obtaining a court order banning the rally.... The nazis asked us to defend their right to hold the rally, and to challenge one of the laws prohibiting it. Though I detested their beliefs, I went into court to defend the First Amendment.

The complex, but classic, issues in the Skokie case require further discussion of the right to assemble in order to fully understand this kind of confrontation.

Less litigated on its own and owing much to the "general" freedom of expression, assembly is one of the situations in which the dangers or threats to public order arise. It has come to include not only the right to gather but also the right to associate for political purposes (Abernathy, 1981). A modern encounter with the freedom to assemble and the issues surrounding it came before the Supreme Court in *Hague* v. *Congress of Industrial Organizations* (CIO) in 1939. In that case, Jersey City had prohibited assemblies in the streets, parks, or public buildings without a permit. When the mayor denied the CIO permission for a rally because he considered it a Communist organization, the labor union challenged the decision and was successful. Justice Roberts ruled that streets and parks have been "held in trust for the use of the public" and that their use may be regulated, but it may not be abridged or denied in the guise of regulation (Pritchett, 1979:317).

In practice, assembly that is viewed as a threat is a micro example of the expression conflict since it is usually applied in terms of the "time, place, and manner" limitations that local officials handle in the conduct of local affairs. Official concern has been about such things as keeping the streets open for travel and preserving the peace and order of the community. Like the other rights to free expression guaranteed by the First Amendment, the right to assemble has tension built into it. Governments can regulate assembly, but the constitutionality of any regulation depends on respect for free expression. In *Cox* v. *New Hampshire* (1941), the Supreme Court upheld conviction of Jehovah's Witnesses who had marched without getting a permit. Nearly three decades later, in *Shuttlesworth* v. *Birmingham* (1969), the justices announced that a procedure for acquiring a permit cannot delegate so much power to public officials that they are able to base their decision on the content of the expression or the purpose of the assembly. Moreover, the actions of public officials are subject to review when they may be discriminatory (*Niemotko* v. *Maryland*, 1951). Content and purpose were fused in a case accepted by the Supreme Court in 1983 (*Watt* v. *Community for Creative Nonviolence*). The case was on appeal from a District of Columbia circuit ruling that demonstrators had a right to sleep in tents in Lafayette Park across the street from the White House as a way of dramatizing the plight of Washington's homeless people. Federal regulations against camping in downtown Washington had been interpreted by the National Park Service to prohibit sleeping in the park, but the appeals court ruled against the government because sleeping out was part of the message that the demonstrators had a First Amendment right to communicate.

A power of local officials is their authority over certain types of public areas or buildings, and therefore their power to proscribe demonstrations in these areas or buildings. Justice Hugo Black, a champion of free expression for speech and writing alone, allowed governments broad regulatory powers where action and conduct were involved. The Court has generally held that "public passages" can be kept open (*Cameron* v. *Johnson*, 1965), noisy demonstrations outside schools proscribed (*Grayned* v. *Rockford*, 1972), the tranquility of federal courts preserved (*Cox* v. *Louisiana*, 1965), and the grounds of a county jail closed to demonstrations (*Adderley* v. *Florida*, 1966). Each of these cases set limits on expression in public places. In 1983, in *United States* v. *Grace*, with only Justice John Paul Stevens dissenting, the Court ruled that the First Amendment gives people the right to picket or distribute leaflets on the public sidewalks surrounding the Supreme Court building. The justices invalidated part of a federal law to open up the public sidewalks around their building. They did not extend the right further than the walkways.

Some of the most difficult "assembly" issues involve quasi-public property, like shopping centers, and run into the next section, which is on institutional situations. The presumption has been that purely private property is not open to public demonstrations. However, in *Logan Valley Plaza* (1968), the Court upheld the right of a labor union to picket a store in a shopping center because there did not seem to be any other way to convey the facts of a labor dispute to the public. The justices relied on a

1946 precedent (*Marsh* v. *Alabama*), where a right to distribute religious literature in a "company" town had been upheld. Eight years later, the other side of the clash between property rights and expression carried the judicial day. In another shopping center case (*Hudgens* v. *National Labor Relations Board*, 1976), the justices nearly overruled *Logan Valley Plaza* by allowing the owners to refuse admission to picketers on the basis of the right to use one's property in support of one's own interests. The Labor Board, however, retained the authority to compel shopping center owners to let picketers in.

In a related case, *Pruneyard Shopping Center* v. *Robins* (1980), the justices of the United States Supreme Court had the opportunity to rule on whether the California Constitution violated that of the United States. The case was somewhat unusual due to this confrontation of constitutional values, but the considerations and the results were well within the traditions of the First Amendment, as well as those of the Fifth Amendment protecting property (see Chapter 5), and of state/federal constitutional relations. The shopping center owner had appealed from a judgment of the California Supreme Court holding that the California Constitution protects speech and petitioning, exercised in a reasonable way, in privately owned shopping centers. The decision by Justice Rehnquist held that the ruling did not deny owners rights under the Fifth Amendment or the free speech rights associated with the ownership of property and alluded to in *Hudgens*. Thus, the decision on the California Constitution was sustained.

In some situations, the act of assembly is said to threaten public order in forms such as use of the streets, public functions, private property, or transportation. Thus, although the local courts in the *Skokie* case issued an order to stop the Nazi march, the appellate court responded with a "stay" of that order. The Supreme Court upheld the right to march on June 15, 1977; the authoritative holding was that action by the city of Skokie had abridged constitutional safeguards. This struggle can only be understood in terms of a commitment to pure tolerance outside of ordinary practice and different from conventional discourse.

Institutional Threats

The previous context presented issues where protest threatened public peace or private rights. The present discussion examines the rights of individuals in an institutional setting. Schools, prisons, public agencies, and union shops have all been subject to free speech litigation. Expression in each case is dependent on the nature of the institution and how its prerogatives are viewed.

When the state governments began providing public education in the nineteenth century, the First Amendment right to expression was applied to the schools. In *Meyer* v. *Nebraska* (1923), the Court ruled that wartime legislation from Nebraska that forbade the teaching of German in schools was unconstitutional. The issue centered around the right to teach this subject as a protected "liberty." Two years later, the justices invalidated a Ku Klux Klan-backed state law that prohibited students from attending private (thus parochial) schools (*Pierce* v. *Society of Sisters*, 1925). The Court based this action on a "property right" to choose a particular form of education (Pritchett, 1979:301). The case is closely associated with freedom in an institutional environment. Thus, both liberty and property rights have contributed to freedom of expression, suggesting corollary interests relevant to how this right is shaped. Moreover, because institutions place special requirements on individuals, matters of conscience often arise in these contexts. For example, compulsory flag salute was invalidated in 1943 (*West Virginia State Board of Education* v. *Barnette*) after such a challenge.

In the 1950s, of course, the perception that there were Communists everywhere was the popular basis for assessing the danger of expression in institutions. The Taft-Hartley Act, the nation's major postwar labor legislation, required a union member to file an affidavit stating that he was not a member of the Communist party. In 1950 (*American Communications Assn.* v. *Douds*), the Supreme Court ruled that the act simply kept those whose beliefs were deemed dangerous from holding office in labor unions. Ten years later (*Konigsberg* v. *State Bar of California*, 1957; *In re Anastaplo*, 1961), the justices focused on the refusal to answer questions which had been a basis for denial of admission to the bar in California in the first instance and in Illinois in the second case. Professional groups have been permitted to impose a higher standard of conduct than might be appropriate in other contexts, yet they have not been granted unlimited latitude.

In schools, free speech has traditionally been balanced against authority over the educational process. Free speech, like due process and equal protection, has been closely associated with the educational setting, but arguably it is uniquely free speech that is "vital" to the contest between views that characterizes the educational enterprise at its best (*Keyishian* v. *Board of Regents*, 1967). The application of the right involved the authority of administration over teaching personnel, as in issues of loyalty oaths, and it involved the authority of administration over student expression. In *Tinker* v. *Des Moines School District* (1969), students had been suspended for wearing black armbands as a protest against the Vietnam War after school officials had forbidden the gesture. The controversy focused on the extent to which official authority had been compromised by the violation of the administrative ban on the armbands. The justices ruled that the authorities in Des Moines had expected too much and reminded them that "state operated schools may not be enclaves of totalitarianism." The Court ruled that preventing a disturbance was not a strong enough foundation to justify suspension and laced the opinion with exhortations to the effect that "It can hardly be argued that either students or teachers shed their constitutional rights to freedom of speech or expression at the schoolhouse gate."

While *Tinker* involved issues of expression versus order in the institution, another body of litigation deals with institutional authority over the curriculum. Like the maintenance of order, institutional decisions over what is to be part of the education process do not usually become clashes over constitutional rights. There are exceptions, however, such as evolution, sex education, and what literature is available in the school library. Following five years of cases in the lower courts, the Supreme Court took up *Island Trees* v. *Pico* (1982) and gave a reading of how the First Amendment applied to this context. In a plurality opinion, Justice William Brennan commented on the limits a school board faced regarding library books that Brennan said would preclude removal simply because the board disapproved of the political ideas or philosophies expressed in the books. Dissenting justices disputed intervention of the courts in this area. Here, we have become used to joining the judicial review and the constitutional rights issue. But the fact is that whether the judiciary becomes involved or not, there is a tradition, under the First Amendment, which should inhibit school boards from overt suppression of political ideas.

Another institutional context is the workplace. Here, a number of conditions and conventions limit individual freedom of expression. These limits are ultimately evaluated by the courts. In 1976, the Supreme Court ruled that even though a union had been designated the exclusive bargaining agent for a group of schoolteachers, this did not bar a union member from giving the employer his own views on upcoming labor negotiations (*Madison School District* v. *Wisconsin Employee Relations Comm.*, 1976). The Court held that, at a bargaining session about wages, a teacher as a union member could not speak directly to the school board as his employer but must allow the union to speak for him, because that arrangement was required by a federal labor law. But the teacher, as a citizen of the town, could speak directly to the school board, as elected officials, at a public meeting called by the board so that it could listen to community sentiments. The teacher was not only a union member bound to obey his union but a citizen entitled to speak to his elected representatives at a public meeting. Here, the context of a public hearing was taken into account, although another arrangement—collective bargaining—presented a challenge to conventional arrangements. Justice

Thurgood Marshall, in a concurrence, pointed out that had this been a collective bargaining session, no such tolerance of expression need have been provided.

Like society as a whole, institutions have particular values and conventional modes of operating. In some cases, as with schools, institutional purposes should enhance freedom of expression. In most cases, however, the prerogatives of an institution limit the amount of expression that is constitutionally protected. This has been a structural dimension of this right.

Unprotected Expression

The prevailing interpretation of the First Amendment views some speech as unprotected because of its substantive content—where society determines that content to be offensive. Its classic expression came in the middle of this century, midway through the development of the modern doctrine on freedom of expression in *Chaplinsky* v. *New Hampshire* (1942). The majority opinion, written by Justice Frank Murphy, the Court's most consistent civil libertarian, found that "certain well-defined and narrowly limited classes of speech" had never raised constitutional problems. For these forms of speech, prevention and punishment had been assumed. They included ". . . the lewd and obscene, the profane, the libelous and the insulting or 'fighting words'. . . ." Justice Murphy reasoned that these "utterances" are neither essential to any "exposition of ideas" nor a "step to truth." Any benefit they might have was outweighed by society's interest in preventing the evils associated with these forms of speech. From this judicial proclamation, this insight into the clash of social values, a distinction has developed that is clear in its outlines, but ambiguous in its details.

The kind of unprotected speech that sparked the controversy in *Chaplinsky*, "fighting words," is the least litigated, although the relevance of the clear and present danger framework is obvious. The initial case involved the Jehovah's Witnesses. A witness by the name of Chaplinsky had been proselytizing in a New Hampshire town and was being taken to the police station for causing a disturbance when he called a town official "a goddamned racketeer" and "a damned Fascist." Mr. Chaplinsky was prosecuted for the references, and conviction was upheld by the Supreme Court. This case identified the category "fighting words." Some of the subsequent cases, like *Terminiello* v. *Chicago* (1949), where a riot really did occur, held the speaker responsible, but more often it has been the audience or the authorities who are expected to keep order in the face of public expression (*Feiner* v. *New York*, 1951). As a matter of constitutional interpretation, "fighting words" have been subsumed within the more general contextual issues surrounding regulation of the time, place, and manner of expression.

Libel has received more attention than "fighting words" throughout the 40 years in which unprotected speech has been considered. Its common law roots exemplify how cross-cutting areas of law create the conflicts that develop the interpretation of the Constitution. This area has been closely associated with press freedoms, where standards for protecting public reputation have been developed that are consistent with the expectation of a free press. "The libelous" will be examined in that context.

Commercial speech has been another area of unprotected expression. At the same time as the *Chaplinsky* case, there was an attempt to bring a commercial handbill under the protection of the First Amendment. The failure gave rise to the concept that the Constitution did not protect "commercial speech." The idea was developed in *Pittsburgh Press Co. v. Pittsburgh Commission on Human Relations* (1973), where newspapers were prohibited from making sex designations in their help wanted column. The Court held that the legislative prohibition did not intrude into protected expression. The problem of commercial speech is that, as part of commerce, it is already more highly regulated than other forms of discourse. It is in this context that a ban on liquor advertising in Oklahoma motivated a cable TV company to appeal to the Supreme Court (*Capital Cities Cable v. Crisp*, 1983). The state had authority over what could be aired on TV, but the introduction of cable systems presented new challenges.

Although there is generally a presumption that commercial speech is expression without political content, the courts have acknowledged such content in certain cases. This was the holding when a newspaper published an ad for abortion services in New York. The publication was allowed because of the political content of the ad. Recent developments have given pharmacists and lawyers the right to advertise under the First Amendment, where restrictions imposed by professional and trade associations had formerly limited free expression. Commercial speech is explicitly protected by these contexts, but that protection is limited and does not apply, for instance, to false and misleading advertising.

Obscenity has been the most fully litigated of the unprotected areas and deserves special attention for that reason alone, but it is also conceptually challenging. It represents the clash between tolerance of expression and the values of a community. The following discussion traces the evolution of a modern doctrine, explores the issue of things considered bad in themselves, and concludes with a discussion of the prospects for a response to obscenity consistent with First Amendment doctrine.

Obscenity

Americans have known limits to expression from colonial times. They had fled persecution but were not themselves a particularly tolerant group. Yet, the colonial leadership faced few challenges to their moral and political authority. It was only as the society diversified that such challenges to morality became an issue. Thus, the first United States obscenity case, *Commonwealth* v. *Holmes* (1821), involved a Massachusetts prosecution of John Cleland's *Memoirs of a Woman of Pleasure* (*Fanny Hill*), a perennial subject of litigation.

Legislative responses and subsequent prosecution increased dramatically in the mid to late nineteenth century due to a more restrictive moral climate and the crusading spirit of moralists such as Anthony Comstock. In the 1890s, prosecutions intensified with publication of a new brand of fiction epitomized by George Bernard Shaw's *Mrs. Warren's Profession* and Theodore Dreiser's *The Genius* (F. Lewis, 1975). The works were frank, and they explicitly examined sexual, as well as moral conduct. While prosecutions were brought on substantive grounds delineating offensiveness, the defense could not yet turn to the pure tolerance of the First Amendment for protection.

Until the middle of the twentieth century, the judicial standard for determining obscenity was the *Hicklin* rule (*Regina* v. *Hicklin*, 1868), which asked whether the material at issue tended to deprave and corrupt the minds of those most open to such influences. This was obviously not a standard that encouraged a wide range of expression. As social diversity in the United States increased the pressure for a more tolerant standard, Judge Learned Hand suggested dropping the *Hicklin* rule as a throwback to Victorian morality (*United States* v. *Kennerley*, 1913). But the influence of this extraordinary judge did not become evident in the higher federal courts for another two decades, when in 1934, a U.S. Court of Appeals substituted for *Hicklin* a concern for "obscenity as the dominant effect" (*United States* v. *Ulysses*, 1934), and the Supreme Court began to drift toward a more generous standard. The obscenity question was first raised before the Supreme Court in *Doubleday* v. *New York* (1948). In this case, the justices were equally divided on the applicability of First Amendment protections. The result of the case was an affirmance of a conviction under a New York obscenity statute for "The Princess with the Golden Hair" from *Memoirs of Hecate County* by Edmund Wilson. This left the obscenity question outside the limits of the First Amendment until 1957. As the reach of constitutional tolerance broadened generally, attention turned to a new standard for distinguishing protected from unprotected expression in the obscenity area.

The *Roth* Test. The constitutional foundation for freedom of expression in this area was established in *Roth* v. *United States* (1957). Roth had a business in New York that published books, photographs, and magazines that federal agents claimed violated the federal obscenity statute. He was accused of publishing ". . . obscene, lewd, lascivious, or filthy book(s) . . . or other publications of an indecent character" (18 U.S. Code 1461). Judge Jerome Frank, one of the dominant legal theorists of his time, writing for the lower court, asked for help from the Supreme Court in setting a standard. When the case was decided, Justice William Brennan, who would speak for the Court for nearly a decade on these matters, wrote the opinion. The logic of his decision and the specific tests he offered established the framework for subsequent discourse about pornography.

Starting where *Chaplinsky* left off, Brennan depicted a history of limited freedom evident in laws against blasphemy or profanity in nearly all of the original states. He noted that it was a crime in the Massachusetts Bay Colony to publish any filthy, obscene, or profane song, pamphlet, libel, or mock sermon in imitation or mimicking of religious services. Brennan's argument was that obscenity "is not within the area of constitutionally protected speech." He defined the obscene as that which involved those lascivious longings associated with a perverse interest in sex rather than a "healthy" predisposition. He believed the obscene was "that form of immorality which has relation to sexual impurity and a tendency to excite lustful thoughts," a subclass of material on sex that offended common decency.

Brennan's second contribution was the construction of a test to safeguard legitimate expression from intrusion by the government. The test would be used by juries in determining the violation of statutes and by legislatures in writing laws on pornography. The new test would look to the average person, rather than the most susceptible (as had been the case under *Hicklin*), and it would apply standards consistent with how the community would assess the material. Which community would be defined later. Prurient interest would be revealed by a tendency to excite lustful thoughts, and it would be considered unprotected speech. According to Brennan's test, the material would have to be taken as a whole, rather than focusing on the most sexually stimulating part. Juries would be the obscenity filter, in lieu of an explicit definition of material not protected by the First Amendment. In each case, the jury would determine what was obscene.

Justices Black and Douglas dissented in *Roth*. They felt that the new standard punished thought that was protected by the First Amendment even though it was offensive. Douglas argued that erotic thoughts were normal, and as a condition for placing the expression that stimulated them outside the protection of the First Amendment, he wanted to be shown that obscene material would cause illegal conduct such as rape. He looked to social research for a connection between sexual arousal and delinquency, although the search was somewhat facetious since he obviously doubted that evidence for the connection existed. This was the beginning of an ongoing debate that is as lively today as it was 25 years ago. The problem is that there are a lot more individuals who get "turned on" than commit sex crimes. For Douglas and Black, the protection of the First Amendment was all the more important when ideas were offensive to the community.

For the majority in *Roth*, all ideas having even the slightest redeeming social importance deserved the full protection of the First Amendment. But obscenity was, by definition, "utterly without redeeming social importance." This became a criterion in *Jacobellis* v. *Ohio* (1964), a case famous for Justice Potter Stewart's claim that although he was unable to define obscenity, he knew it when he saw it. Brennan's argument in *Jacobellis* made the definitional issue a matter of constitutional law. Since only material utterly without redeeming social importance was excluded from constitutional protection (*Jacobellis*, 1964:188), it followed, according to the justice, ". . . that material dealing with sex in a manner that advocates ideas, or that has literary or scientific or artistic value . . . may not be branded as obscenity and denied constitutional protection" (*Jacobellis*, 1964:191). What started out in *Roth* as a premise in Brennan's argument regarding the nature of obscenity had become a test.

The next major case again involved *Fanny Hill*. This piece of early erotica had been banned from Massachusetts. The publishers, anxious to advance the cause of the First Amendment and to sell their book, brought the case to the Supreme Court in *Memoirs* v. *Massachusetts* (1966). The social value claim was the major issue at the trial. Distinguished scholars testified that the book was a minor "work of art" and had "literary merit" and "historical value." The Supreme Court overturned the lower court decision that had found the book to be obscene. It restated *Roth* by requiring that for a book to be considered obscene, the dominant theme of the material taken as a whole had to appeal to a prurient interest in sex, the material had to be patently offensive because it affronted contemporary community standards relating to description or representation of sexual matters, and the material had to be utterly without redeeming social value. The new tests were to be considered separately, and the challenged material had to fail all three tests to be considered obscene. This standard made the earlier distinction a challenge to prosecutors who could be thwarted in their prosecution of obscenity by the existence of even the slightest redeeming "value" in the material under consideration.

The opinion in *Fanny Hill*, perhaps the most vivid example of the relativism coming from the Supreme Court at mid-century, elicited a vigorous dissent from Justice Tom Clark. Clark indicated that his decisive support in *Roth* came because he believed that the test announced in that case did not contain an "utterly without social value" criterion. He reminded his colleagues that the *Roth* opinion even suggested weighing social value against obscenity, and thereby acknowledged that obscene material might have some social value. His concern is evident in a strong commitment to standards of morality. Unmoved by the tolerance of his brethren, he found *Fanny Hill* "dirty" and without social relevance. Clark would not accept the emerging view that sexually stimulating material deserved protection if it was elegant.

The Contemporary Standard. A change in personnel on the Supreme Court between 1968 and 1972 resulted in a new majority that became a significant influence on obscenity law. Nixon appointees Warren Burger, Harry Blackmun, William Rehnquist, and Lewis Powell joined in announcing a new standard in *Miller* v. *California* (1973) and *Paris Adult Theatre* v. *Slaton* (1973). *Miller* involved the application of a state obscenity statute to a mass mailing of sexually explicit advertising material to unwilling recipients. Burger's opinion announced that ". . . we are called to define the standards which must be used to identify obscene material that a State may regulate without infringing the First Amendment. . . ." Emphasizing that some forms of expression are clearly outside the First Amendment, he argued that the *Memoirs* Test had been a shift from *Roth*. This step, according to the Chief Justice, required that the prosecution prove a negative, the utter lack of redeeming social value. In a criminal case, the "beyond a reasonable doubt" standard made this a formidable challenge. To ease the prosecutorial burden, Burger substituted a new standard: pornographic material had to be specifically defined by state law as appealing to the prurient interest, it had to be patently offensive, and it had to lack serious literary, artistic, political, or scientific value.

In the companion case of *Paris Adult Theatre* v. *Slaton* (1973), the Court ruled that the state interest in regulating obscenity was protected even where the movie house had guarded against exposure of juveniles and passers-by. In other words, the quality of life, the "tone of commerce in the great city centers," and the public safety were legitimate objects of regulation. The justices concluded that it is not for the Court to resolve empirical uncertainties in the relation between obscenity and illegal action. Public perception of offensiveness would be an acceptable rationale for legislation. By turning the authority to the state level, the Court sent chills through the publishing community.

The meaning of community standards has been developed further by the Supreme Court. The post-*Miller* decisions give some idea of what the Court had in mind. In *Southeastern Promotions* v. *Conrad* (1975), for instance, the Court held that the play *Hair* could be performed in a municipal theater even if town authorities found that it was not a "clean and healthful" production. Although jurors do not have unbridled discretion—the movie *Carnal Knowledge* could not be banned in Georgia, for instance (*Jenkins* v. *Georgia*, 1974)—they are the relevant community—rather than the state or the nation as a whole—for determining what is obscene.

The Law and Limits

The study of constitutional rights benefits from an occasional probe into the values behind the rights. In the case of unprotected expression, there are countervailing values that place the expression outside the scope of the First Amendment. The public peace is protected from incitement to riot. The value of reputation and, again, the public peace both justify traditional exclusion of libel from protection. In the case of obscenity, there are many claims, but there is no general agreement on the reasons why obscene expression is unprotected. This section looks at those claims. It also examines the feminist anti-pornography movement and constitutional responses to pornography.

Offensiveness. In the middle of this century, civil libertarians portrayed the censor as an ignorant vice squad goon ripping old masters off the museum wall or as a Victorian moralist gluing the pages of literary classics together. Although the characterization is extreme, efforts to eliminate obscene material from public life have been clumsy. The unsophistication of the censors joined with a rhetoric of individualism gave increased stature to the civil libertarian position. By the 1960s, the censors appeared to have been beaten, and a high level of pornographic freedom prevailed in the land. Recently, interest in limits on expression has returned. When the "courageous" publisher of civil libertarian mythology was Larry Flynt of *Hustler* magazine and his "expression" a naked woman being put through a meat grinder, an industry that had flourished under protection by the Supreme Court appeared to be out of control.

A movement to outlaw pornography to guard against crimes of violence is of long standing. The claim is that pornography depraves the minds of those exposed to it, leading to harmful sexual conduct. Justice William Douglas called for evidence of such a connection as early as *Roth.* Yet, it has been difficult to establish. Social science doesn't seem up to this task, and the legality of pornography is not likely to be settled by statistical evidence. The existence of social limits on expression *per se* is a much more significant consideration, and one that deserves attention.

Of the six reasons offered by constitutional scholar Gerald Gunther for the regulation of obscenity (Gunther, 1982), five do not depend on incitement to violent action but stem from the view that obscenity is bad in and of itself. These include protecting moral standards against erosion, improving the "quality of life," improving the "community environment," preventing corruption of individual morals, and protecting against affronts to the senses. Offenses against morality and decency traditionally constitute a category of crime distinct from crimes against persons or property. This is misleading. Murder and statutory rape are illegal because society deems them wrong. Labeling moral offenses in which the participants consent "victimless" mistakenly makes individuals rather than society the basis of criminality. The concern for social morality has a natural place in the criminal law (Devlin, 1965; Brigham, 1980).

The claim that obscenity is inherently offensive requires conceptual clarification. Chief Justice Warren Burger's opinion in *Miller* offered some assistance. He viewed pornography as the subclass of obscenity that dealt with sex. Obscenity, the larger classification, was defined as material that is shocking and has no place in public discourse. It constitutes not simply a matter of intrusion but rather a violation of truths. D. H. Lawrence, himself a target of the censor, was quoted by Justice Felix Frankfurter as having said:

> ... genuine pornography is almost always underworld, it doesn't come out into the open ... you can recognize it by the insult if offers invariably to sex, and to the human spirit. (*Kingsley International Pictures v. Regents of the University of New York,* 1959)

This insult, like most of the reasons obscenity is attacked, reflects interest in preserving fundamental social values.

The obscene arguably includes more than sexual subjects, such as extreme violence, but sex has presented the weakest claims for protection. The new political significance of sexuality may change the views of what is protected discourse since sex and sexual deviance have become core issues in important social movements. Traditionally, the privatization of sex and the embarrassment that resulted fed into the presumption that sexually explicit and stimulating material did not have to be protected. But attitudes toward sex and sexuality have changed. The politics of sex was dramatically elevated by the work of Sigmund Freud. He called attention to the importance of sex in society and associated it with everything from bed-wetting to war. Sex has become a defining criterion in issues that stem from role differences. Housework has had a political dimension at least since the 1970s, and employment is now a sphere of sexual politics. Sex is also political as a defining criterion of life styles, such as homosexuality, that are the source of political interests. Since political discourse includes the sexual, it no longer makes sense to treat sex as a simply private matter.

Although violence may not be convincingly associated with pornography, porn is related to sexual excitement by definition. Treatment of any subject that has stimulation as its purpose, not just sex, has raised judicial eyebrows. Violence has gotten increasing attention where it appears to be a source of sexual excitement. Gloria Steinem (1978) addressed the issue in her distinction between erotica and pornography. She showed how pornography had been associated with prostitution since its Greek origins, and how it has domination and violence at its core. Since most pornography uses women as its subject, women are the objects of the violence, giving pornography a misogynous quality. As a source of sexual excitement, Steinem distinguishes pornography from erotica, which she ties to love, mutual affection, and the absence of domination and violence. This places choice and shared pleasure in the center of the erotic appeal, which would necessarily involve a degree of objectification, but not only of women for male pleasure. *Fanny Hill* is a good example of an erotic novel because it conveys excitement through poetic and metaphoric images. Its harsh treatment in American law on a number of occasions is testimony to the fact that the justices have never distinguished between erotica and pornography. Yet, it is pornography that best fits the definition of obscenity. The glorification of violence and aggression for the purpose of creating sexual excitement is of legitimate concern. In any case, violence is the absence of politics, and such material lacks the characteristics of discourse protected by the First Amendment.

Limiting Pornography. The prevalent "pure tolerance" view of the First Amendment has fostered the idea that limits on expression are both wrong and unusual. The truth is otherwise. Americans have set numerous limits on expression, and there are many ways to legally limit pornography. Most anti-pornography activity has focused on social, economic, and political responses, such as impolite questions, consumer boycotts, picketing, and civil disobedience. These efforts have, in many instances, been effective. An advertisement in the late 1970s for an album by the Rolling Stones, which showed a woman bound in a chair with the caption "I'm black and blue for the rolling Stones and I love it," was taken down only hours after a protest was announced. This action spawned the feminist anti-pornography movement. A few years later, Wendy Kaminer addressed the legal issues in an article entitled "A Woman's Guide to Pornography and the Law" (1980). She claimed that the First Amendment could be preserved only by refusing to involve the government in censorship.

Any group that fails to enlist the aid of the government, however, is at a disadvantage. Political action is less enduring than law, and use of law to set standards of acceptable conduct is basic to the Western tradition. Yet feminist suggestions for legal action have been rare. Robin Morgan, in one of these instances, mentioned invoking a clear and present danger claim and using local ordinances to zone out porn shops and restrict advertising. The clear and present danger standard made the effort to separate protected from unprotected speech the characteristic distinction in constitutional adjudication. This "two level" approach was generally criticized by academics (Kalven, 1960). But, more recently, Frederick Schauer (1979) described the distinction as isolating some material in order to safeguard speech more central to the First Amendment's purpose. Given the difficulty in proving that illegal action stems from pornography, the argument that pornography is inherently offensive and unprotected is more consistent with the constitutional tradition.

The *Miller* standard distinguished protected from unprotected expression by emphasizing community-based offensiveness, with a focus on hard-core pornography. The standard view is that this means "ultimate sexual acts, masturbation, excretory functions, and lewd exhibition" (*Miller* v. *California*, 1973). Violence is not discussed, although sadomasochism would be included in some definitions. Exposure is the "core," but the structure of First Amendment law would not substantially change if there were a shift from exposure to violence and domination as central to the obscene. This redefinition is a first step toward incorporating into law contemporary concerns about the misogynous aspects of pornography.

Regulation short of prosecution is another avenue. An early suggestion along these lines was Justice William Brennan's 1973 dissent in the *Paris* case, where he shifted his focus to when material can be regulated. Based on *Ginzburg* v. *U.S.* (1966), where a conviction was upheld because of the manner in which erotic literature was distributed, Brennan derived the notion that the acceptability of material may depend upon the context of its dissemination. He also found, in *Stanley* v. *Georgia* (1969), where private possession of films showing "orgies of seduction, sodomy, and sexual intercourse" was constitutionally protected, a state interest in protecting children and unconsenting adults on a different basis from the general (or consenting) population. This was ultimately a move away from criminality toward other limitations on objectionable material. In *Erznoznik* v. *City of Jacksonville* (1975), however, the Court did strike down an attempt under nuisance law to protect citizens from nude scenes at drive-in theaters. Nonetheless, stricter limits may be possible where there is no threat of prosecution. Zoning restrictions can also reflect community preferences. In *Young* v. *American Mini Theatres* (1976), the Court upheld a zoning ordinance that restricted the location of adult movies and bookstores without finding whether the material sold was constitutionally "obscene."

Justice John Paul Stevens has contributed to these developments. He supports civil restraints rather than criminal prosecution of obscenity. In his dissent in *Smith* v. *United States* (1977), Stevens argued that a jury determination of standards is not consistent with predictable application of the rule of law. Thus, civil limitations would certainly apply to the obscene but might also be applicable to non-obscene yet offensive displays. Avoidance of free expression concerns almost entirely in *New York State Liquor Authority* v. *Bellanca* (1981), in which public health regulation was relied on to control the environment in which alcohol was served, did not meet Justice Stevens's approval. Dissenting from a short (*per curiam*) decision in the case, Stevens believed the Court had obscured the issue ". . . with irrelevancies such as its mischievous suggestion that the Twenty-First Amendment gives States power to censor free expression in places where liquor is served." He called for the censorship issue to be faced squarely.

Such a confrontation, in the present climate, might allow protection for community standards through measures short of placing people in jeopardy of life or limb and with deference to the constitutional guarantee of free expression. This would allow a shift to substantive concerns, rather than the modern retreat behind the undiscriminating barrier of First Amendment toleration. Then, instead of responding to book burners by claiming people have an absolute right to read whatever they want, there might be room for some substantive debate.

Freedom of the Press

Writers, publishers, and journalists—those we call the press—work with freedom of expression, and they have a special interest in it. The legal practice in this area is defined by, and in turn defines, the parameters within which these professionals function. As with any interest group, the press marshals legal argument and experience to support its interpretation of the Constitution. The claims associated with the First Amendment are derived from past practice. Their resolution has an influence on future possibilities.

Context and the Constitution

Rights take place in a context, in a society of wealth and poverty, education and ignorance, hunger and abundance. The context will not always be considered in this book because this is primarily a story of the rights themselves. The rights sometimes reinforce the values and interests in the society, and sometimes rights are used as tools to change the society. They have a degree of autonomy in how they operate. Yet, the society is the necessary context within which they function, and it deserves consideration. This section on press freedoms provides one opportunity to consider society because, in fact, the context is the material reality of this freedom. Americans romanticize their rights and often forget the context within which they operate. This section is an antidote. Without a press or access to one, the freedom conventionally protected in the Constitution is of little use. The context is called "de facto" freedoms here, and it also serves as limits. These freedoms contrast with the "de jure" freedoms derived from the First Amendment.

De Facto Freedoms. The press operates within a set of economic and social constraints that limit the possibilities of expression. The most obvious limitation on the press is ownership of the machine. A printing press is subject to the same economic laws as any piece of capital equipment. From the small pamphleteer to the nationally syndicated journalist, expression in this domain requires access to the tools by which the written word becomes available to masses of people. Economic power and ownership are of great significance to expression. These socio-legal considerations dictate news gathering as well as editorial policy. It is so obvious as to sometimes go unacknowledged that, well before legal issues are raised by publication of a campaign endorsement or investigative report, some publisher or editor will have taken financial as well as editorial risks. In this arena, the prerogatives and concerns of labor also limit, as well as enhance, freedom of expression. Labor sets the context through negotiation and the willingness to work. On some occasions, workers have refused to set or print material that runs counter to their convictions. While less involved with editorial content, the interests and prerogatives of labor in the workplace serve as another *de facto* limit on expression.

In addition, a good deal of governmental control is exercised on the press indirectly and influences the dissemination and availability of news. Post office regulations contain substantive provisions against sending obscene and subversive material through the mail, and postal rates set by Congress determine which magazines and newspapers will be able to survive. Coverage of governmental activities is also dependent on the cooperation of officials. The White House screens access to presidential news conferences and favors particular journalists when making news available. Although favor has always played a role in the acquisition of news about government, "Watergate" revealed that those closest to the inside may well have diminished capacity to transcend the official line. They may suffer from insiders' myopia.

Modern practice holds that radio and TV present special First

Amendment problems. As the technology developed—during a period of increasing regulation—the government exerted its authority over these forms of expression; it limited access to electronic or broadcast media. According to the theory, the airwaves are finite, and frequencies have to be regulated in order for the forum to function. A concern for the intrusiveness of these media has also been put forth as a basis for regulation. Licenses are restricted and, particularly in the case of TV, very expensive if available. There are rules of conduct, and there is a process of license review that involves official scrutiny unknown to print media. Substantive constraints that apply to radio and TV, but not to print media, include the provision for equal time to candidates for public office and a ban on cigarette advertising. Controversy over Federal Communications Commission regulations led to the "fairness doctrine." Discussed by the Supreme Court in *Red Lion Broadcasting* v. *FCC* (1969), the fairness doctrine requires broadcast media to provide, without charge, time for the victims of public criticism to respond to their critics. Since the doctrine provides for responses to editorializing and not "simple" facts, it has had less impact than it might have, although it remains a threat to the press.

The expanded control over broadcast media was evident in a case involving the comedian George Carlin (*FCC* v. *Pacifica Foundation*, 1978). Regulation in this context concerned indecent, but not necessarily obscene, matter. With radio and television, there is a special intrusive potential to which the Supreme Court has been sensitive. This was evident in Justice Stevens's view that "when the Commission finds that a pig has entered the parlor, the exercise of its regulatory power does not depend on proof that the pig is obscene." In this case Carlin or his speech was the pig, and because he was on the radio, what he said did not have to be obscene to get him into trouble, just a little dirty.

The many ways in which freedom of the press is limited before the First Amendment comes into play demonstrate the constraining influence of the social context and material considerations. These limits also play a part in other First Amendment contexts—from public assembly, in the shopping center cases, to the means to express dissent—and they are often taken for granted. Legal practice, however, remains an important basis through which freedom of the press has evolved.

De Jure Freedoms. Legal or "de jure" influences on the press exist in the criminal process and private law, in addition to the First Amendment. As an institution, the press is a creature of the legal order. For instance, a case in which a former CIA agent broke an agreement not to publish articles about the agency without the agency's prior review of the material was treated by the courts as a matter of contractual obligation, rather than an issue of press freedom (*Snepp* v. *United States*,

1980). The Supreme Court held that former agent Frank Snepp was bound by his agreement. This is a good example of a legal practice from another area of law setting the parameters for a holding on the First Amendment.

In a similar way, press liability for subpoena of news sources stems from the presumption that the government has an obligation to provide defendants with a fair trial. Beginning with *Branzburg v. Hayes* (1972), the mid-1970s saw increasing numbers of controversies between the press and trial judges. One of the more dramatic was the jailing of Bill Farr, a *Los Angeles Times* reporter, because he refused to reveal sources that a trial judge believed might have a bearing on the determination of guilt or innocence. Another stir was caused when reporter Myron Farber and the *New York Times* were fined for contempt because they ignored a subpoena issued in a murder trial (*In re Farber*, 1978). It is clear from these incidents that concern about the criminal process limits the prerogatives of the press. The claim of a professional privilege receives separate treatment later in this chapter.

Judicial authority covers publicity before trial. This has been subject to considerable controversy. In *Rideau v. Louisiana* (1963), the Supreme Court held that a televised confession made it impossible for the defendant to get a fair trial. The press was not strictly limited, because the decision dealt only with the defendant, but it would eventually affect the press, since the norms filter down and are the basis for contempt proceedings against journalists. Publicity during a trial is also subject to constitutional limits. In the 1965 case of Texas "high roller" Billy Sol Estes (*Estes v. Texas*), the Court held that a televised broadcast of the trial prejudiced the case. More recently, the justices ruled that there is no fundamental right to ban television from court when it is permitted by state law (*Chandler v. Florida*, 1981). Chief Justice Warren Burger wrote the opinion. During oral argument, he had suggested that jurors might be criticized by those who had seen the trial on TV. Burger expressed concern about the possibility of prejudice, but he resisted an absolute ban on TV in the courtroom. The tradition in this area reflects the power of the judge to screen a trial from the glare of media attention. The judge's options include limiting reporter access, isolating witnesses, and controlling release of information by counsel, police, and witnesses, as officers of the court. There was also a number of unique mechanisms embedded in the rules of procedure by which the trial is conducted. They insulate the courtroom from outside influences: the *voir dire*, sequestration, change of venue, mistrial, and the voided conviction. Their special meanings are one sign that the trial creates its own reality.

Libel law is another aspect of the legal environment that limits the press. This common law protection of individual reputation existed for centuries prior to the ratification of the First Amendment. The prior existence of this right suggests that constitutional protection of speech and press was not meant to be absolute. In fact, the Sedition Act of 1798 made libel of government officials a crime, indicating that the common law protection would cover government activity. The trend in American constitutional law since then has been in the other direction: toward the protection of individuals. Libel of individuals remains a legal constraint on the press. When public figures or officials are involved, however, the First Amendment provides considerable protection for journalistic zeal.

In *New York Times* v. *Sullivan* (1964), libel of a public official was limited by the Supreme Court to occasions when the media reported something they knew to be untrue that damaged the reputation of a public official or they did not make reasonable efforts to check whether what they were reporting was true or false. This decision widened the sphere of public discourse, making it very hard for public officials to get judgments against the press. Discussion of public figures—people in the public eye who do not hold public office—is also protected under the First Amendment, but to a lesser extent. In *Associated Press* v. *Walker* (1967), a critical description of a retired right-wing general was held not to be libelous because there was no malicious intent or knowing falsehood. Similarly, a newspaper was held not to be liable for reporting that a real estate developer was implicated in a blackmail scheme (*Greenbelt Cooperative Public Assn.* v. *Bresler*, 1970).

While office holding is relatively clearly demarcated, the line between "ordinary" citizen and public figure is fuzzy. In the case of Mary Alice Firestone, who sued Time, Inc., for having said that her divorce trial "... produced enough testimony of extra-marital adventures on both sides ... to make Dr. Freud's hair curl," her award of damages was upheld because she did not have "any role of especial prominence in the affairs of society" (*Time, Inc.* v. *Firestone*, 1976). Nevertheless, the attempt to distinguish in this regard is an aspect of the constitutional commitment to vigorous reporting of public life. Subsequent cases have affirmed that protection against libel must give way somewhat when it inteferes with public debate (see *Edwards* v. *New York Times*, 1977). In the course of a libel suit, however, litigants who believe the press has been malicious can inquire into the editorial processes, including thoughts, opinions, and conclusions bearing on the issue of state of mind, thereby giving those who have been attacked by the press a portion of the common law protection (*Herbert* v. *Lando*, 1979).

The Traditional and the Professional

Two subjects involving the press are given more extensive treatment here. These are slightly curious and certainly important dimensions in the development of the constitutional right of expression for journalists. In the first, concerning prior restraint, the issue is the diminished status of "prior restraint," which had once been the cornerstone of constitutional freedom. The second subject involves the special press claim to constitutional protection and the implications of this claim.

Prior Restraint. "Freedom"of the press from Milton through Blackstone meant freedom from prior restraint, the tradition that a publisher could be punished afterward but not prevented from printing his ideas in the first place. As tolerance of expression expanded in the twentieth century beyond this initial protection, the sanctity of the ban on previous restraint seems to have diminished.

A Supreme Court decision that influenced modern limits on censorship involved previous restraint. Minnesota, in the late 1920s, had made it a crime to publish malicious, scandalous, or defamatory material. It was a misdemeanor—simple nuisance—but the judicial response for abating the nuisance was stopping the presses. The case began with prosecution of a Minneapolis paper that had described the police as permitting "Jewish gangsters" to run illegal operations in the city. Writing for the majority, Chief Justice Charles Evans Hughes argued that the purpose of the statute was suppression rather than punishment, and he concluded that "This is the essence of censorship" (*Near* v. *Minnesota*, 1931). The standard held that prior restraints were legitimate only in "exceptional cases," and the Court did not find this Minnesota case to be exceptional.

While there continues to be sensitivity to previous restraint, there is a countervailing tendency. Expansion of the "first freedom" has resulted in a diminution of the old priority status for previous restraint. This was evident in the "Pentagon Papers" case, called by C. Herman Pritchett "the most significant challenge to press freedom in American history" (Pritchett, 1984:63). The restraint took place when the Nixon administration stopped the *New York Times* and the *Washington Post* from publishing Defense Department documents that examined, sometimes critically, the escalation of the Vietnam War. The legal struggles, which might have taken years, went from the District Court through the Supreme Court in a little over two weeks. The Supreme Court ruled that the government had failed to meet the heavy burden required to justify a continued ban, but prior restraint had already taken place. The old absolute protection had become conditional. Prior restraint was all right when there was a danger. This explains the temporary injunction issued against *The Progressive* in 1979 for an article on defense secrets that told how to make a hydrogen bomb. When it became clear that the information was readily available to the public, perception that there was a threat diminished, and the injunction was lifted.

Special Privileges. Due to its unique mention in the First Amendment, the press has sought special protection *in addition* to that guaranteed under freedom of speech. Believing it should have special privileges, the press has sought immunity from subpoenas and grand juries, privileged access to government information, relief from libel laws, and protection from police searches. The claim to special protection has also been associated with the other values in the First Amendment connected with the role of publishers and reporters in disseminating the information on which public policy decisions are made. The promise, in the First Amendment, of freedom for "the press" has been read as a description of journalists, instead of a reference to the written as well as the spoken word.

Some scholars have argued that the press would be better off if it did not seek special privileges (Dworkin, 1980). With its claim the press may be perceived as simply another special interest. But a stronger claim for the press would lie in the principle of open public discourse that is guaranteed to all citizens.

Ronald Dworkin has recently addressed these issues in the context of the decline in free speech protection from the Burger Court. He has described the press as taking the First Amendment "as a kind of private charter" and using it to attack judicial recalcitrance in the light of expanding claims to protection (Dworkin, 1980:50). Again there is the warning that such a strategy is a poor one that may turn attention away from concern for public discourse and public information by relying too heavily on a privileged position. The implication is that the First Amendment, in referring to "the press," means simply published speech. It is a promise to protect what comes out in print.

Dworkin has also characterized the implications of journalistic claims to special protections as compromising the rights of all citizens by treating free expression as a policy issue rather than a matter of principle. Policy arguments inevitably involve balancing speech against other issues of social policy. Principles would provide a basis for a public right of access that could not be waived. Principles have, of course, been the characteristic feature of constitutional rights. The power of principle, however, has seemingly been missing in such failures of press claims as *Zurcher* v. *Stanford Daily* (1978), where the police were permitted to make an unannounced search of a newspaper room, and *Houchins* v. *KQED, Inc.* (1978), where the press was refused permission to investigate and film a part of the Alameda County jail at Santa Rita. Instead it has been in conjunction with public rights that the press has had its greatest success of late, as in the issue of public reporting on a criminal trial in Virginia (*Richmond Newspapers, Inc.* v. *Virginia*, 1980).

Freedom of Religion _____

The Bill of Rights begins with religion. Joined with the right to speak, publish, and assemble, these protections were the first to be added to the Constitution. Religion and expression had been interwoven since before the founding of the nation. The heritage of the religious battles that stimulated colonization was well known to those who would draft the Bill of Rights. It had been religious belief that motivated John Milton's speech in Parliament opposing extension of the censorship laws in England. And at the same time, in the colonies, Roger Williams was preaching against persecution of religious expression. Thomas Jefferson, James Madison, and those of the founding generation who placed freedom first among the constitutional amendments were children of an age of reason (Cox, 1981). They feared that the new government would act in behalf of an established religion, and that this would be a threat to reason and the practices they had been living under.

We should not go too far, however, in seeing the initial project of the First Amendment protection as being close to contemporary views. In the nineteenth century, the First Amendment was directed against acts of Congress, in part to block Congress from disestablishing existing official state churches (Tribe, 1978:814). This and the fact that the freedom in the rest of the amendment allowed punishment for expression suggest differences from contemporary views and some of the considerations that are important to a modern perspective on these protections. For, since they became applicable to the states in the 1940s, the challenges posed to the distinctive clauses that constitute freedom of religion have been influenced by the newer pure tolerance conception that pervades the constitutional protection of freedom.

The structure of the freedom of religion clause of the Constitution indicates that the government shall not establish or become involved with supporting a particular religion. Under the growth of the welfare state and pressure for public assistance, however, the "establishment clause" has been a source of tension in the last half of the twentieth century. This is a classic constitutional confrontation potentially pitting the services of the government to citizens against the rights on which the government was instituted. The other area is a stipulated concern for the free exercise of religion. This dimension of constitutional protection inevitably raises some puzzling problems at the heart of public policy, such as whether people can refuse to fight in war due to their religious beliefs. Free exercise also presents some problems for its companion, the establishment clause, such as when the government accepts the claims of members of one church and not another for conscientious objector status. We begin with that aspect of constitutional protection for freedom of religion that is closest to freedom of expression: the free exercise provisions.

Free Exercise

The constitutional right to free exercise of religion is invoked in support of challenges to laws that limit religious practice. Often, the judicial response is that it is not clear what constitutes a religious observance. The first significant free exercise case, *Reynolds* v. *United States* (1879), involved federal statutes that outlawed polygamy, the taking of multiple wives, a practice engaged in by the Mormons. Lawyers for the Mormon Church defended the practice on free exercise grounds. Although revealing an expectation about the reach of the constitutional right, the assertion failed and the federal legislation was upheld. The justices found that polygamy involved more than belief and anticipated a later distinction between belief and action that became important to the development of the First Amendment (Emerson, 1970). More significant than the distinction between belief and action, however, seems to have been the fact that the Mormon practice was not viewed with equanimity by the rest of the population, which included the Supreme Court.

Another religious group, the Jehovah's Witnesses, which was also founded in the nineteenth century, has brought First Amendment challenges at every level of government. This group takes proselytizing for their faith as part of their religious obligation, which has made them familiar in many a neighborhood as well as in the halls of justice. When the Witnesses practice their religion, society has often seen their practices as challenging and threatening. The result was sometimes arrest for breach of peace or expulsion from school for not saluting the flag. Another distinguishing feature of this sect has been their capacity and commitment to struggling for their rights in the legal arena. It is, perhaps, an extension of their faith: the commitment to "witnessing." The first of these cases to reach the Supreme Court came in 1940 (*Cantwell* v. *Connecticut*) after Witnesses had been convicted for "soliciting without approval" and "breach of the peace." The Court upheld their claim that the convictions violated their right to freely exercise their religion. The case was the first to apply the protection of the First Amendment in this area to the states. Justice Owen Roberts's opinion in the case provided an appearance of the distinction between belief and action. This was a period of balancing interests in this, as in other areas of the First Amendment, and the opinion reflected an attempt to balance in its holding that society's interest in religious conduct "remains subject to regulation for the protection of society."

Soon after the Supreme Court began interpreting the standards of religious toleration, it ran into difficulty in the flag salute cases. In the first, *Minersville School District* v. *Gobitis* (1940), two children had been expelled for refusing to participate in a required flag salute ceremony in the public schools of Pennsylvania. The children were Jehovah's Witnesses, and they equated saluting the flag with paying homage to false gods. In an appeal, the children's father was successful in the federal district court, and then in the circuit court of appeals. In the Supreme Court, the Witnesses were supported by a committee of the American Bar Association and by the American Civil Liberties Union. *Gobitis* is an interesting case, which has become important in part for decisions that followed but also because of the heat that it generated. In *Gobitis*, the lower courts were overturned in an 8-1 decision by the Supreme Court. The opinion was written by Justice Felix Frankfurter. Frankfurter was an immigrant and Jewish, but he argued for the universal symbolism of flag and country over the individual commands and beliefs of religion. There was also a considerable degree of judicial restraint in his opinion, as he deferred to the local school board which was enforcing the policy.

The *Gobitis* case and one that came three years later, *West Virginia State Board of Education* v. *Barnette* (1943), form a seminal pair for students of the politics on the Supreme Court, for they dramatically depict the Court's ability to change its mind. The lone dissenter in *Gobitis*, Justice Harlan F. Stone, who said in his opinion that the Constitution required withholding "... from the state any authority to compel belief or the expression of it where that expression violates religious convictions...," was elevated to the Chief Justiceship the next year. Along with two new appointments and three of the justices in majority in *Gobitis*—Black, Douglas, and Murphy, who thought better of their earlier view—the majority shifted in the 1943 case to protect religious objection to the flag salute. The Court held for religious freedom over an older symbol of political unity: the flag. By modern accounts, the tolerance of the First Amendment is a far better mechanism for binding a polity together than the more primitive, yet certainly evocative, instruments of patriotism, such as the flag. Thus, the justices do change their minds, although seldom this dramatically, for with intelligible claims on either side they have that opportunity, with the internal politics and personalities determining the outcome.

Since the justices began to monitor the free exercise of religion in the nation they developed a standard that "... any inroad on religious autonomy be the least restrictive means of achieving a compelling end" (Tribe, 1978: 846). The standard links the *Cantwell* case with *Murdock* v. *Pennsylvania* (1943), where the imposition of a fee for distributing religious pamphlets was considered too prone to abuse to be permissible, and *Schneider* v. *Irvington* (1939), where the requirement of a police permit for proselytizing was considered excessive regulation. Laurence Tribe describes the situation as one where, if the harm is grave enough, as in vaccination against communicable disease, the state can intervene and regulate risk taking. But, he maintains that if the harm is "ill-defined or plainly not serious," there must be an exemption for the religious practice (Tribe, 1978:858). This was the conclusion of the California Supreme Court in *People* v. *Woody* (1964),* when they sruck down the conviction of American Indians for using peyote in their religious practices. Thus, where the instruction from the state is directed at an individual's soul, and not at public welfare or individual health, the justification for infringing on religion is weak.

Free exercise has developed as one of the classic "negative" liberties. It is a right not to do something that one would otherwise have to do but for the immunity derived from religion. Perhaps the best example of this immunity is the right to claim exemption from military service and the opportunity to become a conscientious objector (C.O.). Having a longstanding place in the American tradition due to the prominence of the Society of Friends, or Quakers, in the colonial period and during the Civil War, the right has always come up when there is a policy of mandatory armed service.

In the statutory provision for conscientious objection to the draft, the Supreme Court's interpretation of crucial issues, such as what constitutes a religion and the degree of toleration mandated by the Constitution, have had a bearing on the statutes. Both issues have arisen with regard to conscientious objection. The tradition had been that the source of the immunity from the draft was religious conviction. But in a case arising out of the Vietnam War, for instance, the Court defined a "sincere and meaningful belief" as occupying a place "parallel to a belief in God" (*United States* v. *Seeger*, 1965). This liberalizing rule extended the mantle of religion to "a belief that is equally paramount in the lives of their possessors" as God is in the belief of a member of an organized religion. It was, however, a statutory intepretation. Five years later, the Supreme Court again took up the reach of the C.O. provision (*Welsh* v. *United States* (1970). The case involved an individual who was opposed to war on historical, philosophical, and sociological grounds. He had been denied a C.O., but in an opinion by Justice Hugo Black, the

---

* There is a general truth about constitutional discourse that might be mentioned in conjunction with *Woody:* the classification for a case goes a long way toward determining the outcome. Thus, if *Woody* is considered a religion case, it is a good bet the Indians will be permitted to use peyote. Similarly, Bob Jones University wanted to call its dispute with the IRS over racial discrimination a freedom of religion case. It lost both the classification issue and the case (see Chapter 6).

conviction was reversed based on the *Seeger* precedent. The consequence was a reading of the law that would exempt ". . . all those whose consciences, spurred by deeply held moral, ethical or religious beliefs, would give them no rest or peace if they allowed themselves to become a part of an instrument of war." This, the Court would later say, was not the same as selective conscientious objection.

Non-Establishment

Government in the United States is prevented by the Constitution from making laws "respecting an establishment of religion." This is the provision associated with the separation of church and state in American experience, although it was once thought to protect establishment in the states by preventing Congress from setting up a national religion. Debate over this limitation has focused on the meaning of establishment. While in its broad outline it has been clear that this protection is part of the concern with religious liberty just discussed and that it prohibits the naming of an official national church, it is not so clear what forms of involvement with religion constitute establishment. Given the many facets of modern life the government has entered, it is inevitable that issues will arise over which services and benefits offered generally should also go to religious institutions. Although tolerance is again the basic standard, here the issue is *not* whether individuals or churches can be exempt from a particular policy, as was the case in the protection for free exercise, but rather whether a policy such as free textbooks provided to religious schools, is permissible given the requirement that the government not establish religion. This situation inevitably leads to heated confrontations.

The idea of a "wall of separation" between church and state, of a barrier dividing the two spheres, was first articulated in the Mormon polygamy case discussed in the last section (*Reynolds* v. *United States,* 1879). In order for that religious practice to be carried out, the state would have had to absent itself from regulation in the area of marriage and family life. By allowing a degree of intervention, the Constitution set limits on religious expression. In the middle of the twentieth century, higher standards of toleration began to press for increased separation of church and state as well. In *Everson* v. *Board of Education* (1947), the issue was provision by the State of New Jersey of bus fares for all school children—including those going to parochial schools. Government support of education had become a fact of modern life. In this case, the Supreme Court upheld the principle of a "wall" between church and state, but it indicated that where New Jersey had provided support to take children to parochial schools, the "wall" was not breached. The test announced in the case was:

... what are the purpose and primary effect of the enactment? If either is the advancement or inhibition of religion then the enactment exceeds the scope of legislative power as circumscribed by the Constitution. That is to say that to withstand the strictures of the Establishment Clause there must be a secular legislative purpose and a primary effect that neither advances nor inhibits religion *(Everson v. Board of Education, 1974)*.

Thus, the basis for this decision, that the support for buses was without a religious purpose, became one of the tests or considerations in determining when church and state had become involved with religion in an unconstitutional fashion.

Perhaps the case that provides the best summary of the constitutional standard in this area is *Lemon v. Kurtzman* (1971). In this case, the Supreme Court examined the Rhode Island practice of paying part of the salary of parochial school teachers. In upholding the payment—for teaching nonreligious subjects—the justices added the idea that the state should interpret the non-establishment clause with sensitivity to avoiding "excessive entanglements" in the religious business, by using the tests described above in *Everson*.

Government funds finding their way to religious coffers would seem, on the surface at least, to be a violation of the principle of separation of church and state. In 1983, after a lower federal court had determined that it was unconstitutional for a state legislature to pay for a chaplain to open its lawmaking sessions, the Supreme Court reversed the decision (*Marsh v. Chambers*, 1983). This is a practice of long standing, yet the intervention by the justices to uphold it led to rhetoric inevitably undercutting the tradition of separation. In the words of the Chief Justice, "To invoke divine guidance on a public body entrusted with making laws is not, in these circumstances, an 'establishment' of religion. . . . It is simply a tolerable acknowledgement of beliefs widely held among the people of this country." Acknowledgment in some official way by the government of widely, but not universally, held religious beliefs is, however, what the non-establishment clause has traditionally been about.

In this area of the expenditure of public funds, a much more significant and predictably more heated debate surrounds the issue of tax credits for parents who send their children to parochial schools. In many cities throughout the country, the provision of religiously based education, predominantly Roman Catholic, by organized churches has removed a large financial burden from state and local governments. This fact and the interest of parents who send their children to such schools as well as pay taxes has led to continued pressure for some sort of compensation. The latest Supreme Court decision on this issue came in 1983. A 5-4 ruling in *Mueller v. Allen* endorsed a form of tuition aid to parochial schools for the first time. The aid came in the form of a Minnesota tax credit amounting to $700. This development was tempered somewhat because the justices held that the benefit must at least be nominally available to parents of public school children as well.

School prayer had also been a source of ongoing controversy in the area of religion. It is perhaps the most dramatic source of tension, not only "in" the Constitution, but for the Court itself, which has come to provide the last word on its meaning. The issue involves many forms of religious observance in public institutions, but it has been epitomized by the controversy 20 years ago over a non-denominational daily prayer designated by the New York Board of Regents for use in the public schools of New York State. The prayer which went, "Almighty God, we acknowledge our dependence upon Thee, and we beg thy blessings upon us, our parents, our teachers, and our country," was recommended for reading at the beginning of each school day. The decision of the Supreme Court in *Engel* v. *Vitale* (1962), invalidating the use of this prayer in the public schools, became a lightning rod for opposition to the liberal constitutional interpretations handed down by the Supreme Court while Earl Warren was the Chief Justice. Justice Hugo Black wrote for the majority that in using its public school system for the recitation of a prayer, New York had adopted a practice "wholly inconsistent with the Establishment Clause." Only one justice dissented from a decision that went on ". . . it is no part of the business of government to compose official prayers for any group of the American people to recite as part of a religious program carried on by government." Similar decisions upholding the basic principle have continued to be handed down while the controversy rages.

In January of 1983, for instance, the Court decided not to take an appeal by a school district in Texas from a ruling in the Court of Appeals that had struck down the district's policy of permitting student religious groups to meet on school property before and after regular school hours (*Lubbock* v. *Lubbock Civil Liberties Union*). The Court refused to change its general proclivities in this area, even though the appeal had been supported by a legal brief filed by 24 U.S. senators reminding the justices of congressional efforts to strip the federal courts of jurisdiction over subjects such as school prayer.

Religious authority has come a long way from the mighty institutions of the Massachusetts Bay Colony, which once reigned supreme in the sacred and the secular realm. The non-establishment clause sometimes rides and sometimes nudges that declining authority. In a Massachusetts case that came to the Supreme Court in 1982, an establishment that went by the name of Grendel's Den was able to employ the constitutional standard to strike down a state statute that supposedly gave a veto power to churches in the state over the granting of nearby liquor licenses (*Larkin* v. *Grendel's Den*, 1982). Justice William Rehnquist and his clerks offered a clever dissent in which they took the majority to task for making so much of the case. Taking off from the old adage that "hard cases make bad law," the dissent suggested that "silly cases also make bad law." But there is not much law being made here in any case, at least not much of ideological significance is being added to the Constitution. It is nonetheless a colorful example of the rather large circle we have traveled from those religious beginnings over 300 years ago.

The treatment of some areas of constitutional protection for expression, such as religion, has been brief by comparison with our treatment of unprotected speech and the extensive focus we have provided on obscenity. The determination of what to emphasize in this chapter has been based on two considerations. First, the choice has been to concentrate on areas of legal action that best exemplify the structure of constitutional ideology. In presenting the pure tolerance interpretation of the First Amendment, obscenity is more instructive than religion because the issues there (which have a religious dimension) appear to cut more deeply into the constitutional fabric. In the second place, there are some aspects of constitutional law that are so technical that to fully describe all the ins and outs would take a book in itself. This is true of criminal procedure, which is presented in broad outline in the next chapter. It is also the case with freedom of religion, as the last few pages have indicated. Religious freedom is an issue of compelling belief (Arons, 1983), and its twists and turns are byzantine. To account for the nuances of this byzantium in anything like a comprehensive fashion would be to focus on policy decisions and their consequences. It would not provide greater insight into the ideological structure of constitutional freedom.

We now turn to a discussion of due process. In the next chapter, we take up, in turn, criminal procedure and civil procedure, and explain the rights of due process from the ideological point of view.

Due Process 3

The rights that Americans possess when they are threatened by the government can be traced back to twelfth century England. Early sovereigns offered new forms of justice and promised superior procedure for settling disputes, as a way of consolidating authority over the realm. The enticement to fealty was an alternative to private mechanisms for settling disagreements that had a propensity to degenerate into interminable feuding and bloody acts of vengeance. The procedural guarantees that evolved from the law as applied in the King's courts were given a boost in the Magna Carta. There, the King himself was constrained by the promise of due process. The resulting fundamental right as it developed in America is derived from these efforts first to extend royal authority and then to limit the way it is exercised. Constitutional due process is "... ingrained in our national traditions and is designed to maintain them," Felix Frankfurter said in *Anti-Fascist Refugee Committee* v. *McGrath* (1951:161). Reflecting its heritage, this constitutional right has a dual nature.

Twin Functions

Process is a mechanism for determining truth and for showing respect for individuals, which is supposed to cause them to identify with the system. Both functions serve to legitimize the state in the eyes of those who might come under its purview. The forerunners of conventional procedures, mechanisms such as dunking and trial by combat, seem bizarre today. They do not conform to either acceptable methods for determining truth or the ways in which we conventionally show respect for individuals. The shift to standards of scientific inquiry and Renaissance humanism supports and explains what is appropriate today.

Fundamental rights in this area, as with other civil liberties, find doctrinal footing in the Bill of Rights. That document, along with the Declaration of Independence, reflects a commitment to human dig-

85

nity—at its height around the founding of the American Republic. Indeed, the system of authority that supports the government depends on conformity with accepted practice. The requirements are so deeply embedded in procedural guarantees that they sometimes require participation on the part of the citizen that he or she might prefer to forfeit. Whether or not a person desires to appear at trial, for instance, the process expects it. Judges have bound and gagged defendants in order to satisfy this requirement—thereby defeating its purpose. For the most part, however, the rights associated with due process are protections that serve the interests of defendants, as well as the state.

The standards reveal a concern for humanity that goes beyond science and is sometimes at odds with the expectation that the process should result in a "true" determination. The processes were not developed with only pursuit of truth in mind. The robust, uncompromising model, which is idealized as critical inquiry and associated with scientific investigation, is often a challenge to the due process model, which is concerned with the rights of the individual. Legal guilt is a compromise between the competing claims of a humanitarian exercise of authority and the expectation that truth will win out. But with such mechanisms as prohibition against searches and seizures, the rules of evidence, and double jeopardy, the government gives up some of its truth-determining capacities in favor of protection for the defendant. Nevertheless, the model holds that an exchange between interested parties with determination by a neutral judge will produce a result that is not too far from our idea of the truth.

The significance of procedural guarantees is reflected in the eloquence of the rhetoric that it has elicited. Justice Benjamin Curtis's discussion in *Murray's Lessee* v. *Hoboken Land and Improvement Co.* (1855) is an early example. In his opinion, Curtis developed the meaning of the Fifth Amendment in terms of the tradition of the Magna Carta. "The law of the land," he observed, indicates the importance of safeguards both general and specific. In approaching the idea, he looked first at the Constitution to determine whether any particular process is "... in conflict with any of its provisions..." and "if this not be so, we must look to those settled usages and modes of proceeding existing in the common and statute law of England." The process that Curtis held up to the measure of settled usages is that no summary proceeding could be carried out without the person in jeopardy being given the opportunity to "show himself to be acquitted." This is the general justification for procedures that are not always explicitly delineated in the Constitution and the Bill of Rights. (See also *Grannis* v. *Ordean*, 1918.)

Justice Benjamin Cardozo's 1937 discussion of how Bill of Rights protections should be made applicable to the states is another eloquent expression of due process standards. Cardozo's view, in *Palko* v. *Connecticut* (1937), was that only protection which was "implicit in the concept of ordered liberty" would be applied to the states. In this case, the issue was whether appeal of a sentence by the prosecution was a violation of double jeopardy. By his formulation, the justice evoked the image of a meaningful tradition that would serve as guide in specific cases. In Palko's sad case, however, it may be that the very grandness of the principles ". . . at the base of all our civil and political institutions" made it hard to see their specific application and allowed Connecticut prosecutors to try again for the death sentence. (The case is remembered for its contribution to the ideology of due process and not for the outcome.)

Perhaps the most eloquent of the classic arguments for due process in the constitutional setting came in a concurrence by Justice Felix Frankfurter in *Anti-Fascist Refugee Committee* v. *McGrath* (1951). The Committee, one of the Cold War's casualties, had been designated "communist" without notice, justification, or the chance to confront the evidence, without, as Frankfurter argued, the fundamental fairness that is due process. "Fairness of procedure," he said in the opinion, is "due process in the primary sense." Though the case turned on the administrative context, the learned justice was able to summarize the twin functions with his characteristic precision.

> No better instrument has been devised for arriving at truth than to give a person in jeopardy of serious loss notice of the case against him and opportunity to meet it. Nor has a better way been found for generating the feeling, so important to a popular government, that justice has been done.

Thus, at the height of national paranoia over the communist threat, the pursuit of truth and respect for the individual combined to preserve due process from the passions of the moment. In such times, the grand statements need to be called up.

Procedure, perhaps more than any of the civil liberties, depends on context for a determination of what is appropriate. Originally associated primarily with the criminal sanction, the idea has grown as the functions of government and its obligations in the modern state have increased. Since due process guards against unjust deprivation of a person's freedom or benefits from the government, attention to context is part of the following analysis. Americans may now call for procedural fairness in schools, prisons, and welfare agencies, as well as courts. This discussion begins with criminal procedure. The specifics are most fully developed there, and the constraints on prosecution epitomize the promise of due process. Substantial attention will also be paid to the less fully developed due process protections, where the deprivation that results is not a consequence of a crime. Although the substance is less well defined, expansion of procedural guarantees in this area affects far more people than criminal procedure. We will conclude with a discussion of how both criminal and civil due process contribute to the legitimacy of the government.

Criminal Procedure

The power of the government to maintain order through the criminal law is a function long established in the liberal state. Criminal procedure thus antedates protection for the individual faced with loss due to the actions of some other institutional authority. Well before the government was providing student loans, food stamps, or social security benefits, it was bringing people to trial for breaches of the peace and order of the community. The process invoked in instances such as this stems from fundamental rights at the heart of the constitutional tradition. The "deep structure" of criminal procedure is found in the Fourth, Fifth, Sixth, and Eighth Amendments to the Constitution—the core of the Bill of Rights. (This is suggested by Table 3-1.)

The process begun by the police, carried out by the prosecutor, and concluded by the judiciary has three main stages: the period prior to trial when the investigation, arrest, and initial appearance before a magistrate take place; the period of the trial, including the selection of a jury and the evidentiary matters that constitute the business of the trial; and the post-trial period, which focuses on sentencing, punishment, and the appellate process. Looked at as a flow of the case through its various stages (see Figure 3-1), it is evident that the process takes its structure from the constitutional protections in the Bill of Rights. These protections shape the criminal process and, in substance, they are evident in the actual operation of the system. The motivating force behind prosecution may be "crime control" in which "repression of criminal conduct is by far the most important function to be performed . . ." (Packer, 1964). The manner in which this takes place, however, is conditioned by the need to maintain respect for the state and the legal system. The result is a liberal "due process model" that functions as crime control over the long run.

Plea Bargains in the Shadow

Before developing the elaborate guarantees that are the expressions of constitutional protection in the criminal process, it is essential to explore one rather large tangent because most cases never go to trial. The tangent is the "plea bargain," an arrangement between the prosecutor and the accused for a plea of guilty in exchange for concessions in the charge and sentencing. In most jurisdictions, around 90 percent of

Table 3-1 Constitutional Criminal Procedure

4th Amendment	5th Amendment	6th Amendment	8th Amendment
Search and seizure (exclusionary rule)	Indictment Double jeopardy Self- incrimination Due process	Speedy trial Impartial jury Information Confrontation Counsel	No excessive bail or fines No cruel or unusual punishment

criminal cases are settled this way. Given this situation, it is crucial to consider whether constitutional protections have an effect on these pleas. We begin with the legal status of the plea bargain and conclude with attention to research that explores whether the bargain is conditioned by the procedural setting.

Plea bargaining or "trading out," the disposition of criminal cases short of trial, is not new. References to plea bargaining appeared in *United States* v. *Ford* (1898), where the Supreme Court ruled that the government was without authority to negotiate a plea. Subsequently, the Court held that the negotiated plea "...is itself a conviction; nothing remains but to give judgment and determine punishment" (*Kercheval* v. *United States,* 1947). Yet, it has only been since the due process revolution of the 1960s that the justices have brought the practice under the umbrella of constitutional legitimacy. As they have said, "Only recently has plea bargaining become a viable practice accepted as a legitimate component in the administration of criminal justice" (*Blackledge* v. *Allison,* 1977:1630). Thus, plea bargaining has been a central feature of the bureaucratic administration of justice because there are not enough resources allocated to the criminal justice system to be able to try all the cases that arise.

Beginning its supervision of the guilty plea in the late 1960s, the Supreme Court held due process to require that a negotiated plea be given voluntarily and knowingly (*McCarthy* v. *United States,* 1970). The decision required that a judge not accept a plea of guilty unless he was satisfied that the plea had some factual basis—that it was at least partially true. Such "satisfaction" meant that the judge had to confront the defendant rather than "a silent record." Suspicion of abuse in the informal process of negotiation led to calls from the legal community for formality, uniformity (Michelman, 1969), and active supervision of the process. From its inception, the Burger Court has been concerned about efficiency in the criminal process. Consequently, it has appeared reluc-

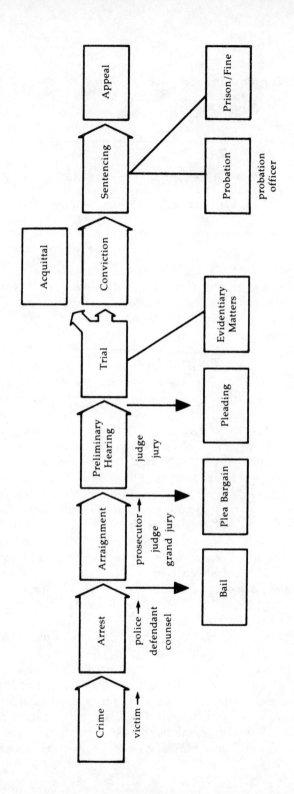

Figure 3-1 Criminal Procedure Institutions

tant to upset negotiated pleas (Conlyn, 1973), but it has been attentive to the practice.

In *Brady* v. *United States* (1970) and the two cases decided along with it (*McMann* v. *Richardson; Parker* v. *North Carolina*), the Court heard appeals from defendants who claimed that they had not pleaded guilty voluntarily. Charged with kidnapping, Brady faced the death penalty. This, he felt, was a coercive element influencing his plea. The justices considered the circumstances and held that since Brady's co-defendant was about to testify against him it was to his advantage to plead guilty. The Court had begun to treat the plea not as a practice to be ignored but as one in which the context might be examined. In *Parker* v. *North Carolina* (1970), a black man tried to have his indictment declared invalid after he had pleaded guilty because blacks had been excluded from the grand jury that indicted him. Under North Carolina law, an objection to the composition of the grand jury must be raised prior to the entry of the guilty plea, so the Court ignored Parker's plea. This outcome was attested to in *McMann* v. *Richardson* (1970), where defendants were unable to challenge the voluntariness of their confessions because they had already pleaded guilty. Although the Court had actually limited the admissibility of confessions after the defendants in this case pleaded, they were not allowed to take advantage of the change. In dissent, Justice William Brennan lamented this extreme commitment to the sanctity of the plea. In *Tollett* v. *Henderson* (1973), the Court summarized its position that "the voluntary plea insulates prior constitutional defects" from appellate review.

Santobello v. *New York* (1971) set the parameters for a policy of judicial deferral in matters of substance, with reinforcement of due process. The Court held the plea bargain to be "an essential component of the administration of justice" that was to be "encouraged" (*Santobello,* 1971:260). The appeal involved a broken agreement, and the majority sent the case back to the state to determine whether the agreement should be enforced or whether the plea could be withdrawn. They held that "when a plea rests in any significant degree on a promise or agreement of the prosecutor, so that it can be said to be part of an inducement or consideration, such promise must be fulfilled" (*Santobello,* 1971:262). In 1977, a conviction was again overturned where the courts failed to keep adequate records of the plea and the sentencing promise (*Blackledge* v. *Allison,* 1977). Here, concern for the finality of the plea would ultimately be preserved by cognizance of the bargain. That same year, the Supreme Court let stand a circuit ruling requiring a federal trial judge to accept a bargain even where he had not felt it was "in the best interests of justice" (*Woodruff* v. *U.S.,* 1977).

Prosecutorial attempts to increase the charges after a refusal to plead guilty had been considered vindictive (*North Carolina* v. *Pearce*, 1969; *Blackledge* v. *Perry*, 1974). But when the "bargaining" environment was accepted as part of the process in *Bordenkircher* v. *Hayes* (1978), greater freedom was granted to the prosecutor. In this case, the prosecutor added a repeat offender charge to a misdemeanor offense, increasing the sentence to life. The give and take, with the prosecutor giving threats and the defendant taking what he could get, had become constitutionally recognized as consistent with the due process clause of the Fourteenth Amendment. The justices treated the bargain much as the law has treated contracts, with little attention to the substance of the arrangement. Having set these parameters, the Supreme Court has kept its distance from the process. When the Eighth Circuit ordered a district judge to resentence in accordance with a plea agreement because he had added a requirement of restitution that was not in the original agreement, the Supreme Court declined to review the decision (*Runck* v. *U.S.*, 1980). Constitutional requirements are satisfied without review of the context or attention to whether the defendant got a sentence comparable to what he would have received if he had gone to trial.

Two perspectives govern the process and the literature on it. The first is that most defendants plead guilty prior to trial because most defendants are guilty (Heumann, 1978), and the second is that because not going to trial saves the expense and time of a trial, the bargain should be weighted in favor of the accused (Haney and Lowy, 1979). There is little in the massive literature on plea bargaining about the significance of the legal environment for the plea, that is, the possibility that the defendant would have been acquitted if the case had gone to trial (Feeley, 1979a). Thus, in a great deal of criminal justice literature, the premise is that criminals plead, not defendants. This is particularly evident in the appellate process, where the admission of guilt stops the review of evidentiary matters and cuts off the possibility that errors in the state's case would show up at trial (*Tollett* v. *Henderson*, 1973). While Malcolm M. Feeley (1979b) has argued that "vigorous negotiations between defense and prosecution often appeal to 'the law' and take place 'as if' they were being umpired by a judge" (Feeley, 1979b:13), there is little evidence to support Feeley's contention in the literature on the bargaining process (Feeley, 1979a). The other side of the picture, a perception that the adversary process is disappearing (Blumberg, 1967), is a sobering possibility that casts a shadow on the forms to which we now turn.

Pre-Trial

The pre-trial period begins with the investigation, leads to arrest, and ends with arraignment. During the investigation, the Fourth

Amendment protects a citizen against unreasonable searches and seizures. The amendment guarantees that people will be "secure in their
persons, houses, papers, and effects." In contemporary terms, one's
"space" will not be violated without cause and the consent of a neutral
authority. At arrest, the "Miranda" warnings further protect the defendant by alerting him of rights derived from constitutional provisions.
The Fifth Amendment sets the parameters for indictment, guarantees
that the defendant will not be forced to assist in his own prosecution,
and provides assurances that there will be no violation of double
jeopardy.

    Investigation. The constitutional issues are most closely tied to
"search and seizure." The basic rule in preliminary investigations is that
a warrant, that is, an official authorization for some action, is necessary.
It must be from a disinterested magistrate and show "probable cause"
that the named items will be found. The warrant provision reflects the
concern about prior justification when the government undertakes a
search to collect evidence against an individual. The warrant requirement need not operate in every instance in order to have meaning as a
constitutional protection The requirement has significance as the institutions and even the exceptions develop around it. As with other areas of
constitutional law, the exceptions delineate the constitutional right.

    There are six major exceptions to the basic warrant requirement: (1)
consent, where an individual has agreed to let the police search; (2)
searches provided for by statute, such as those at borders to minimize
the spread of insects and disease (some wiretaps also fall into this
category, see *Biswell,* 1972; *U.S.* v. *Giordano,* 1974); (3) non-testimonial
personal evidence, such as lineups and fingerprints (on the related issue
of blood alcohol tests, see *South Dakota* v. *Neville,* 1983); (4) volatile
situations in which police officers in the field are suspicious—based on
their claim of expertise and the particular situation, the police have the
right to search, or at least "stop and frisk" under such circumstances
(*Terry* v. *Ohio,* 1968; *Penn.* v. *Jones,* 1978); (5) searches of automobiles,
where probable cause exists in a volatile situation (*Carroll* v. *United States,*
1925; *Delaware* v. *Prouse,* 1979; *Rhode Island* v. *De Masi,* 1981); and (6) a
search subsequent to a valid arrest. The courts often have delineated the
right to search connected to an arrest, and from these cases comes the
doctrine of "plain view" (*Chimel* v. *California,* 1969; *Matlock* v. *U.S.,* 1974;
Cardwell v. *Lewis,* 1974), which means that what the police see while
searching incident to an arrest can be used in a trial.

    The case of a narcotics dealer known as "Bandit" linked the
automobile exception with that of search incident to arrest and provided
Justice John Paul Stevens with an opportunity to demonstrate some key

characteristics of the constitutional requirements for warrantless searches while enlivening the United States Reports with another true life police drama (*United States* v. *Albert Ross, Jr.,* 1982). In this case District of Columbia police had followed a tip that identified "Bandit" as selling narcotics out of the trunk of his "purplish maroon Chevrolet Malibu." The police arrested the individual, and searching the car without a warrant, they found heroin in a "lunch-type brown paper bag" in the trunk and cash in a red leather pouch. The decision by the Court was that when police had legitimately stopped a car and had probable cause to believe that it contained "contraband," they could conduct a search as thorough as a magistrate could authorize by warrant. The limitation, as important as the rule in this case, was that "the search is limited by its object." For example, as Justice Stevens pointed out, if a van is being searched for illegal aliens, the police would have no justification for examining the contents of a small suitcase in the vehicle.

Warrantless searches authorized by special circumstances or statutory provisions were the focus of extensive attention in 1983. The Court struggled with the constitutional questions surrounding a "drug courier profile" used by narcotics agents to pick out likely suspects at airports. The ruling was that even where an agent is justified in intercepting the passenger, the suspicion does not provide a basis for more prolonged interrogation (*Florida* v. *Royer,* 1983). This is at the margin of the warrant requirement. In another case dealing with contraband, customs officials were allowed to make random inspections of ships on inland waterways without any suspicion that a crime was being committed (*U.S.* v. *Villamonte-Marquez,* 1983). The use of random inspections has been a way of getting around the requirement that individuals be protected from the arbitrary use of legal authority. Finally, also along these lines, the Court held that exposure of luggage to a dope-sniffing dog is not a "search" and requires no previous suspicion of wrongdoing (*U.S.* v. *Place,* 1983). The politics of the cases put the outcomes squarely behind law enforcement although, with reference to the ideology of search and seizure, the cases add little to the Constitution.

The specter of technological intrusion holds a special place as a threat to human autonomy and dignity. The right not to be subject to such intrusions is grounded in the web of constitutional concerns uniting the Fourth and Fifth Amendments to form the penumbras associated with privacy. An exception raising a compelling threat in this regard is that for statutory wiretaps. The first such wiretap case (*Olmstead* v. *U.S.*) came to the Supreme Court in 1928. Because it was a tap outside the home and there was no intrusion or physical seizure, the justices found no violation of the constitutional requirement. The concern for privacy, however, was introduced to the Court through a dissent in this case by Justices Holmes and Brandeis. They argued that protection from warrantless telephone wiretaps was part of the Fourth Amendment. The conjunction of the Fourth and the Fifth Amendments, that is, the protection for the individual that came with the Fifth Amendment, laid the foundation for a broader due process protection from wiretapping. In *Katz* v. *U.S.* (1967), the justices threw out the old requirement that there had to be a trespass and that some physical object had to be seized for constitutional protections to come into play. They extended the safeguards to bugging devices, wiretaps, and other forms of electronic eavesdropping that either didn't require a trespass or didn't produce a physical object as a result of the investigation.

The issue of statutory exemptions from the Constitution's warrant requirement was considered in *U.S.* v. *U.S. District Court* (1972). These statutory exemptions are laws passed by legislatures exempting certain people from needing to use a warrant, due to various reasons of public safety. In this case, the justices rejected a claim by the president of the United States, Richard Nixon, that he had an inherent power in domestic security cases to order wiretaps without a warrant, and the Court also turned down the president's claim that warrantless wiretaps had been authorized by the Omnibus Crime Act of 1968. Due to the special circumstances surrounding President Nixon's status, and his considerable involvement in the use of "national security" wiretaps, Nixon had asked the courts to protect him from personal liability for damages stemming from a warrantless wiretap ordered while he was in office. The tap, on the home telephone of National Security Council staff member Morton Halperin, had lasted 21 months and had been part of the White House effort to stop information leaks. The district court ruled that the president and his top aides had violated Halperin's constitutional rights. The court of appeals rejected the damage award and found the federal wiretap statute to apply. An equally divided Supreme Court, with Justice William Rehnquist not participating, left the court of appeals ruling intact (*Kissinger* v. *Halperin*, 1981).

In a case appealed to the Supreme Court by the American Civil Liberties Union on behalf of a Michigan lawyer, the justices refused to review a ruling from the Sixth Circuit Court of Appeals which allowed the National Security Agency to furnish summaries of telegrams to the FBI. The agency monitors worldwide electronic communication without warrants and had turned some of the information it had collected over to the FBI, which was investigating attorney Abdeen Jabara. This national security exemption thus amounted to domestic surveillance (*Jabara* v. *Webster*, 1983). But the distinction between criminal and civil proceedings seems to be more basic than that between agencies. Two 1983 decisions (*Sells Engineering* v. *U.S.* and *Baggot* v. *U.S.*) restricted the use of grand jury evidence by the Internal Revenue Service, which sought information on back taxes, or by the civil attorneys at the Justice Department, who sought information concerning government damage suits. In the first case, a Navy contractor had pleaded guilty to conspiring to defraud the government. The Court made it clear, for the first time, that the government was required to obtain a court order to send the records of the grand jury investigation from prosecutors to its civil attorneys. The Internal Revenue Service claimed that the rulings put at risk about $500 million in civil tax cases involving grand jury materials.

Interrogation. Another part of the pre-trial investigation takes place while the defendant is in custody. Fifth Amendment protection covers the related aspects of custodial investigation: interrogation and immunity. There has been a right to remain silent during interrogation by state law enforcement officers since *Malloy* v. *Hogan* (1964). In the same year, rough treatment of Danny Escobedo by the police in Illinois was the basis on which the Supreme Court required counsel during questioning (*Escobedo* v. *Illinois*, 1964). This brought the adversary process into the interrogation room. The implications of these cases were spelled out in *Miranda* v. *Arizona* (1966), where the Court announced a series of rules known as "Miranda warnings." These rules require the police to notify an arrested subject of the following: (a) that he has the right to remain silent, (b) that what he says may be used against him in court, (c) that he has a right to counsel, (d) that counsel will be provided for him without charge if he cannot afford to pay an attorney, and (e) that any information that he gives must be given voluntarily. These warnings came to represent the "due process revolution" of the 1960s in which the state governments, which do most of the criminal law enforcement, were subjected to constitutional review of their actions. Specifically, the right to remain silent and to obtain counsel stem from the inherent coerciveness of custodial interrogation. The *Miranda* ruling was subject to persistent attack—from *Harris* v. *New York* (1971) to *United States* v. *Mandujano* (1976). The attacks dealt with peripheral matters, such as whether an illegally obtained confession can be used to impeach the testimony of a defendant. After over ten years of decisions siding with prosecutors who wanted to use statements obtained without *Miranda* warnings, the justices restated the authority of the warning requirement in *Estelle* v. *Smith* (1981) and *Edwards* v. *Arizona* (1981). In the first case, Texas had violated the defendant's rights when it admitted into evidence, at the penalty phase of a capital murder trial, testimony based on psychiatric interviews conducted without *Miranda* warnings. In the second, the justices held that the police could not initiate any questioning until an attorney had arrived, if the defendant requested counsel. Somewhat weakened, the *Miranda* ruling has survived because in the end it is not simply a matter of police procedure, but a reflection of the constitutional standards of due process as they bear on criminal justice.

Respect for the individual during the interrogation process is also evident in the requirement for voluntary confessions. Traditionally a source of guidance in other areas of the criminal process—like consent for a warrantless search—this area of law raises compelling social and philosophical questions. Modern attention to voluntariness here stems from *Brown* v. *Mississippi* (1936). This case out of the South involved the way the arm of the law was laid on black Americans. As reported by Justice Charles Evans Hughes, "... defendants were made to strip and they were laid over chairs and their backs were cut to pieces with a leather strap with buckles on it..." in order to gain a confession (*Brown*, 1936:282). Subtle issues of voluntariness are hardly relevant in this case, but it serves as the basis for the requirement of freely given consent to confessions. For Justice Felix Frankfurter, 20 years later, the test became whether a confession was "... the product of an essentially free and unconstrained choice by its maker" (*Culombe* v. *Connecticut*, 1961). He described a three-phased analysis involving "crude historical facts," inferential "psychological" facts, and a combination that became the rule of law. The result he called "an amphibian" because "it purports ... to describe an internal psychic state and to characterize that state for legal purposes" (*Culombe*, 1961:605). Now, the totality of the circumstances provides the basis for determining voluntariness, and the Constitution encourages inquiry into the context of an interrogation. But determining voluntariness remains a challenge. The Burger Court has been rather generous to the prosecution. It has allowed uninformed consent to stand in a decision that Justice William Brennan argued was "... supported neither by 'linguistics,' nor 'epistemology' nor indeed by 'common sense'" (*Schneckloth* v. *Bustamonte*, 1973:227). Yet, verbal assent to a confession by the defendant does not end the constitutional inquiry.

Voluntariness as a key to the interrogation process must also be understood with reference to the overlay of considerations that stem from due process generally and in particular from the variety of procedural requirements that now constitute acceptable police practices. These range from provisions bearing largely on police conduct, like the *Miranda* warnings—which provide protection independent of voluntariness—to the provisions for immunity from prosecution—which are for prosecutorial advantage and cancel the Fifth Amendment protections. It was with reference to the issue of *Miranda*-mandated warnings that the Supreme Court most recently offered a definition of interrogation. The issue again involved the coerciveness of the interrogation process. In upholding the conviction of Thomas Innis for armed robbery, over concerns expressed by the Rhode Island Supreme Court for his rights,

Justice Potter Stewart and his colleagues in the majority demonstrated very little sensitivity to protections from coerciveness that had been associated with the interrogation process for two decades. Although not under the glaring lights of the station house, the defendant was tricked into revealing where he had hidden his gun (*Rhode Island* v. *Innis*, 1980). He was told that handicapped children in a nearby school might find the weapon and hurt themselves. This was condoned under a definition of interrogation extending "only to words or actions on the part of police officers that they should have known were reasonably likely to elicit an incriminating response."

Immunity. The Fifth Amendment right not to be compelled to be a witness against oneself does not amount to a right to remain silent, not, at least, since the introduction of prosecutorial immunity. The grant of immunity from criminal prosecution was determined in *Ullman* v. *United States* (1956), to satisfy the constitutional requirement against self-incrimination while still forcing the defendant to testify under penalty of contempt. The position was upheld in *New Jersey* v. *Portash* (1979). *Portash* was a case where a municipal official testified before a state grand jury under immunity. He was later charged with misconduct in office and extortion. At the trial, he was told that if he testified, his grand jury testimony would be allowed into evidence to impeach his credibility. He didn't testify and was convicted. On appeal, the Supreme Court held that the testimony could not have been used against him and because the reading of the law by the trial judge turned out to be wrong a new trial was ordered.

The interpretation of constitutional protection giving this kind of immunity has particular significance in the context of grand jury investigations where cooperation with the prosecution can be required under penalty of criminal sanctions. The situation is such that if the subject of an investigatory net refuses to testify, he or she can be held in contempt. Along with the immunity provisions, the procedure for contempt circumvents the respect for individual autonomy in relation to the state. However, it even tips the balance expected to characterize the pursuit of truth in that it does not require the prosecutor to prove a case on the basis of evidence.

In addition to the limited reading of the Fifth Amendment protections in the modern period, there has also been erosion of constitutional protection from self-incrimination in another sense. Since the early 1970s, federal and state legislation has limited the scope of the immunity promised in exchange for testimony. This limitation has been in the form of "use" immunity; it prohibits the use of testimony but does not prevent prosecution in regard to an entire "transaction," that is, the circumstances that surround the testimony. This more limited immunity was upheld by the Supreme Court of Chief Justice Warren Burger soon after the legislation was passed (*Kastigar* v. *U.S.*, 1972). Thus, the immunity that authorized compelled testimony is more limited than it had been when such compulsion was introduced.

The "exclusionary rule" links the pre-trial period and the trial. This rule stems from the general principle that if the police or prosecution have failed to obey the laws governing the criminal process, or have twisted them to their own advantage, the illegal evidence or extra-legal procedure cannot be used for a conviction. It has applied in federal courts since 1914 (*Weeks* v. *United States*). The rule was made applicable to the states in *Mapp* v. *Ohio* (1961), a case in which the police broke into the home of Mrs. Dolree Mapp—allegedly in pursuit of a fugitive—and used obscene literature which they found in Mapp's home to get a conviction. To some, the principle has represented the sanctity of the due process sytem; to others, it has represented the system's propensity to "coddle criminals."

The rule has undergone intense scrutiny since the early 1970s when Richard Nixon made his appointments to the Supreme Court. One of the broadest and most puzzling in constitutional interpretation, from an ordinary observer's point of view, the rule excluding illegally obtained evidence has seemed destined to be excluded itself. The politics of constitutional adjudication has focused on this issue, while its place in the ideology of constitutional due process is marginal. It is a mechanism for preserving the integrity of the criminal process by excluding illegally obtained evidence and it has been an instrument used by the judiciary to deter unlawful police conduct (*Stone* v. *Powell*, 1976). The first goal has a formal rationality to it and the latter is appealing even where it may be ineffective. The rule has been a convention in constitutional interpretation of surprising resiliency. After twenty years of supervision by the justices of the Supreme Court, it appears most subject to dilution where its implications are irrelevant to either of its goals and where the benefit to the defendant is gratuitous. This is the situation with what has been called "good-faith exception" where evidence is acquired in the belief that constitutional standards have been met. The Court has indicated its interest in this question, while reserving "for another day the question whether the exclusionary rule should be modified" (*Illinois* v. *Gates*, 1983).

Trial

The Sixth Amendment promises no undue delay in a case being brought to trial, an impartial jury and a public trial, notice of the accusation, and confrontation of witnesses and supporting witnesses by the defendant. It sets the stage for trial. As in the pre-trial setting, it is from the Sixth Amendment that specific institutional practices and particular rights have emerged. For instance, the requirement of impartiality creates the possibility of a change in the site of the trial (venue), determines how jurors are called (venire), and how they are chosen (voir dire). The right to an impartial jury results in an amalgamation of institutional practices rooted in the constitutional requirement of procedural fairness. The ideal is a combative process balancing the search for truth and respect for the individual. This is epitomized by efforts to have the accused present at trial to confront his or her accusers. Transcribed testimony will not satisfy the requirement of confrontation (*Pointer* v. *Texas*, 1965; *Chambers* v. *Miss.*, 1973).

Knowledge of the accusation, along with the other protections, addresses horrors vividly depicted by Franz Kafka in his book *The Trial*, where the defendant not only has no opportunity to face his accusers but is not told such simple details as what he has done and the evidence against him. Knowing the charges is a fundamental due process right that reaches back in constitutional history (*Connally* v. *General Construction Co.*, 1926)—although it must be continually supervised (*Rose* v. *Loche*, 1975).

Delay. While the right to a public trial has been guaranteed since the 1940s and subject to relatively little controversy, the right to a speedy trial is of more recent vintage and has been an issue of considerable controversy and legislative as well as judicial action. The Constitution's provision was applied to the states in *Klopfer* v. *North Carolina* (1967), a case arising out of civil rights struggles in which the defendant Peter Klopfer—a professor at Duke University—was tried for participating in a sit-in at a segregated restaurant. Klopfer was brought to trial for trespass. The trial was suspended, and Klopfer faced the threat of renewed prosecution at North Carolina's discretion *any time it chose.* The Supreme Court judged this to be a denial of the speedy trial right, which had already been recognized by most of the other states.

The courts were initially reluctant to specify exactly or "quantify" the length of time allowed by the constitutional provision. Willie Mae Barker's case, however, appears to have stimulated such a quantification of the permissible delay. Initially scheduled in 1958, Barker's trial was postponed 11 times while the prosecution sought a conviction of his partner. Barker objected to the 12th continuance, which would have brought him to trial five years after he was arrested. Writing for the Court, Justice Lewis Powell did not consider the speedy trial time clock relevant until the defendant objected, which, in Barker's case, was well after he was arrested (*Barker* v. *Wingo*, 1972). The Federal Speedy Trial Act of 1974 was a partial response to this case (Pritchett, 1984:227), and generally, it has been through statutory authority rather than judicial decision that the parameters of access to timely justice have been delineated.

Jury. The right to an impartial jury also protects the individual from governmental oppression; this right is closely associated with due process guarantees. Although jury trials are the exception rather than the rule in the criminal process, they set the framework in which more common plea negotiations take place. The jury has long been a subject of judicial commentary. It was first mentioned by the Supreme Court in 1795, when Justice William Paterson wrote that jury trials were protected by the Pennsylvania constitution (*Vanhorne's Lessee* v. *Dorrance*, 1795). The idea of a jury was developed further in 1830 by Justice Joseph Story, who described trial by jury as "...justly dear to the American people" (*Parsons* v. *Bedford*, 1830:446). Writing in his opinion that trial by jury was to be required in all suits that were not of equity or admiralty jurisdiction, Story made clear in this case that the unique role of the jury as finder of facts would limit the range of appellate inquiry into a case. It was also clear before the turn of the century that the jury spoken of in the Constitution was the traditional common law jury (*Thompson* v. *Utah*, 1898). What precisely that was, on the other hand, was not fully amplified until well into the twentieth century, when pressure on the traditional jury began to mount.

In *Williams* v. *Florida* (1970), Justice Byron White argued that the jury must place itself "between the accused and his accuser." White wrote that the number of people on the jury had to be large enough "...to promote group deliberation free from attempts at intimidation, and to provide a fair possibility for obtaining a representative cross section of the community." The common law jury of tradition had been twelve persons strong. It is against this standard, and by using the test suggested by Justice White, that the smaller and allegedly more efficient juries of today are measured. Six has been the lower limit, since *Williams*. Thus, a misdemeanor conviction by a five-person jury that reached the Supreme Court in 1978 was reversed (*Ballew* v. *Georgia*, 1978). Social science research investigating the nature of the jury process and the question of how large is large enough has contributed to resolution of the constitutional questions (Kalven and Zeisel, 1966; Lempert, 1975).

The traditional jury has worked under the requirement of unanimous agreement. This requirement has existed for some time in federal courts (*Patton* v. *United States*, 1930). In state cases, the constitutional provision was applied in 1968 (*Duncan* v. *Louisiana*). The attack on unanimity came in the early 1970s, when this unique requirement was treated as something of a historical accident. Like size, the decisional matrix began to be viewed in functional terms as necessary for determining "reasonable doubt" (*Johnson* v. *Louisiana*, 1972; *Apodaca* v.

Oregon, 1972). Since the 1970s, fewer persons have been needed for conviction—nine or ten—on the grounds that having fewer persons would not limit the possibility for assembling a cross-section of the community. Dissenting justices, and a number of scholars, have argued that, independent from the common law tradition, majority juries would be less sensitive to minority views than unanimous juries. The tradition for interpreting the decision matrix demonstrates the difficulty of line drawing in general, since "... it requires attaching different consequences to events which, when they lie near the line, actually differ very little" (*Duncan*, 1968:161). But the justices have drawn the line, and in *Burch* v. *Louisiana* (1979), they held that a nonunanimous six-person jury for a petty criminal offense was not constitutional. The majority opinion by Justice Rehnquist who, while not passionate in his commitment to the common law jury, was not willing to yield the constitutional provision for a jury in favor of the state's interest in saving money and time. The decision is evidence of the significance of the idea and its limits.

The capacity of the jury to represent the community is also related to the selection process. There, the defendant is protected against bias by the impartiality requirement, by the right to challenge those who would serve, and by how the jury pool is constituted. The make-up of the group from which the jury is chosen (pool) must be a cross-section of the community, although the Court approved confining jury service to males as late as *Strauder* v. *West Virginia* (1880). Women were made eligible later, although in a number of instances, statutory exemptions, such as allowing mothers to stay home with children, made it easy for women to avoid jury service (*Hoyt* v. *Florida*, 1961). In 1935, the "Second Scottsboro Case" (*Norris* v. *Alabama*) struck down systematic exclusion of blacks. Concern over racism and more subtle exclusion of minorities was the cutting edge of the impartiality issue until a requirement that the jury represent a cross-section of the community was established in 1975.

Counsel. The right to have counsel assigned to those who cannot afford to hire a lawyer is discussed here in the context of the trial. It is not only at trial that the issue of representation arises (see *Brewer* v. *Williams*, 1977), but it is here that the need is most vivid and it was in this regard that the constitutional requirement for the provision of representation first came to the fore. Although not a stage in the process like the other subsections of the criminal process developed here, the issue of representation is central to due process. For years, the federal courts have recognized that counsel is the key to fair treatment. The expansion of the right of representation into the states bears special note because it reveals some characteristics of doctrinal shifts—such as the professional commitments at the center of procedural fairness—that give the appellate courts such concern for adequate representation.

The federal duty to assign counsel in capital cases stems from the Federal Crimes Act of 1790. In the states, it is associated with the first Scottsboro case, *Powell* v. *Alabama* (1932), where nine young black men, ranging in age from 12 to 19, were prosecuted for the rape of two white women. Often viewed simply as a right to counsel case, the Scottsboro case also raised the issue of whether there was a right to adequate counsel. The trial only lasted a day, the trial judge had virtually appointed no counsel by appointing all members of the bar to represent the defendants, and the sentence was death. The initial premise on the Supreme Court was voiced by Justice George Sutherland, who began with the fact that even the ". . . educated layman has small and sometimes no skill in the science of law." The holding was that in capital cases where the defendant is unable to employ counsel the court must assign one, and the assignment must be in time for the provision of ". . . effective aid in the preparation and trial of the case." It is the latter finding that indicates the relevance of the issue of adequacy.

From capital cases, the provision of counsel was expanded to felonies in the federal courts (*Johnson* v. *Zerbst*, 1938). When the Supreme Court expanded this protection to the states in *Betts* v. *Brady* (1942), the justices ruled that counsel was not essential to a fair trial in all cases, although there might be circumstances like incapacity of the defendant or complexity of the trial that would require that counsel be provided. Because *Betts* required counsel in "special circumstances," it led to a series of ad hoc decisions in which the justices of the High Court determined what were and what were not circumstances requiring the provision of counsel. When the justices tired of these ad hoc decisions, they brought up the case of *Gideon* v. *Wainwright* (1963). This case was dramatized by Anthony Lewis, who covered the Supreme Court for the *New York Times*, in the book *Gideon's Trumpet* (1964). Clarence Earl Gideon was a hapless petty offender who, nevertheless, had a strong sense of his rights. Charged with felony breaking and entering in Florida, he requested a lawyer because he could not afford to hire one. His request was turned down at the trial and in the state appellate courts, but it was accepted by the Supreme Court. The ruling was a high point of Warren Court jurisprudence in the criminal law, and it established a new requirement for court-appointed counsel for indigents in serious criminal trials.

A later advance in the right to counsel came when the Burger Court made counsel a requirement where imprisonment is possible (*Argersinger* v. *Hamlin*, 1972), with the subsequent interpretation that review of the right would have to be based on an actual prison sentence (*Scott* v. *Illinois*, 1979). Exactly where the right begins and ends gets into another level of constitutional discourse, and there are enough differentiated stages and events in the process to keep appellate courts busy for as long as they choose to monitor this area of the due process right. The cost to the state for this right is often substantial. In June of 1981, Chicago paid $133,000 for the defense of mass murderer John W. Gacy. In this, as in other due process expenses, the state's costs in conducting a trial are balanced against the benefits of guaranteeing a *fair* trial.

Although related to fairness, the adequacy of counsel has been less successfully adjudicated. Since *Powell*, "adequacy" has rested on a standard of "reasonable competence" (*Tollett* v. *Henderson*, 1973). Justice Thurgood Marshall has suggested a higher standard of "competence in law." But no one has successfully raised the equal protection issue at the heart of the fairness question. Such a concern might consider whether counsel provided to an indigent was comparable to that for a person capable of paying. The justices have been reluctant to accept this claim, but if the Constitution is to really achieve equal protection it might be in this arena of criminal due process. Here, procedural justice is uniquely attuned to charges of bias.*

Post-Trial

The conclusion of a trial presents the opportunity for appellate review, but this stage generally results in the imposition of sanctions. These sanctions are governed by the Eighth Amendment, which protects against excessive bail, as well as against penalties that are cruel and unusual. The post-trial stage also embodies protection against double jeopardy, an area of procedural protection against being twice put in jeopardy of life or limb. By setting up a system of federal courts with the Supreme Court at the top having "appellate jurisdiction," and then by extending this jurisdiction to state action under the due process clause of the Fourteenth Amendment, the Constitution promises judicial supervision over the criminal process. Although only a portion of convictions are appealed, these appeals are one source of the decisions delineating constitutional due process.

Appellate Review. Post-trial constitutional protection is, first and foremost, the very existence of process subsequent to conviction, the right to appeal. Embedded in the structure of the criminal law, the provision of these levels of appellate review are fortified by the constitutional stature of common law processes in the Seventh Amendment, which guarantee that ". . . no fact tried by jury, shall be otherwise

---

* Note that the right to defend oneself, although not to be taken for granted, was upheld in 1975 in *Faretta* v. *California*. Knowledge of the law is central to procedural fairness, but the courts have also realized the importance of participation in one's own defense.

reexamined in any court. . . ." Appeals concern law which affects outcomes. The right to appeal itself has been less subject to review than access to this process. The right to a trial transcript for indigent defendants arose from the Warren Court's concern about equal access to appellate review (*Griffin* v. *Illinois,* 1956). More recently, the Court has said that alternatives to full free transcripts might be acceptable where the state shows that these alternatives are adequate (*Mayer* v. *Chicago,* 1971). The right to counsel, which had been extended to the pre-trial and the trial period, also came to be required for the first appeal, sentencing, and probation revocation hearings. In *Douglas* v. *California* (1963), Justice William O. Douglas commented that "where the merits of the one and only appeal which an indigent has of right are decided without benefit of counsel . . . an unconstitutional line has been drawn between rich and poor." The Burger Court extended attorney assistance to prisoners where appeals are matters of right, but made an exception for petitions to the Supreme Court itself (*Ross* v. *Moffitt,* 1974). There, counsel is provided after the justices decide to hear a case.

Double Jeopardy. This is a confusing right without clearly demarcated coverage, but at a more general level it is a core principle of constitutional due process. While the defendant has a right to appeal a criminal conviction, the prosecutor cannot appeal if the defendant is acquitted. The basis for this is the right not to be tried twice for the same crime, or the protection against double jeopardy. From the Fifth Amendment, the clause reads "nor shall any person be subject for the same offense to be twice put in jeopardy of life or limb." Due to this right, trial judgments that go against the prosecution cannot be attacked. This has had a marked impact on the development of the constitutional law of criminal procedure. The tradition also holds, however, that once the defendant begins an appeal, the prosecution can defend his position (*U.S.* v. *Ball,* 1896) and sentences may be reviewed by higher courts (*U.S.* v. *DiFrancesco,* 1980). In *Palko* v. *Connecticut* (1937), however, Justice Benjamin Cardozo found that "double jeopardy" was not necessary to "the concept of ordered liberty." In *Palko,* state review of a verdict that resulted in a retrial and a death sentence was not considered a violation of double jeopardy. Because it was not held central to the due process at that critical juncture and because it is a highly complex realm, double jeopardy holds a particular fascination. It was not until 1969, in *Benton* v. *Maryland,* that the double jeopardy protections were considered fundamental enough to be applied to the states.

Related issues have been described by C. Herman Pritchett (1984:237) as surrounding what constitutes "jeopardy" in a legal proceeding and the meaning of "sameness" in an offense. On the first issue, it is jeopardy and not being tried twice that triggers the Constitution. It is not necessary for a trial to reach the verdict stage for double jeopardy protection to apply. If this were the case, trials might be stopped when they appeared to be going against the prosecution (*U.S.* v. *Jorn*, 1971), and then started all over again. On the second, offenses are viewed as the same where identical evidence is required to prove them. The event itself does not determine sameness (*Morgan* v. *Devine*, 1915). Thus, a number of charges may stem from one event and may even result in repeated trials (*Ciucci* v. *Illinois*, 1958; *Ashe* v. *Swenson*, 1970). Since 1976, the government may appeal when a trial judge reevaluates his own conduct and overturns a conviction in light of a Supreme Court decision (*U.S.* v. *Morrison*, 1981). In *U.S.* v. *Martin Linen Supply* (1977), however, the Court held that if a jury deadlocks in a federal criminal case, and the trial judge acquits, the government may not appeal. Although the Chief Justice dissented, the key to double jeopardy is still acquittal. Once the defendant has been acquitted, the government's case is finished. A defendant can be certain of having "once" been put in jeopardy of life and limb if he or she has been acquitted. Support for this view came in *U.S.* v. *Scott* (1978), where a pre-trial dismissal was reversed on appeal, the action being "prior to acquittal." In *Crist* v. *Bretz* (1978), the Court divided 6-3, holding that double jeopardy protection begins in state cases once the jury is impaneled. In federal court, the protection begins when the first witness is sworn in. In related cases, six justices held that a defendant cannot be subjected to a second trial if an appellate court reverses a conviction because of insufficient evidence (*Burks* v. *U.S.*, 1978) and that a Massachusetts man could not be tried a second time even though the Court of Appeals erroneously said the charges had been dismissed (*Greene* v. *Massey*, 1978).

Punishment. A tragic case links double jeopardy to post-trial protection from cruel and unusual punishment. *Louisiana ex rel. Francis* v. *Resweber* reached the Court in 1947, after the state had attempted to execute a convicted murderer. Because of mechanical difficulty, the electric chair failed to work. Lawyers for Francis tried to stop a second attempt on the grounds that it would constitute double jeopardy and be cruel and unusual punishment. Both claims were rejected, and Francis was executed. Recently, the Court held that the Constitution prohibits the state from asking for the death penalty at a retrial of defendants whose first jury, following sentencing proceedings that amounted to "trial" on the issue of punishment, declined to impose that punishment (*Bullington* v. *Missouri*, 1981).

Generally, the Eighth Amendment has provided a conventional standard of reasonableness with regard to cruel and unusual punishment. There are, for instance, equity issues in punishment that prevent the government from turning a fine into a prison term for those unable to pay (*Tate* v. *Short*, 1971; *Bearden* v. *Georgia*, 1983). Since 1910, in *Weems* v. *U.S.*, the expectation has been that punishment would be proportionate to the offense. In *Weems*, a case coming from the Philippines—which was under U.S. authority at the time—the Court found that 12 years in chains at hard labor for altering an official document did not meet these standards. Generally, the Court has deferred to legislative determination and judicial imposition of sentence. Thus, although there has been agreement that a proportionality requirement exists, some rather disproportionate results have survived, like forty years in prison for a marijuana conviction (*Hutto* v. *Davis*, 1982). However, in 1983, a life sentence without the possibility of parole for a series of nonviolent petty offenses was ruled "cruel and unusual" (*Solem* v. *Helm*, 1983). Punishment has been also viewed as cruel when it seemed inappropriate, as being jailed for drug addiction (*Robinson* v. *California*, 1962). Inappropriateness was also raised as an issue with reference to criminal sanctions for public drunkenness, although the appeal was unsuccessful (*Powell* v. *Texas*, 1968). Capital punishment for rape was held to be unconstitutional because the seriousness of the punishment did not match the seriousness of the crime (*Coker* v. *Georgia*, 1977).

Efforts to hold some forms of punishment inherently barbarous, though rare recently, draw a disproportionate amount of attention. Torture went out of fashion with the "enlightenment" penology embedded in the Constitution, and different forms of execution have been examined with reference to a modern sensibility. Public execution by firing squad (*Wilkerson* v. *Utah*, 1878) and electrocution (*In re Kemmler*, 1890) were upheld in the nineteenth century. Lethal injection has withstood legal challenge more recently.

Capital punishment, whatever the form, draws the most attention to the Eighth Amendment these days. It can be distinguished from all other forms of punishment when considering its finality. Since it was barely suggested by earlier cases on the death penalty, the 1972 decision in *Furman* v. *Georgia* was a bombshell. By a vote of 5-4, the Court held the death penalty to be a violation of the constitutional ban on cruel and unusual punishment. Justices Douglas, Stewart, and White based their opinions on the capriciousness with which the death penalty is imposed and its excessive impact on minorities. Justices Brennan and Marshall, the other members of the majority, focused on execution's "affront to human dignity," characterizing it as the ultimate denial of that respect for the individual traditionally associated with due process. The capriciousness of this ultimate penalty, rather than the death penalty per se, made it cruel and unusual. Many states revised their statutes, and these statutes began to reach the Court by the middle of the decade.

In the appeal by Troy Gregg of his death sentence, under a

reconstituted Georgia death penalty statute, the Court was asked whether a "non-capricious" death penalty was constitutional (*Gregg* v. *Georgia*, 1976). Gregg was convicted of having killed two men who had given him a ride while he was hitchhiking. His trial was divided, or "bifurcated," so that guilt was determined first, followed by a separate process for determining the penalty. Death was a possible penalty when the case involved "aggravating circumstances" such as aircraft hijacking, treason, prior conviction of a capital felony, commission in the act of another capital felony, or when the murder was "horribly vile." Gregg's case was held to include all of the last three circumstances. On automatic appeal to the state supreme court, another mechanism that sought to minimize arbitrariness, the verdict was monitored for the influence of "passions, prejudice or any other arbitrary factor." The justices found the Georgia death penalty statute constitutional, and Gregg was sentenced to die. But, in the same year, "mandatory" capital punishment statutes— passed after *Furman* in response to the charge of capricious application— were struck down (*Roberts* v. *Louisiana*, 1976).

By the 1980s, the death sentence was on the rise, although it was still rarely carried out. While the federal government sought the penalty for treason, espionage, and presidential assassination, 35 states enacted new statutes to meet constitutional requirements set by the Supreme Court. In 1981, there were 780 people on death row in the United States. Opponents of the death penalty claim that the same arbitrariness and racial discrimination that led to its temporary abolition in 1972 still exist. Supporters, like Justice William Rehnquist, criticize the procedural protection that allows imposition of the sentence to be delayed. As part of the continuing split over exactly how to treat capital punishment, the Court upheld in 1983 the use of expedited procedures by the courts of appeals to review habeas corpus petitions from death row inmates (*Barefoot* v. *Estelle*, 1983). The 5-4 decision reflected the division over capital punishment itself. The aura around the death penalty, amplified by its infrequency as a punishment, gives special meaning to due process in this area. Since the death penalty cannot be revoked, the search for truth is more significant here, and pressure to eliminate the penalty as the ultimate indignity is likely to remain strong.

Most people will not use the criminal due process guarantees, although these are among the best known constitutional rights. There are times when we may wish to invoke some constitutional right in order to let the police or other authorities know that we are aware of limits to their authority, even if they are not. The rights may not stop determined authorities without a struggle and in an administrative context of plea bargains the rights that delineate the criminal process are generally well in the background. Criminal due process rights are a resource and the institutions of the criminal law have been set up to reflect guarantees which carry the enlightenment humanism behind the Bill of Rights. It is as an affirmation of that tradition that these rights are known best.

Civil Procedure

Criminal procedure epitomizes the application of constitutional safeguards to individuals in jeopardy. We feel safer because the criminal procedure protections exist, yet they affect relatively few people. Civil due process, or procedure, is different. It is newer, the protections are less dramatic, and its impact, at least quantitatively, is far broader than criminal due process. With expansion of the roles and services provided by the government, substantial issues arise outside the criminal sphere to which due process may be applied. Whatever the object of struggle, whether it be an education or a welfare benefit, procedural guarantees set standards for how people are to be treated when government action threatens them with a loss.

"Imperialism" of the Due Process Model

Legal concepts evolve in different ways. One way comes from changes in meaning. This was true of due process in the late nineteenth century when the justices, using the concept broadly, offered protection for corporations from legislation concerning such matters as baking and child labor on the basis of "substantive" due process protection. Concepts can also expand their application. This was evident in the "due process revolution" that applied the protections of the federal system to the states in the 1960s. This second kind of change is political and can be described in terms associated with that realm. Due process in such institutional settings is almost imperialistic. When it moves into new settings, the procedure alters the structure of power as old ways of doing things, and the interests they served, give way to new ways and new interests.

C. Herman Pritchett has called due process "perhaps the most expansive and adaptable of the Constitution's many broad phrases" (Pritchett, 1948:587). It is an idea that sets the parameters of relations between persons and institutions. Even in its most specific provisions, such as the right to assistance of counsel, due process determines how social institutions will operate. Its requirements change the nature of the institutional setting. Where it is applied to a new institution, it brings with it forms of interaction and authoritative sources of meaning. The degree of procedural imperialism is impressive when the range of institutions where due process has become influential in the last two decades is considered. Beginning with public employment, due process challenged the old distinction between a right and a privilege. The higher federal standard of procedural guarantees fueled early developments in criminal rights, but after a decade of incorporation in that area, there followed the application of procedural safeguards to other institutional settings. Due process was accompanied by the recognition of entitlements as a matter of settled expectations. Public assistance was perhaps the most dramatic example. Here the effect was on how decisions were made. In prisons and schools, however, the institutional setting began to look different as it was influenced by new standards.

It is inadequate to look at due process, especially the sort associated with noncriminal situations, without addressing the relationship between constitutional ideas and the institutional settings in which they are applied. Institutions are constituted by people bound together by ideas. New ideas change the substantive nature of that bond. In the area of freedom of expression, the new standard of protection came after the First World War. The result was an expansion of what could be said by the press or on the street corner. In the case of the criminal process, the enthusiasm for procedure reached new heights after the Second World War, as part of a nationalizing effort. The result was new police procedures. In the civil setting, where changing norms and reliance on the legal process have swamped family courts with child custody battles, constitutional standards have been invoked to preserve parental rights (*Santosky* v. *Kramer*, 1982). The result in all of these cases has been new institutional settings.

Like the specific provisions that transformed the criminal process, a broader due process, associated with fundamental fairness, has been extended to major social institutions. Prisons and schools are two settings with strong institutional commitments that reveal another facet of the interactive transformations that have taken place. Prisons are settings where little faith in the human spirit exists and where the inhabitants least exemplify those aspects of the ideal citizen that are the foundation for due process. Schools are a good comparison because there greater faith can be found, although the structure of authority is remarkably similar. Due process has changed both areas in fundamental ways.

Prisons: Due Process Issues

Due process governs some prison disciplinary proceedings. In this setting, due process refers to internal (civil) proceedings, rather than the external (criminal) context. This is clearly not a civil setting in the ordinary sense. It is influenced by the larger penal environment.

Nevertheless, the due process issues that follow are sufficiently civil to provide insight into this dimension of the constitutional right. The general ideal of due process applies to administrative hearings affecting those in confinement, although the scope of specific rights enjoyed by inmates is limited. The decisions of the courts, delineating the extent to which traditional due process applies to prisoners, have narrowly interpreted constitutional requirements. In these cases, the search for truth is being balanced against correctional goals and security. Prison due process will therefore be treated as a link. It has a connection to both criminal and civil standards of justice. This angle is unique enough to justify attention here.

Balancing. Constraints imposed in prison disciplinary cases have traditionally followed from the doctrine that the process due depends on the severity of the sentence and the belief that "one cannot automatically apply [guarantees] designed for free citizens in an open society to the very different situation presented by a . . . prison" (*Wolff* v. *McDonnell*, 1974:953). This ruling came in a case where prison officials guarded against contraband by opening mail from an inmate's attorney. The balance struck by the institution and approved by the courts in order to preserve constitutional rights required that the inmate be present when the mail was opened. The courts conceded that imprisonment justifies the denial of certain rights available to free citizens and that the nature of the institution legitimizes restrictions on due process.

Court involvement with prisoners' rights has swung from a "hands-off" policy to an interventionist approach in the last two decades. Historically, the courts found that a prisoner's "fate is by law in the hands of administrators whose acts . . . may be presumed legal" (*Landman* v. *Royster*, 1971:643). As early as 1899, however, extreme cases evoked judicial intervention. In that year, a prisoner who had been chained at night by the neck so that he could neither sit nor lie down was found to have had his constitutional rights violated (*In re Birdsong*, 1899). This ruling came from a lower federal court, and it would be over 50 years before widespread constitutional supervision of the rights of prisoners would develop. This is at least in part due to the uniqueness of this sphere, where the person in jeopardy has already forfeited some of his or her rights.

The mid-1960s saw a dramatic increase in the application of constitutional protection to prisoners' rights (Cole, Hanson, and Silbert, 1981). Since *Cooper* v. *Pate* (1964), where statutory protection under the Civil Rights Act of 1871 was accorded to prisoners, the number of suits has risen from 218 in 1966 to 13,000 in 1980 (Cole, Hanson, and Silbert, 1981:1). The suits were for injunctive and compensatory relief over a variety of issues—from the brutality of guards or abuses by other prisoners to inadequate care and the loss of personal property. Although the attention reflects a concern for prisoners rights, the outcomes have not always been in the prisoners' favor. In cases where the courts have intervened, the decisions generally reflect a pro-institution stance. In assessing the application of constitutional standards to institutional proceedings, the courts consider the feasibility of due process rights and the impact that certain provisions could have on prison administrations. This is the institutional balance: ". . . that a prisoner retains rights under the Due Process Clause in no way implies that this right is not subject to restrictions imposed by the nature of the regime to which he has been lawfully committed . . . there must be mutual accommodation between institutional needs and objectives and the provisions of the Constitution that are of general application" (*Wolff* v. *McDonnell*, 1974).

Early judicial intervention in the administration of prisons was closely tied to physical brutality and the degradation of being stripped, beaten, and exposed to severe and threatening conditions (*Jordan* v. *Fitzharris*, 1966; *Wright* v. *McMann*, 1967; *Jackson* v. *Bishop*, 1968). Occasionally, deprivations of more general "civil" rights—such as correspondence privileges—have been viewed as cruel and unusual. More often, however, challenges have raised less sweeping due process claims. Recent due process cases in prison conditions address three questions: Has the discipline imposed on the inmate violated a constitutional right? Does the state have a legitimate charge? Did the inmate's actions warrant the punishment meted out (Hirschkop and Millerman, 1969)?

Hearings. The processes by which administrative hearings are conducted in prisons can be compared to the constitutional protections outside the walls. There is a parallel since accuracy and legitimacy are still issues, although in the prison context the process is limited by punitive and security considerations. The due process right to a hearing includes a timely and adequate notice of the action and charge, an opportunity to present a defense, and an impartial decision maker. In 1979, in *Greenholtz* v. *Inmates of the Nebraska Penal and Correctional Complex*, the Supreme Court reviewed the process by which Nebraska determined eligibility for parole on the basis of a constitutionally protected "conditional liberty" interest held by the inmates. The Court found that a reasonable entitlement to due process is not created whenever a state provides for the possibility of parole and that the procedure provided by statute—which included notice and hearing— was adequate. However, in *Hewitt* v. *Helms* (1983) Justice Rehnquist reaffirmed the tradition whereby a liberty interest requiring due process considerations can be created by a state through legislative supervision of its prisons. The interests range from systems of good time credits to freedom from solitary confinement.

Of equal import are those rights not generally believed to be constitutionally guaranteed to prisoners: the rights to cross-examine and confront adverse witnesses, to remain silent without unfavorable inferences being drawn, to representation by appointed or retained counsel, and to knowledge of reasons for denial. Due process in administrative proceedings outside prisons requires that defendants have the right to cross-examine and confront adverse witnesses. This right is important in cases where people challenge a charge as "resting on incorrect or misleading factual premises or on misapplication of rules or policies to the facts of particular cases" (*Goldberg* v. *Kelly*, 1970:299). This contributes to fair adjudication and a means for finding the truth. Lower courts, since 1971, held that in prison disciplinary cases, "the right to confront and cross-examine witnesses is essential . . ." and that "the ultimate decision be based on evidence presented at the hearing, which the prisoner has the opportunity to refute" (*Landman* v. *Royster*, 1971:653). But in *Wolff*, the Supreme Court nullified the *Landman* decision and offered the view that cross-examination of adverse witnesses would jeopardize the security of institutions and unnecessarily burden administrations. Since guards are usually the witnesses against inmates, the Court held that cross-examination would place guards on equal terms with inmates and thus threaten the officers' authority. Furthermore, the Court worried that institutions would require larger staffs to monitor cells during hearings. In some institutions, inmates are permitted to confront adverse witnesses; however, if the administrators choose to rescind this right, they are not constitutionally compelled to provide an explanation for such a denial (*Baxter* v. *Palmigiano*, 1976:823). In 1983 the court limited the protection even further when it held that anything more than a written statement from a prisoner contesting charges that he was a security threat and needed to be segregated would be at the discretion of the prison administration (*Hewitt* v. *Helms*, 1983).

The self-incrimination provision of the Fifth Amendment does not apply to prisoners who refuse to testify during disciplinary proceedings. Adverse inferences may be drawn from the refusal to testify, contrary to the *Miranda* ruling applicable in criminal cases (*Baxter*, 1976:821). Similarly, the Court adjudged in *Wolff* that inmates do not have the right to appointed or retained counsel during disciplinary hearings. If the administration identifies an inmate as being incompetent, however, another prisoner may assist the defendant in preparing evidence for the hearing; but otherwise, inmates are not guaranteed the right to assist one another. After this decision, a rehearing of *Clutchette* v. *Procunier* (1974) was held to amend the original decision in accordance with the provisions outlined in *Wolff*. Judge Shirley Hufstedler, sitting on a three-judge panel, refuted the *Wolff* standard, claiming that "any guarantee of process due is empty if the particular inmate is incompetent to avail himself of it" (*Clutchette*, 1975:616). Finally, even in cases where a disciplinary infraction violates state law, inmates do not have a right to appointed or retained counsel at disciplinary hearings (*Baxter*, 1976:811).

Measured Impartiality. The courts place limitations not only on testimony and the right to counsel but also on the type of adjudicator. Although prisoners have the right to an impartial decision maker, the only stiplulation ensuring impartiality is that "the hearing be conducted by some person other than the one initially dealing with the case" (*Morrissey* v. *Brewer*, 1972:497). In practice, correctional administrators, serving as adjudicators, decide disciplinary cases. In fact, in *Hewitt* v. *Helms* (1983), the prisoner's only opportunity to respond to charges and influence an administrative decision must be addressed to the official making that decision. Outside institutional settings, this would be a clear violation of the neutrality provision, but as we will see in looking at schools, due process does have a different meaning in institutions. The restrictions on specific due process rights affect the ability of arbitrators to determine the truth "beyond reasonable doubt." Instead, the disposition of inmate cases is made by weighing the evidence presented and deciding which side has a more valid case. The fact that inmates are rarely allowed to cross-examine witnesses, coupled with the fact that correctional officers with a stake in the outcome act as judges, diminishes the likelihood that truth will surface, no matter what standard for weighing the evidence is employed.

After hearing officers make determinations, prisoners do not have a right to administrative appeal. An impediment to appellate review stems from the holding in the *Wolff* case that inmates need not be given a written statement as to the evidence relied upon in determining the disciplinary action. Without this knowledge, inmates have difficulty finding grounds for appeal.

The courts have established guidelines for internal prison hearings. Many of these guidelines remain subject to revocation, however, if administrators feel their implementation could threaten the security of the institution. This qualification, and the fact that the courts consistently defer to prison administrators in disciplinary hearings, emphasizes the difference in the scope of specific due process inside these institutions. Although the level of deference to administrative expertise in prisoners' rights cases has changed in the last two decades, the Supreme Court showed its hesitation to transgress administrative authority in *Meachum* v. *Fano* (1976:454) in writing that

> To hold . . . that any substantial deprivation imposed by prison authorities triggers the procedural protections of the Due Process Clause would subject to judicial review a wide spectrum of disciplinary actions

that traditionally have been the business of prison administrators rather than of the federal courts.

As a consequence of such judicial deference, the capacity of due process for determining truth in prisons is limited.

When courts apply the Constitution to cases involving prisoners, the right to due process is considered, although it is balanced by the concern for institutional efficiency. Justice Byron White, writing for the Court in *Wolff*, accounted for the establishment of specific rights as representative of "a reasonable accommodation between the interests of the inmates and the needs of the institution" (*Wolff*, 1974:960). It is partly a function of the limited claim that a prisoner may make that he or she remains a citizen, from which due process flows, that procedural guarantees have been so circumscribed in this realm. But it is due to the spirited application of procedural formalism that civil liberties protections were introduced into prisons. This is a development that is, as we have seen, not simply a charitable response to the less fortunate, but one of the ways that procedural protections present the authority of the government in a humane light.

Schools: Three Models

In schools, the relationship between students and administrators has also come to be affected by the due process guaranteed by the Constitution. Here the right follows from the liberty and property interests associated with an education. As with prisons, the institutional situation goes a long way in determining the nature of individual rights and the due process required. In this section, the focus will be on college students. Their rights involve procedural guarantees that shield students from the arbitrary exercise of administrative power (see Van Alstyne, 1977). With these issues, the context in which the rights are applied is as crucial as it is in other due process cases.

Since we will be approaching constitutional rights in a sphere where they have only recently been applied, it is instructive to look at the prior models in order to illuminate the nature of institutional incorporation. Since the colonial period, and well before the development of our present system of public schools, there have been essentially three models of administrative authority: (1) the *in loco parentis* model; (2) the contract, or market model; and the (3) due process, or rights model.

In Loco Parentis Model. The earliest model, *in loco parentis*, stemmed from analogy to parental authority. Its manifestation in legal doctrine came to symbolize the perception administrators had of their authority—its nature and limits. The doctrine developed out of tort law, the law of private conflicts, for those suits brought in behalf of minors seeking damages from teachers for assault and battery resulting from corporal punishment. Parental authority was the standard and the model back to the early part of this century, when state courts held that whether rules or regulations were wise, or their aims worthy, is a matter left to the discretion of the authorities or parents. Cases from state courts throughout the country have held that courts have no more authority to interfere than they have to control the domestic discipline of a father in his family.* The legal principle resulted in extreme deference by the courts to academic administrators out of respect for the challenges they were thought to face in running the schools.

The governing principle grew as a model for general academic authority. Thus, the validity of rules prohibiting students from spending time and money in certain ways, living in certain places, or associating with particular people was tested by analogy with whether parents could maintain such a rule. Often, even the substance of the model reflected that of a rather strict and protective parent. As an example, there was a time, up until the late 1960s, when women were allowed in male dormitories for only a few hours on Sunday afternoons. During that highly charged period, doors had to be kept open and the occupant and visitor had to keep three feet on the floor at all times, epitomizing the rule of "in loco parentis" in residential institutions. It may come as no surprise that this was also a period in which the authorities were more protective of girls than "men." Women had curfews, 10:30 P.M. on week nights, 12:30 A.M. or 1:00 A.M. on weekends. In some places of course they still do, but no longer at the state universities. In the 1960s men could stay out as long as they wanted. This represented a difference in attitude toward men and women that appears in related forms today, as in the prosecution of men, but not women, for statutory rape. (See Chapter 6.)

Contract Model. Standards began to change in the 1970s, and the impetus came from both the courts and the culture. The U.S. Supreme Court directed a dramatic period of liberal activism that raised awareness of rights and expanded protection to the powerless. At a cultural level, especially in higher education, it became evident that institutions of 30,000 students or more had little of the warmth and hominess of the family. Moreover, in 1970, students had gotten older; the average college student was likely to be an adult. The old standards differentiating faculty from students began to break down out of the pressure to be treated as equals. By the late 1960s, courts showed signs of abandoning

---

* See *Santosky* v. *Kramer* (1982) for a recent holding on procedural issues concerning the state's power to intervene in family disputes.

in loco parentis. As an Alabama court cautiously put it in 1968, "college does not stand, strictly speaking, *in loco parentis* to its students."

In each of these models, the historial period is an approximation and there is considerable overlap between models. The standard for this period during which students began to see themselves as mature individuals is the "contract" model. Contract is associated with common law protection for business agreements. As a model for institutional responsibility, it has even less substance than *in loco parentis* and holds that the obligations of an administrator stem from the terms of the relationship that existed when a student entered the institution. There would be little recourse to notions of justice and fairness if they were not stipulated. The issue to come before the courts would be whether there was a rule in effect and whether the student had followed it. This, of course, suggests a propensity to "go by the book" in order to remain relatively safe from the litigation that inevitably followed a model derived from economic exchange.

The doctrine can also be associated with "consumerism" among college students. In this sense, it reflects the inclination to consider education a product. Administrators are seen in the role of managers responsible for efficiency and quality control. Some results from operating in this fashion were greater dissemination of rules and regulations, and publication of student guides to teacher quality. At some institutions students even began to relate the quality of the course and the salary a professor earned. Although the model, and the movement which spawned it had some impact, one serious problem with this attitude was that it reinforced the ideas that students were not responsible for getting educated, and that they would receive a product for their tuition much like buying a bag of chips at the market.

Legal scholars also pointed out that the model's protection for students had been minimal from its inception because the institution set the terms of the contract. This was evident in a 1923 case involving Bryn Mawr College. There the courts upheld a clause in the college rules and procedures that said "the college reserves the right to exclude at any time students whose conduct or academic standing it regards as undesirable." Because the contract model had little substance, students were expelled and disciplined with minimal attention to their rights and even where the institutions had written rights and obligations into their codes of student conduct, these were often ignored. The contract model did, however, produce some unusual challenges to teacher competence.

Due Process Model. The third model is derived from civil liberties, and its greatest impact is in the area of due process. This model is a recent phenomenon that stems from the demise of *in loco parentis* and from the due process revolution since the 1960s. The sources of the law are, for the first time, clearly outside the institutional context. Yet, in all cases, the context has influenced the form that due process has taken. The early civil liberties applied to schools were actually statutory protections, such as those of the Civil Rights Acts. First employed in 1961 (*Dixon v. Alabama*, 5th Cir.), they signaled a shift to new substantive conceptions of how institutions should operate. This decision ordered that students be reinstated where they had been dismissed without written specification of the charges and a hearing. The privacy and freedom of information acts also significantly altered the context of students' rights in the schools. Other major sources in this area have been constitutional rights such as equal protection—with its concern for discrimination—and freedom of expression—with its unique association to the school environment. In one expression case, for example, students wearing black armbands in opposition to the war in Vietnam had been summarily suspended by school authorities, but they were vindicated on appeal to the Supreme Court (*Tinker v. Des Moines School District*, 1969).

In 1975, in *Goss v. Lopez*, due process rights were provided to students who had been temporarily suspended from their high schools without a hearing. Having found that the state of Ohio promised the students an education, Justice Byron White held that this benefit could not be taken away without due process. The process "due" (*Morrissey v. Brewer*, 1972) came to be treated as a function of the right in jeopardy. In this case, due process would apply because the guaranteed education was threatened. Basing his argument on *Cafeteria and Restaurant Workers Union v. McElroy* (1961), White emphasized the practical nature of the procedural requirement. The minimal standard was "the opportunity to be heard" (*Grannis v. Ordean*, 1918) or "notice and opportunity for hearing appropriate to the nature of the case" (*Mullane v. Central Hanover Trust Co.*, 1950). As White summed it up, the students had to be given "some kind of notice and afforded some kind of hearing."

In this decision, the Court considered the burdens that due process required in relation to the interests of school authorities in carrying out their institutional functions. The requirement for suspensions of 10 days or less was "an informal give-and-take" between the school authorities and the student in order to preserve the essence of due process, an opportunity to get at the truth while respecting the individual. Although confrontation in a high school corridor has few of the trappings of formal hearings, it does reflect the twin functions evident in the concept employed by Justice Frankfurter in *Anti-Fascist Refugee Committee v. McGrath* (1951). In addition, Justice White wrote that if the student denies the charges, he or she deserves an explanation and an opportunity to present his or her side of the story (*Goss*, 1975). This might help keep the exchange open, although White did not require any delay between the notice and the opportunity to respond.

As with due process in other institutional settings, *Goss* linked the procedure to the weight of the deprivation. This pragmatic approach was evident again in *Board of Curators of the University of Missouri* v. *Horowitz* (1978), where the fact situation produced an important distinction between disciplinary and academic judgments. *Horowitz* demonstrates the extent to which civil due process in the academy has been influenced by a penal model resulting in considerable deference to institutional functions. In the *Horowitz* case, a medical student had been dismissed on the basis of "erratic attendance at clinical sessions, poor performance around patients and poor personal hygiene" (*Horowitz*, 1978:81). She claimed that she had been unconstitutionally deprived of liberty and property. Justice Rehnquist considered the claim in his opinion for the majority on the Supreme Court. According to Rehnquist, the liberty interest that Ms. Horowitz was entitled to invoke was the opportunity to continue her medical education and gain employment as a doctor. Rehnquist deferred to faculty and administrative prerogatives where educational evaluations were at stake. Since the school had informed her of its dissatisfaction and the final decision was believed to be "careful and deliberate," the disappointed medical student was found to have been awarded "at least as much due process as the 14th Amendment requires." Because there had been "deliberation," the Court found that the institution met the minimal requirements due when the issue is purely academic. In the justice's words, it was "Like the decision of an individual professor as to the proper grade for a student in his course . . . and is not readily adapted to the procedural tools of judicial or administrative decision making" (*Horowitz*, 1978:90). His concern was over transforming the situation into an adversary one. The distinction may have broad consequences. By recognizing the liberty interest, but requiring little because of the setting, the Court diluted the value of due process itself in deference to the traditional prerogatives of the academy.

Academic judgments have traditionally involved deference to expertise. It would be odd to call a jury to find out whether a student would make a good doctor or would deserve an A in a civil liberties class. Discrimination on the basis of sex and religion, however, such as Ms. Horowitz claimed, taint any evaluation process. Charges of bias are exactly the sort of thing for which neutral adjudication and procedural safeguards were developed. To dismiss them as "substantive," in the fashion of Justice Rehnquist, is to ignore the tradition of procedural fairness. Due process emerged as a hedge against arbitrary state action, for the purpose of honoring the individual and getting at the truth. The requirement of a fair hearing historically would include a procedural protection against bias. This "political" due process becomes operative when some claim, about which the society is particularly sensitive, is made. Because of such claims, due process may be appropriate where ordinarily "expert" judgment could not be challenged. For instance, when hiring or promotion decisions are made, the articulated criteria are inevitably job-related, no matter what the "real" reasons. In the university, judgments about grades always involve expertise, yet it is now recognized that racism and sexism can affect expertise. It is in this regard that sexual harassment, as an emerging political issue, is closely connected to due process.

Sexual Harassment: Due Process Issues

Sexual harassment is a social phenomenon that amounts to the abuse of power for personal sexual pleasure. Like such abuses in pursuit of financial gain, sexual harassment is an activity of long standing. Unlike abuses that have money as the object, such abuse has not been publicly sanctioned until recently. Because an early demand in the battle against sexual harassment was for "grievance procedures" and because the response from those charged with harassment is invariably a call for procedural protection, this area is fertile ground for discussion of due process. This has been particularly true in the academic environment in the early 1980s. On the one hand, the volatility presents the classic challenge to due process: the confrontation between an outraged and single-minded public and the object of their scorn and fear. On the other hand, the current attention to this issue serves as an opportunity for examining the impact of legal and formal structures in traditional spheres like colleges. In these environments, traditional modes of proceeding have sometimes been out of phase with the law. Although the issue has become a significant one on college campuses, however, it is of course not limited to this realm.

The tactical moves in the battle over sexual harassment have also not been limited to due process protection, and the protection itself has not always been attributed to the constitutional protections. Some of the initial energy, stimulated by the women's movement, raised issues of equality and equal protection based on the treatment of women in the workplace. Similarly, the right against sexual harassment is not a procedural due process right. In fact, it probably does not make much sense to see that right as a constitutional right at all. Rather, the right against sexual harassment is a social and moral right that derives from the way we define appropriate behavior in this society. The due process right is a response to harassment and, in that sense, it is a strategic consideration for those who would minimize such activity. Like due process generally, the appeal to due process in this context is a resource in a political struggle, a tool that is provided by the state to maintain its own position of authority.

The most common definition of sexual harassment comes from Equal Employment Opportunity Commission (EEOC) regulations (45 Federal Regulation 74676-77, November 10, 1980), and it emphasizes the special setting that makes unwelcomed sexual advances a problem of this sort.* There are broader definitions of the conduct that include "... sexist remarks about a woman's clothing, body or sexual activity, unnecessary touching, patting or pinching, leering or ogling a woman's body, constant brushing against a woman's body ..." (AAUP, 1980). Part of raising consciousness concerning a problem consists of describing it; such description necessarily results in a broad definition. The context is also a matter of debate, with questions arising as to whether sexual harassment can occur between persons of the same status, such as two students. The most likely response to this is the part of the EEOC guidelines that addresses unreasonable interference and creation of an intimidating atmosphere. In such cases, even people of the same status are capable of abuses of power. Although it is generally portrayed as a condition where men are the aggressors, this is at least partly a function of their greater access to positions of power in the past.

There is nothing new about employers or faculty members responding to the sexual tension that exists because of our humanity. Without a degree of such tension, the human race is clearly less likely to perpetuate itself (given present technology anyway), and such a degree of tension is the happy product of physical relations, which many of us quite enjoy. It is the abuse of power, not sex (just as it was violence and not sex when we discussed pornography), that presents a social problem. Not all agree on the extent of this problem. Phyllis Schlafly, leader of the anti-Equal Rights Amendment forces, for example, calls the sexual harassment issue a basis for unscrupulous persons to file mischievous complaints. "The most cruel and damaging sexual harassment taking place today," she said in 1981, "is the harassment by feminists and their federal government allies against the role of motherhood and the role of the dependent wife." Her view is that for the virtuous woman there is not a problem, that men hardly ever ask sexual favors of women from whom the certain answer is "no." This perspective, although it is meant to trivialize the issue, should not be dismissed entirely, since the messages we send each other must clearly be taken into account.

---

* Unwelcomed sexual advances, requests for sexual favors, and other verbal or physical conduct of a sexual nature constitute sexual harassment when: (1) submission to such conduct is made either explicitly or implicitly a term or condition of an individual's employment, (2) submission to or rejection of such conduct by an individual is used as the basis for employment decisions affecting such individual, or (3) such conduct has the purpose or effect of unreasonably interfering with an individual's work performance or creating an intimidating, hostile, or offensive working or academic environment.

The issue of sexual harassment was first articulated in the law as a form of sex discrimination (Mackinnon, 1979). Appeal was to the provisions of the 1964 Civil Rights Act. Other avenues of legal response have been considered, such as criminalization, civil actions, and new statutes; but, the most significant one is perhaps that of the fundamental right to due process. This is not only the most powerful response because it exists as a constitutional right, but it is the right traditionally employed to stem abuses of power. Since power comes from the place one occupies in the institutional structure, the significance of due process is that it reconstitutes the power relationships in the institutions that need watching.

Due process, in a sexual harassment case, serves both parties as well as the institution within which the harassment takes place. Its importance to the aggrieved party (the person who has been harassed) is in the chance to be heard and perhaps to focus attention on the conduct as well as the general issue. Due process makes it harder to ignore the conduct; consequently "grievance procedures" have been a major part of the claim. The person charged with doing the harassing has the more traditional claim to due process. Finally, the institution within which the harassment has occurred gains to the extent that a problem that would otherwise poison the work environment is aired in a regular and controllable way.

Legitimation

Idealism may not be a requisite for attaining public office, but the law that governs official behavior has its own idealism. Due process is such an ideal, and its importance reaches beyond its application in particular instances. Originally tied to a public promise extending the range of sovereign power by providing superior mechanisms for settling disputes, the twin functions of a search for truth and respect for the individual reflect the interests operative at the "founding" of the American Republic. The constitutional rights to due process are the parts of the larger legal structure that contribute to its authority by guaranteeing fairness and settled procedure. They have become a basis for economic and political relations. Process is not only a central tenet of liberalism, it is the institutional principle on which liberal democratic regimes have been constituted.

Procedural guarantees strengthen public authority because they contribute to the structural autonomy of the legal system. A rising middle class in the seventeenth century used law to eliminate the "... arbitrariness and dead weight of ascriptive status distinctions from its profit making activities" (Balbus, 1973:4). This involved separating the prosecutorial from the judicial functions, thereby symbolizing the separation of the law from the immediate influences of politics (Kircheimer, 1961:120; Balbus, 1973:20). Thus, among other things, due process means that the court proceedings must be isolated from direct interference by political executives and legislatures, and by powerful groups in the society. It also means that judgments must not favor wealthy, well-connected, socially prominent, politically powerful litigants over the less favored. Due process also means that no one will be punished except in accord with principles of law that are accepted as legitimate and that are applied even-handedly to all. Thus, we speak of the legal system as having a certain autonomy from the social, political, and economic systems. Only then can litigants expect fair treatment, no matter how much they are disliked by various social and political powers.

The name given to this rationalization of public authority is "legitimation." The term emphasizes the social function of legal practices beyond the resolution of disputes. A regime that accords its legal system such autonomy is more likely to be considered legitimate by its own citizens than one that does not provide fair legal process. Like the formal rules of which it is a part, due process legitimizes public authority in a society where there are inequities. Its promise cuts across these inequities to provide a practice more egalitarian than the society generally, and its provisions serve as an ideal to which transformative appeals can be tied. Its promise, however, also perpetuates systemic inequality and minimizes critical attack on the system. In short, differences in wealth and power will appear more acceptable to the poor and powerless in a society that treats everyone fairly and equally in court than in a society that does not. A well-publicized acquittal, like access to law books in prison, makes things seem less desperate.

The provision of lawyers for the poor, romanticized in print and film in such productions as *Gideon's Trumpet*, while it equalizes the power of people *before the law*, provides hope based on an untenable distinction between the legal and the social sphere. Given the different resources of the rich and poor, it seems clear that "if the law is indifferent to the distinction between rich and poor, it follows that the law will necessarily tend to support and maintain this distinction" (Balbus, 1973:5). In the studied indifference to privilege that remains after formal equality before the law has been established, legal autonomy works at cross purposes, preserving privileges while it denies their relevance, and attacking oppression while it serves as its instrument.

Like the pressures on the search for truth and respect for the individual within due process, there are pressures on the whole institutional apparatus. During the uprisings in the inner cities in the

1960s, for instance, less severe penalties were imposed on participants than for comparable offenses in "normal times." This was a practical accommodation for the system under stress. It served the long-term interest in the law, but it appeared to go against the immediate interest in maintaining order. Thus, preservation of the procedural promise is necessarily somewhat beyond the control of those with power. Sometimes the powerful must sacrifice their particular interests in order to preserve the larger ideals. For example, when the system of procedural guarantees gives a mental patient an opportunity to gain release or a minority defendant a more deliberative forum than he or she might otherwise receive, the interests of those in power may not appear to be served. But their place in the system is dependent on its continuing operation, and these procedures are essential to that continuity. They give people a reason for hope and an opportunity for change.

Finally, even where a regime perpetuates inequalities in part through procedural guarantees, the fact that the regime must then itself defer to these guarantees in order to maintain its credibility often results in fairer treatment for the powerless. In other words, a government that seeks to gain popular support by claiming to be fair often must actually be fair. Due process sometimes allows citizens to successfully challenge arbitrary government action, and it sometimes even compels more equality of treatment. Because due process insists that all citizens be given the same procedural treatment by government, it is more clearly consistent with a democratic vision than some other traditional liberties, like property, which acknowledge that some citizens are to be far better off than others. In spite of its potential for excusing and legitimating social and economic inequalities, the vision that everyone should have a full, fair, and equal day in court remains a very attractive one.

We now leave the realm of due process, and turn to constitutional liberty. In the next chapter, we will cover application of the right to reproductive privacy and "lifestyle" privacy and to protection for autonomous action.

Liberty | 4

To some, constitutional liberty is a collection of claims that have been fabricated at different times to serve political interests. To others, it is the essence of law drawn from the texts of liberal democracy and critical for its survival. Not surprisingly, an accurate description of this right must incorporate a little of both views. Liberty has been relied on heavily in constitutional interpretation, and its use has been marked by more than the usual amount of judicial creativity. The right is also, however, well integrated into the structure of the constitution and a fine example of the inevitable social influences on fundamental rights.

The Tradition

In an 1823 case (*Corfield* v. *Coryell*), Supreme Court Justice Bushrod Washington took the position that the Constitution contained fundamental rights that went beyond those explicitly mentioned. "Privileges and immunities" were initially where the more general and unstated constitutional rights were placed. These were ideas about law and how it should function that transcended procedure. Not long afterward, the view that due process in the document meant more than what was specifically written in the Constitution was announced by Justice Benjamin Curtis in *Murray's Lessee* v. *Hoboken Land and Improvement Co.* (1856). The dispute before the Court involved when and how the government could take land from an individual. Justice Curtis argued that an individual could claim protection under a general due process right or "law of the land" that had its roots in the Magna Carta.

After passage of the Fourteenth Amendment, the general protection that had been associated with privileges and immunities and "law of the land" ideas found a doctrinal ground in due process when life, liberty or property were threatened. "Life" came to be associated with the particular protections in the Constitution outlining criminal procedure. "Property" has had such significance in constitutional interpretation that the next chapter will be devoted to it. Here, we direct attention to protection for "liberty" in the Fifth and Fourteenth Amendments. Although a decision on the Fourteenth Amendment in the *Slaughterhouse Cases* (1873) initially limited its application to newly freed slaves, subsequent expansion including the treatment of corporations as "persons" accompanied the demands of business during the Industrial Revolution and association of constitutional liberty with business interests continued until after the fight over the New Deal.

Beginning near the end of the nineteenth century, and evident in *Hurtado* v. *California* (1884), the idea of fundamental rights guaranteed to all was the basis for dissemination of procedural rights to the states. Central to "incorporation," or application of the Bill of Rights to the states, was the notion that the principles of a free and democratic nation were guaranteed to all citizens. Thus, a constitutional liberty interest is both the doctrinal basis for procedural protections and their precursor. As a doctrinal basis, constitutional liberty anchors the specific due process protections; as the precursor to incorporation of the specific rights, constitutional liberty held out the promise of fundamental fairness on which incorporation was based.

Substantive Due Process

Chapter 3 was about due process in the sense of the procedures that must be used by police, courts, and other governmental bodies when they are deciding whether an individual will be deprived of something by government. In the tradition of American constitutional discourse, there is another kind of due process called substantive due process. The distinction between substantive and procedural due process is confusing. By convention, substantive due process is not about the specific steps a government has to follow before it takes someone's rights or liberties away, it is about those rights and liberties in general. Procedural due process holds that a citizen may not be put in prison and thus deprived of his right to go where he pleases unless first he has been convicted by jury trial. The belief that he had a right to go where he pleased before he lost that right at trial is associated with no specific provision but with due process generally. The more general right is referred to as a substantive due process right.

Since the shift of judicial protection away from economic rights for the New Deal, certain rights have been obscured by the shadow of "substantive due process." The shadow resulted from the battles during the Depression over judicial capacity to limit legislative regulation in the economic and social sphere. The triumphant camp had been critical of the judicial use of substantive due process, whereby the courts had negated legislation to curb the abuses of capitalism. A whole body of jurisprudence was built on this criticism of substantive due process. The implication was that due process was particularly susceptible to self-interested abuse on the part of interpreters of the Constitution. As "substantive due process," constitutional liberty had fallen into disfavor.

Although substantive due process was traditionally associated with property rights, other rights not explicitly stated by the Constitution have been funneled into the word "liberty" in the due process clauses of the Fifth and Fourteenth Amendments. Because these rights are not expressed in so many words in the Constitution as written in 1789 or in the amendments, the justices are sometimes accused of creating them. Yet for the most part, constitutional liberty simply involves protections based on general principles. The Constitution does not say in so many words that you have a right to move from one town to another or to have children if you desire a family. But laws that forbade us to move or have children would certainly appear to deprive us of a constitutional liberty.

Thus, substantive due process is associated with natural law and the idea of the law of the land. Although it had been used by the Supreme Court to strike down economic regulation, after it fell into disfavor, substantive due process came to describe suspect or excessive constitutional creativity on the part of the justices. The result is an implication of arbitrariness when this general due process is compared with the more specific procedural protections. Yet, an aspect of constitutional liberty has the elimination of arbitrariness as its object. For instance, the "void-for-vagueness" doctrine ". . . requires that a penal statute define the criminal offense with sufficient definiteness that ordinary people can understand what conduct is prohibited and in a manner that does not encourage arbitrary and discriminatory enforcement" (*Kolender* v. *Lawson,* 1983). Justice Sandra O'Connor's words in this case set a substantive requirement about the sort of laws that are permitted. It came in response to a California statute which stipulated that:

> Every person who commits any of the following acts is guilty of disorderly conduct, a misdemeanor . . . Who loiters or wanders upon the streets . . . and who refuses to identify himself if the surrounding circumstances are such as to indicate to a reasonable man that the public safety demands such identification. (Cal. Pen. Code 647)

The justice linked her opinion to maximizing individual freedom ". . . within a framework of ordered liberty." In this form, constitutional liberty is not just about the criminal process, it is a protection against laws that are too vague.

Ideological implications have also been connected with the broader due process claims. These implications were suggested by Justice Oliver

127

Wendell Holmes in *Lochner* v. *New York* (1905), where he described the majority as having decided the case "upon an economic theory which a large part of the country does not entertain." Clearly, political attitudes have played a role here. For the first third of the twentieth century, the ideological bent of the Court ran to laissez faire in economic matters. For a period afterward, the Court directed its efforts toward advancing political liberties. Yet, there is nothing uniquely substantive about the due process applications. They simply involve protections based on general principles, rather than on specific procedural stipulations. The general principles of due process provide an open classification system, a framework within which shared values find an expression. This is most evident when there is controversy over the outcomes and when doctrinal references are general and without specific foundations, as in the right to privacy.

Paradoxically, the core "libertarian" values associated with individual freedom and privacy have been viewed as lacking in doctrinal foundation, and decisions protecting them have been criticized as political. Although some liberties do lack clear textual foundations in the Constitution and are not explicitly stated in a particular amendment, their development by the judiciary is a central feature of modern constitutional law. It is in terms of this development that liberty must be articulated. There need not be any less clarity about the meaning of constitutional liberty than the meaning of any other right. Liberty is more than a euphemism for substantive due process; it is the doctrinal basis for a body of general due process guarantees. In this sense, the concept is "fundamental" to the ordered processes that are part of the constitutional heritage. The chapter looks at various guarantees grouped under the heading of "privacy" and constitutional "autonomy," that is, the freedom of self-directed action without interference by the government.

Developing since the turn of the century, interpretation of the right to privacy reveals judicial creativity, but it also shows the constraints imposed by the Constitution where new rights are fashioned. The application of this right to birth control and abortion is portrayed in this chapter. Privacy came into prominence due to the make-up of the Court and the tenor of the times. This is a familiar story, and it preceded the decline of the privacy right as a subject of constitutional interpretation. It is easier for a right to pass away than for it to achieve sensible status in discussion of the Constitution.

Complementing the privacy right protected by constitutional liberty is an autonomy for the citizen stemming from the Renaissance humanism of the Founders and incorporating their idealism as well as their commercial inclinations. This autonomy is reflected in the economic, social, and political spheres. It has no single doctrinal base. Autonomous action existing as a matter of right is evident in the right to be treated as an individual, a right to travel, and a right to receive care when designated mentally ill. All of these rights are derived, by structure and implication, from the constitutional tradition. They amount to an expressive or positive aspect of liberty.

As with its "companion" freedom, that relating to expression, the discussion of liberty brings into focus the nexus between state and individual as a source of constitutional doctrine. The concept of liberty, as it has existed in the legal context, is not the stuff of empty rhetoric, but rather the consequence of adjudication and the resolution of conflict over important guarantees. We see here the construction of legal reality as a reflection of the inclinations, perceptions, and aspirations of a people filtered through the professional practice of law. The result has the significance and the many facets of a central element in legal ideology. Thus, where we take for granted the freedom to travel about, constitutional protection is relatively limited. It is strongest where it is buttressed by interstate commerce and weakest where it comes up against national security interests.

Privacy

One hundred years ago, there was no right to privacy as such in the Constitution. The constitutional right to privacy emerged as a consequence of the twentieth century preoccupation with this value. Privacy has been an object of debate throughout this century, with legal arguments, judicial dissents, and ultimately majority opinions finding their way into constitutional interpretation. As the century progressed, the right became attached to the due process clause of the Fourteenth Amendment (Rubin, 1982:63), until by the early 1970s, the Supreme Court ". . . recognized that a right of personal privacy, or a guarantee of certain areas or zones of privacy, does exist under the Constitution . . ." (Roe v. Wade, 1973). The change in the ordinary or common law concept of privacy with its introduction into the Constutition reveals the structure of that body of law and its conceptual significance. Privacy in the Constitution is not simply the common law right with a different reference point; it is a different right in important respects.

Privacy has been institutionalized by the opinions of the Court. It has become a part of the common understandings to such an extent that it now has a stature comparable to some of the specific procedural protections in the Bill of Rights. Without a particular doctrinal reference, like that for double jeopardy, people know what it means to refer to constitutional protection for privacy. Creative developments of this sort tell us something about constitutional discourse. They reveal where the boundaries are and how they change. A concept can enter the domain of the Constitution and become intelligible. We see this in the way privacy is referred to, even by those who do not like its implications. In *Roe v. Wade*, Justice William Rehnquist claimed ". . . a difficulty in concluding, as the Court does, that the right of 'privacy' is involved in this case. . ." (*Roe*, 1973), but he certainly knew what the majority was talking about in this landmark abortion case. He acknowledged the existence of a right, if not its particular application, where no right had existed less than a century before. We begin our discussion of constitutional privacy by showing where the concept of privacy has come from and how it entered the constitutional frame.

A "Right to Be Let Alone"

Judge Thomas Cooley, an influential state judge and law professor, provided the seed, and distinctive phrasing, in articulating a right "to be let alone," in 1888. Advocacy of this notion as a "right to privacy" by Samuel Warren and Louis Brandeis in 1890 launched the concept. These advocates anticipated that "political, social, and economic" forces would support the inclusion of a new right in the common law. They concluded that "the right to liberty secures the exercise of extensive civil privileges, and the term 'property' has grown to comprise every form of possession—intangible, as well as tangible." These proper Bostonians were responding to a new technology, the instantaneous photography then becoming available to mass circulation newspapers. The traditional limitations existing in the law of libel and slander were too limited. Seeking a broader right "to determine the extent to which thoughts, sentiments and emotions will be communicated," Warren and Brandeis argued in their article that:

> The principle which protects personal writings and all other personal productions, not against theft and physical appropriation but against publication in any form, is in reality not the principle of private property, but that of an inviolate personality (Warren and Brandeis, 1890:141).

They hoped to establish the "right to be let alone." Their successful law review article is closer to being the source of this legal concept than any judicial opinion. Prior to the article's publication, the right was not recognized in English or American law. By taking concepts from property and other rights, the authors established as a fundamental principle "the inviolability of an individual's privacy."

The first reference to the article by a higher court came early in the century in a New York case, *Roberson v. Rochester Folding Box Co.* (1902).

The issue of compensation for humiliation arose when a young woman from New York had her picture used to market flour—without her consent. She sued and she lost because the courts of New York found there was no common law right to privacy. This was not a popular decision. On August 23, 1902, the *New York Times* editorialized against the New York State Court of Appeals for holding that "the right to privacy is not a right which in the State of New York anybody is bound to respect." The editorial resulted in a New York State statute directed against the commercial use of personal information and images. The right, developing at the turn of the century, was a new one.

Between 1890 and 1960, the individual's right to privacy developed into an accepted principle of American law. It was recognized in 31 states, and over 300 cases relating to privacy were decided in the appellate courts (Westin, 1967:347). The only resistance came on "the general grounds that it deals with a state of mind and recovery is difficult." Whether it was due to the "social status" that Warren and Brandeis are said to have given to it or because of "its compelling social attractiveness," privacy became a very popular legal claim (Davis, 1959:7). Although not all commentators could find a single tort or legal wrong (Prosser, 1960; O'Brien, 1979:7-10), among the claims associated with privacy, the right had become a part of American law.

The concept has roots in the ideology of American politics. It is compatible with individualism, limited government, private property (Westin, 1967), and the specific protections in the Bill of Rights, all of which gave support to the developing interpretation of the constitutional right to property. Alan Westin viewed the ideological basis for privacy as evidence that it is not a modern legal concept:

> Thus, the notion put forward by legal commentators from Brandeis down to the present—that privacy was somehow a "modern" legal right which began to take form only in the late nineteenth century—is simply bad history and bad law (Westin, 1967:337).

Yet, there is no reference to "privacy" as a legal right prior to the end of the nineteenth century. There are differences in the ideological and the legal spheres of discourse. The notion of privacy is implicit in the ideology, the American tradition, and even in the common law. But, its articulation as common law or as a statutory right is a modern contribution. Like tort law, which owes much to the Industrial Revolution (Friedman, 1973:409), the law of privacy may be laid at the door of the technological revolution. From telephone and instantaneous photography through the intrusions of wiretaps and bugging devices, the concept of privacy has advanced along with the technology that has redefined the nature of American social life. Indeed, it was eavesdropping, sensing devices, and later data banks, that prompted the Committee on Science and Law of the Association of the Bar of the City of New York to study the relationship between modern technology and privacy.

Constitutional Development

A statutory right to privacy thus appeared in the last century in America. Rooted in the ideology of liberalism and reflected in the common law, the right developed as a protection against technological threats to private life. In its form and content, the articulation of these concerns accompanied privacy into the constitutional setting. In that sphere official commentary determined the sort of right that constitutional privacy would become. Judge Cooley's conception of privacy was evident in a decision of the Supreme Court in 1891 (*Union Pacific v. Botsford*). In that case, it was decided that a plaintiff in an injury claim did not have to submit to surgical examination on the basis of "the right of every individual to the possession and control of his own person" (*Botsford*, 1888:251). Potential indignity was considered "an assault and a trespass." The Court's references were to the common law and Cooley's interpretation. Although it introduced privacy to Supreme Court deliberations, this case did not lead to privacy being considered a claimable constitutional right.

Beyond the Procedural Protections. The constitutional right to privacy required a conceptual integration into the Constitution's framework, a conjunction of the protection against "intrusions" in the Fourth Amendment and the immunity from "disclosure" or self-incrimination in the Fifth Amendment. In his dissent in *Olmstead v. United States* (1928), Justice Louis D. Brandeis suggested the path to be followed in order to bring privacy into the Constitution. The case itself was closely associated with developing technology since it involved electronic taps on telephone lines. Since there was no trespass in appropriating the conversations, the issue was whether the Fourth Amendment protections applied (O'Brien, 1979:51). A majority of the justices did not believe wiretaps violated the protections in the Constitution against searches and seizures. Justice Brandeis, on the other hand, saw the wire taps as evidence of the "subtler and more far-reaching means of invading privacy that have become available to the government," and he argued that the Founders had provided a protection against the government in "... the right to be let alone." This, for Brandeis, was "the most comprehensive of rights and the right most valued by civilized men (*Olmstead*, 1928:473). In his opinion, Justice Brandeis thus expanded on the concept he had introduced in his seminal law review article almost 40 years before.

As important as this conceptual link to the law review article was an authoritative link to the constitutional past. Justice Brandeis's opinion in *Olmstead* relied on an 1886 decision that ". . . the Fourth and Fifth Amendments run almost into each other" (*Boyd* v. *United States*, 1886). By this reference, Brandeis was able to add significantly to his contribution by joining the protections against warrantless searches with those for self-incrimination. Until this time, the privilege against self-incrimination had been limited to criminal prosecution, and attempts to expand its reach to the protection of "reputation or private affairs" had failed (*Brown* v. *Walker*, 1896).*

Building on the conceptual foundation provided by Brandeis, Justice Frank Murphy took constitutional privacy a step further in 1942 in *Goldman* v. *United States*. The case involved use of a detectaphone by federal agents investigating a lawyer's conspiracy to defraud creditors in a bankruptcy case. The device allowed conversations to be heard through a wall without "intrusion." Murphy's dissenting opinion recognized that physical entry was no longer necessary for a search ". . . for science has brought forth far more effective devices for the invasion of a person's privacy." Justice Murphy advocated capturing the essence of traditional protection, whether or not the doctrine seemed to apply literally. He cited Brandeis's 1890 law review article and indicated that "one of the great boons secured . . . by the Bill of Rights is the right of personal privacy guaranteed by the Fourth Amendment" (*Goldman*, 1942:136). Justice Murphy's opinion thus linked concern over searches and seizures in the Bill of Rights with the conception of privacy being introduced into the Constitution.

Justice Felix Frankfurter was a subsequent contributor to the development of this right when he described privacy as a constitutional liberty. Privacy, he said, was part of the conception of liberty through which the Bill of Rights could be incorporated. He wrote:

> security of one's privacy against arbitrary intrusion by the police—
> which is at the core of the Fourth Amendment—is basic to a free
> society. It is therefore implicit in the "concept of ordered liberty". . .
> (*Wolf* v. *Colorado*, 1949).

Reliance on privacy and its relation to things fundamental, like ordered liberty, had become commonplace.

In *Frank* v. *Maryland* (1959) Justice Frankfurter acknowledged "the right to be secure from intrusions into personal privacy," but he considered it insufficient to preclude a search where there was no threat

---

* A particularly perspicacious dissent in *Brown* v. *Walker* (1896) by Justice Stephen Field would anticipate Brandeis's suggestion in *Olmstead*. "It is contended, indeed, that it was not the object of the [Fifth Amendment] Constitutional safeguard to protect the witness against infamy and disgrace . . . but I do not agree. . ." (*Brown*, 1896:631-632).

of prosecution. The opinion in *Frank* contains a review of the protection afforded by the Fourth and Fifth Amendments, and Frankfurter's conclusion that "giving the fullest scope to this constitutional right to privacy, its protection cannot be here invoked" (*Frank*, 1959:366). Justice Douglas's dissent in *Frank* attacked the requirement of criminal proceedings as a limitation that was inconsistent with the American tradition outside the constitutional sphere. Douglas had indicated his sympathy with the Brandeis position some years before. When a lower court held radio programs on federally supervised buses to violate the liberty protected by the Fifth Amendment, in that they constituted "forced listening," Douglas supported the decision, writing:

> The case comes down to the meaning of "liberty" as used in the Fifth Amendment. Liberty in the constitutional sense must mean more than freedom from unlawful governmental restraint; it must include privacy as well... (*Public Utilities Commission* v. *Pollak*, 1952:467).

On this basis, the Supreme Court came up with "a new concept of constitutional privacy" between 1956 and 1966 (Westin, 1967:330). The Warren and Brandeis article was mentioned three times during this period; each time the reference was to the common law roots of privacy and each time there was a push to expand the concept into a constitutional right. The article was first referred to in a dissent by Justice Douglas to an unsuccessful birth control appeal (*Poe et al.* v. *Ullman*, 1961). Then the article was cited in a concurrence, as support for the proposition that "the philosophical foundations" of privacy are rooted in the common law (*Gibson* v. *Florida*, 1963). Finally, the article was mentioned by Justice Brennan in 1963 in *Lopez* v. *United States*, when Brennan criticized what he saw as the Court's encouragement of electronic searches and seizures. "The right of privacy would mean little," he argued, "... if it were limited to a person's solitary thoughts" (*Lopez*, 1963:449). The reference to privacy had again united protection from "disclosure" with that of "intrusion" by means of electricity.

The last structural dimension to the constitutional development of the concept of privacy involved freedom of expression. The First Amendment freedoms expanded privacy related concerns beyond the criminal process, but protection associated with freedom of expression cut two ways. It was a source of strength to the new right with serious limitations. With regard to the common law right, the First Amendment impinged on the "right to be let alone" since it fostered and protected an aggressive press corps. The First Amendment, however, also protected political privacy (*Watkins* v. *United States*, 1957) and the related "right of associational privacy" (*NAACP* v. *Alabama*, 1958), which was far more positive in its orientation than the common law right. These aspects of the right to privacy prohibited the government from interfering with the private space that was also protected by common law privacy.

Thus, the foundations for constitutional privacy lay in creative adjudication incorporating protection against warrantless searches and seizures, self-incrimination, and providing for freedom of expression. The result was a right that went well beyond any of these and took on quite a different character from the common law roots to which it can be traced.

Polite Penumbras. Except for the limited Fourth Amendment holdings and a few connected with the First Amendment, constitutional privacy claims were not successful until 1965. Yet, privacy had become a possible claim well before it received authoritative support from a majority of the Supreme Court. Acceptance of the right by the Court is only the most obvious evidence that a concept is intelligible, that the idea "has arrived." *Griswold* v. *Connecticut* (1965) was that benchmark in which the constitutional right to privacy was recognized. In this case concerning a statute which limited the use of contraception in Connecticut, the majority opinion by Justice Douglas was grounded in constitutional privacy. The case involved "likely invasions of the privacy of the bedroom." (Ely, 1973). Although Douglas referred to "penumbras, formed by emanations" from the First, Third, Fourth, Fifth, and Ninth Amendments (*Griswold*, 1965:484), the Connecticut contraceptive use statute was held to be unconstitutional by the Supreme Court on the grounds that to enforce it would require prying into the privacy of the home. The basis for the decision was thus a more limited right to marital privacy, "a right of privacy older than the Bill of Rights. . ." (*Griswold*, 1965:486). Justice Black dissented from the opinion of the Court because he desired the holding to be based on "some specific constitutional provision." In his opinion, Black paid homage to the early collaborative efforts of Samuel Warren and Louis Brandeis, but objected to the elevation of the phrase "right to be let alone"—from the law review article—to the level of a constitutional rule. The view was consistent with Black's general disdain for more flexible interpretation. In his reaction to the holding, Black saw a larger development than that undertaken by Douglas, who limited the right to marital privacy.

A great deal of legal commentary subsequent to *Griswold* was directed toward the new right (Dixon, 1971). Constitutional privacy had become the point of contention (Emerson, 1971:37). In the decade that followed, privacy was often appealed to as an independent constitutional right (*Paris Adult Theater* v. *Slaton*, 1973), but this appeal was successful only where it was applied to the search and seizure context (*Katz* v. *U.S.*, 1967), the privacy of the home (*Stanley* v. *Georgia*, 1969; *United States* v. *Reidel*, 1971), or to the realm of sexual or marital privacy (*Eisenstadt* v. *Baird*, 1972). In short, the successes were all linked very closely to the elements of privacy that had brought the right to its constitutional status.

The development of the constitutional right to privacy is an example of conceptual change that has continuing doctrinal significance. In 1896 and for nearly half a century thereafter, the justices could not have ruled that prohibitions on abortion violated a constitutional right to privacy. There are many reasons for this, but the most dramatic was the absence of privacy as a constitutional right at that time. The way a new constitutional concept is introduced is an important dimension of the process of "making sense," which we discussed in Chapter 1. Once articulated, legal concepts may be enlarged, limited, or maintained. They constitute the subjective space in which judges act, the "artificial" but very significant forms of reason in the law. Consequently, concepts are the basis of legal action and choice. The role of constitutional privacy in judicial interpretation is the subject of the next sections.

Reproductive Privacy

This area examines the privacy right in a volatile policy arena and considers the capacity of the Supreme Court to articulate policy that reaches well beyond the scope of past decisions. Reproductive rights acquired constitutional significance at the juncture where privacy as a constitutional doctrine and feminist political power were at their peak. The result was a ruling which challenges the convention that dispute ceases once the trip has been made "all the way to the Supreme Court."

Griswold had elevated the "right to be let alone" to constitutional stature in the context of the marital relationship. In *Eisenstadt* v. *Baird* (1972), contraception was the basis for an extension beyond the marital relationship of the right to privacy. The opinion by Brennan stated:

> If the right of privacy means anything, it is the right of the individual, married or single, to be free from unwarranted governmental intrusion into matters so fundamentally affecting a person as the decison whether to bear or beget a child (*Eisenstadt*, 1972:453).

The fact that contraceptives could be legally distributed to married persons made denial of contraceptives to unmarried persons a violation of equal protection. The decision in *Eisenstadt*, although on equal protection grounds, provided a link to the 1973 abortion decision by proving particularly sensitive to marital privacy.

***Roe* and *Doe*.** Of the subsequent holdings to deal with constitutional privacy, none more clearly demonstrates the new status of privacy than does the 1973 abortion ruling, *Roe* v. *Wade*. In *Roe*, the right to privacy became embedded in a major controversy but use of the concept also made it clear that this right was included in the justices' tool box.

Justice Harry Blackmun seemed less concerned about the source of the right in his abortion opinion than with the fact that privacy had been recognized as a right. He wrote:

This right of privacy, whether it be founded in the Fourteenth Amendment's concept of personal liberty and restriction upon state action, as we feel it is, or, as the District Court determined, in the Ninth Amendment's reservation of rights to the people, is broad enough to encompass a woman's decision whether or not to terminate her pregnancy (*Roe*, 1973:153).

Blackmun's opinion treated the case as "just one of the many cases that recognized the right of privacy" (Epstein, 1973:169).

In *Roe v. Wade* (1973), the Court held unconstitutional a nineteenth century Texas statute that made abortion a crime, at any stage of pregnancy, except to save the life of the mother. In *Doe v. Bolton* (1973), a Georgia statute was also held to be unconstitutional. This statute had required abortions to be conducted in hospitals, had interposed a hospital abortion committee, had required confirmation by other physicians that the abortion was necessary, and had limited abortion to Georgia residents. The Court's two rulings covered state abortion policy from the century-old anti-vice legislation of Anthony Comstock to the more recent formulation by the American Law Institute. Like the reformers at the American Law Institute, Justice Blackmun seems to have approached the decision by trying to bring the law in line with social custom.

Roe and *Doe* stimulated more controversy and subsequent litigation than any decisions since the desegregation cases in the 1950s. Confronted with laws in effect for over 100 years, as well as more modern statutes, the Court employed the right to privacy to provide a choice for pregnant women over the interests of the states in limiting abortion. The effect of the decisions was to hold as unconstitutional abortion laws in all 50 states and the District of Columbia. Those decisions marked the peak of the political power of the women's movement. They are remembered with special fondness by some and as a moral outrage by others.

The decisions were not simply a commentary on the Constitution; they set the framework for national policy on abortion. The policy mandate from the Supreme Court in a constitutional case stipulates what shall legitimately stand as law. The public policy in the abortion decisions was a directive to state legislatures limiting their lawmaking capacity. *Roe* and *Doe* held that: (1) states shall not regulate abortion in the first three months of a pregnancy; (2) subsequent regulation of abortion during the second trimester must relate to the preservation and protection of maternal health; and (3) with the viability of the fetus in the last three months, the state may proscribe abortion except when it is necessary to preserve the life or health of the mother. These were the parameters handed down by the Court. They set limits for subsequent action regarding abortion, which have been monitored by courts in individual challenges aimed at antiabortion legislation passed by the states after the Supreme Court's decision.

Policy Consequences. When states make new laws, they must conform to the Constitution as interpreted by the Supreme Court. The Constitution sets the framework. Supervision by lower courts implements the law. Thus, the policy consequences of Supreme Court opinion can be traced through decisions by the judiciary. The Supreme Court's original opinion was sweeping enough that nearly all of the legislative issues that would come before the lower courts sought to curb the Court's holding. Appeals thus constituted a request that the courts determine whether legislative action was consistent with the Supreme Court's mandate (Ulmer et al., 1972). There are two levels of response worth distinguishing, that of the lower courts and that of the Supreme Court itself.

Between 1972 and 1982, there were 116 abortion cases appealed to the High Bench. This 10-year run included 37 summary actions* and 12 full opinions. (See Table 4-1.) In the first term after *Roe* and *Doe* were decided, there was a high of 21 cases dealt with by the Court. The 17 of these that were decided by summary action* reflect the immediate impact of *Roe* and *Doe* and the Court's commitment to supervising a transition to the new policy. Subsequently, a pattern was established in which petitions and appeals piled up, leading to a full opinion and followed by another spate of summary action. There is an ebb and flow in the implementation process, whereby issues are raised with increasing persistence, leading to an authoritative decision. Supervision of issues by the justices is evident in major opinions such as *Planned Parenthood* v. *Danforth* (1976), *Maher* v. *Roe* (1977), *Bellotti* v. *Baird* (1979), and *Harris* v. *McRae* (1980). Opinions such as these are handed down periodically, and at least in this policy area, they are correlated with increased appeals.

Most lower court decisions that were appealed to the Supreme Court presented unexpected or unenvisaged cases, such as advertising, parental consent, and public funding. (See Table 4-2.) In addition, the licensing of practitioners accorded the right to perform abortions, the licensing of facilities, death certificates, and custody all involved legisla-

---

* Summary actions are decisions by the Court based on prior holdings and, consequently, reasoning that has already been announced.

Table 4-1   The Pattern of Abortion Appeals by Supreme Court Term

	1972	1973	1974	1975	1976	1977	1978	1979	1980	1981
Petitions/Appeals	2	7	7	8	3	5	7	10	7	11
Summary action	17	0	2	4	8	1	2	3	0	0
Full opinion	2	0	2	2	0	0	2	3	1	0

tive responsibilities that transcended the initial abortion question. The federal courts consistently struck down these limitations in the early years, extrapolating from *Roe* with attention to their rulings' impact on access to abortion. State courts responded differently than the federal bench in the period after the landmark decision, siding with the legislative bodies in their states in all cases that eventually reached the Supreme Court. In 53 out of 56 cases decided by federal courts, however, legislative responses to *Roe* had been struck down. Intervention by federal judges to expand the availability of abortion was the norm, at least for the first five years following the decisions in *Roe* and *Doe*. In addition, where federal judges upheld legislative limitations on the availability of abortion, the Supreme Court was more likely to step in. Two out of the three appeals that involved viability (that is, whether or not the fetus could survive on its own) were given a full hearing by the Court (*Beal* v. *Franklin*, 1975; *Planned Parenthood*, 1976). In both cases, the lower courts had upheld state regulations, which was unusual for federal district courts.

The abortion opinions contained a certain amount of imprecision, because in establishing the trimester periods, the justices used both the three-month division and also delineated the periods according to traditional understanding of the stages in pregnancy. These stages were inherently imprecise. (The line between the second and third trimester is a gray area, at least in part because it is attached to viability, which is a medical rather than a legal concept.) This imprecision is a kind of "open texture" in the law rather than simply vagueness (Hart, 1961; O'Brien, 1980). The room to maneuver that is left open is part of the policy process, and subsequent abortion cases arose where this room existed. These cases included issues of parental or spousal consent, the licensing of treatment facilities, and legislative provisions attached to public health statutes. In short, like most judicial policies, the abortion decisions had an open texture (Brigham and Burns, 1980).

The first major restatement of the initial abortion decision came as controversy over the holdings mounted. In this case, *Planned Parenthood*

Table 4-2   Abortion Appeals: The First Decade*

Term	1972	1973	1974	1975	1976	1977	1978	1979	1980	1981
ISSUES RAISED										
Advertising for abortion services	1	2			1					
Rights of unborn fetus	5	2		1			1	1		
Regulation of practitioners	2	1	1	2						2
Defining fetal viability			2	1			1			
Criminal penalties governing abortions			1				2			
Regulation of facilities	1	2	2	1	2			2	1	3
Public funding for abortions	3		2	4	4	1	2	8	2	
Spousal/parental consent or notification		3	1	4	3		3	1	1	2
Miscellaneous provisions for fetus			2				2	1	2	3
"Informed" consent requirement				1	1		3		1	1
Publication of abortion records			1				2			
Custody of live births			1				2			
Standing to challenge				1					3	1

* Appeals to the Supreme Court, some of which have produced more than one issue. (Constructed with the assistance of Diane Burns.)

v. *Danforth* (1976), Justice Blackmun's opinion again treated constitutional privacy as a given. The case considered a state requirement for spousal or parental consent for an abortion. This complicated the privacy issue, and in striking down spousal and modifying parental consent, Blackmun reiterated his view that privacy was conditioned by state regulation.

Some cases, like *Bigelow* v. *Virginia* (1975), were adjudicated so squarely on other issues that they very nearly ceased to be abortion cases. *Bigelow* was first sent back (remanded) to the state court in light of *Roe* v. *Wade* before it again went to the Supreme Court for determination. The Court's second consideration of *Bigelow* revealed the relation between freedom of expression, the abortion issue, and privacy. In *Bigelow*, the justices were asked to decide whether Virginia could restrict advertisements for abortion clinics. They held that in matters of commercial speech there should be a balance between the purposes of regulation and the public interest in receiving the advertisement. In holding for the abortion ad, the justices made it clear that commercial speech had not been stripped of its constitutional protection, but the case also indicated that the privacy on which protection for abortion rested was as political and associational as it was personal.

The public assistance for abortion cases, *Maher* v. *Roe* (1977) and *Harris* v. *McRae* (1980), are excellent examples of how tradition in constitutional discourse influences decisions in particular cases. Although it is never possible to show that the tradition determines the outcome, in these cases the implications of having chosen a particular line of argumentation for the abortion holdings is clear. Because abortion rights had been associated with the discourse of privacy—with its protection against government intrusions—the case against the denial of governmental funding for abortions was weakened. In *Maher* v. *Roe* (1977), the Supreme Court held that a state could choose not to pay for nontherapeutic abortions, even though it did pay for childbirth. Here, the federal district court had ruled that the presence of a fundamental right to abortion required careful scrutiny of the distinction between abortion and childbirth. But when the case was before the Supreme Court, Justice Powell held that the lower court had "misconceived the nature and scope of the fundamental right recognized in *Roe* ... [in that] the right protects the woman from unduly burdensome interference with her freedom to decide whether to terminate her pregnancy." This is testimony to privacy as a liberty based protection.

The abortion cases did not call the government to account for equal protection of its laws, although these cases might easily have been dealt with along equal protection lines. In the early 1970s, because of variation in state laws, wealthier women had an access to abortions that poor women could not even dream of affording. At the time, there were many publicized instances where women were flying to other states or even other countries to obtain abortions prohibited to them by the laws of their own states. Had the abortion cases been decided on equal protection grounds, with its implications of a positive right to equal action by government, the Supreme Court might have found it easier to reach the conclusion that to deny public funds for abortion was a violation of the Constitution. In *Maher*, the justices did listen to some equal protection arguments, but they found that financial need was not enough to identify an unconstitutional denial of equal protection. Three years later, the decision was reaffirmed in *Harris*, where the justices held that the liberty in *Roe* includes the freedom of a woman to decide whether to terminate a pregnancy but does not include a public obligation to make the choice a reality. If the Court had decided *Griswold* and *Roe* and *Doe* as equal protection claims by poor women for the same abortion liberties as enjoyed by middle-class women, then they would have found it much harder to decide *Maher* and *Harris* the way that they did.

There is some evidence in recent abortion cases that the strength of the privacy concept has waned while the right to abortion has been affirmed. *H. L.* v. *Matheson* (1981) came from Utah on a statutory requirement for parental notification prior to an abortion being performed on a minor. From the traditional perspective, it would seem that a statute of this sort trades away the element of protection for personal privacy in favor of the policy concerns of the State. Although perhaps a minor inconvenience when measured against reproductive rights, in the context of the privacy interest, which was the doctrinal ground for the initial abortion decision, the holding was decidedly and dramatically a negative step. Chief Justice Warren Burger, in presenting the majority view, distinguished the case from *Planned Parenthood* and *Bellotti*, since in both those cases statutory provisions amounted to an absolute veto over the abortion decision. At least in one case where grounds other than privacy were presented, however, the justices seemed more willing to resist state legislation limiting the abortion right. This was *Colautti* v. *Franklin* (1979), in which the Court invalidated a Pennsylvania law designed to protect fetuses "potentially able to survive." The law was held unconstitutionally vague. Ultimately, the Court's commitment to abortion became very clear in the 1983 case of *Akron* v. *Akron Center for Reproductive Health*, where the only comfort to anti-abortion groups was the support they received from Justice Sandra O'Connor. The Court's decision surprised many by striking down a local ordinance which required a 24-hour waiting period for abortion, that all abortions after the first three months of pregnancy be performed in hospitals, and a detailed informed consent provision that required doctors to lecture on the antiabortion view of fetal life and the consequences of abortion.

Judicial policies will inevitably fail to fully circumscribe the implementation process. The clearest articulation of a new policy will leave some doubt and generate cases that could not have been anticipated. But some decisions are more successful than others. When the level of controversy over a decision becomes as intense as it has been over legal abortion, we have evidence that judicial or legal rationalization has failed. The burden of undercutting the constitutionality of so many state statutes may have been more than the concept of constitutional privacy could handle. The legal standard was of such a unique professional caste that the rhetoric of privacy or even personal autonomy that it generated failed to legitimate the decision to a broader audience. In addition, constitutional privacy was a weak and individualistic foundation for abortion compared to the moral outrage of the "Right-to-Life" challenge. Ultimately, in its failure to convince a wider audience, the Supreme Court has left open a dramatic and highly charged policy issue.

"Lifestyle" Privacy

"Lifestyle" will be used here to cover choices about how to live that arise from the varieties of culture and fashion in the United States. The term covers reputation and sexual preference, areas that require a barrier of protection from public exposure and its consequences. In this chapter we distinguish this aspect of constitutional privacy from "lifestyle autonomy," where there is less concern with public exposure and more focus on issues arising over freedom to act (Karst, 1980). Autonomy will be discussed later in the chapter. Both "lifestyle" areas will thus be treated as part of constitutional liberty.

The nexus of privacy with reproductive rights that linked the contraception and abortion cases to the Constitution has implications for issues of lifestyle as well. The cases that carried the privacy right beyond the criminal law also protect various ways of living. These are instances where enforcing the preferences of the majority would intrude into a private sphere. In *Griswold, Eisenstadt,* and *Roe,* the right to privacy came to full flower in matters of sex. While *Roe* (1973) is the take-off point for reproductive privacy, *Eisenstadt* (1972) was an early expression of lifestyle privacy concerns, dealing with contraception in a way that made it a bridge to subsequent cases. The constitutional tradition made problematic the policy distinction between married and single persons in the Massachusetts statute at issue. In *Eisenstadt* v. *Baird,* family planning activist William Baird was convicted in a Massachusetts court of exhibiting contraceptive articles and giving a young woman a package of contraceptive foam. The state statute prohibited distribution of these devices to single persons. Based on First Amendment grounds, the Massachusetts Supreme Court set aside Baird's conviction for exhibiting the articles, but it allowed his conviction for distributing the foam to stand. Using a standard requiring only minimal rationality on the part of the legislature (see Chapter 6), the justices of the Supreme Court determined that if the statute was for the purpose of regulating morality it would be cruel to prescribe pregnancy as a punishment for fornication, and they argued that if the statute was a health measure the state should be as interested in single persons as in those who are married. Although treated as an equal protection case, this decision indicated increased sensitivity in state courts to choices concerning sexuality and marriage. Thus, although it encompassed reproductive rights, *Eisenstadt* linked privacy to protection from discrimination, and the decision increased the number of possible appeals that could be brought concerning lifestyle.

Reputation. In *Paul* v. *Davis* (1976), the Supreme Court considered a case in which a person who had been arrested for shoplifting, but not prosecuted, found his name and picture on an "Active Shoplifters" flyer distributed throughout his community. Justice Rehnquist wrote in the opinion of the Court:

> . . . the Court has recognized that "zones of privacy" may be created by more specific constitutional guarantees and thereby impose limits on government power (*Paul*, 1976: 1166).

Rehnquist then went on to describe the "fundamental rights" protected by privacy, and "declined to enlarge them" in the manner suggested by the case. In dissent, Justice Brennan asserted:

> . . . privacy notions appear to be inextricably interwoven with the considerations which require that a state not single an individual out for punishment outside the judicial process (*Paul*, 1976:1177).

For both the majority opinion and the dissent in *Paul*, privacy is the focus of interpretation. The concept is the link between the opinions; there is a shared discourse about the concept, although its implications are contested. The conception of privacy associated with this adverse publicity is close to the original right to be left alone and nearer to the common law meaning of the right than it is to the reproductive rights cases. Thus, as an aspect of *constitutional* privacy, this case is an important example of the relevance of the right to reputation.

Sexual Preference. Issues relating to sexual preference are treated as part of constitutional privacy, even where the consequences go beyond public exposure, because so much of constitutional privacy is sex. An instance of the Supreme Court's refusal to even hear a claim to a more expansive holding in the area of privacy occurred in 1976 in the case of *Doe* v. *Commonwealth Attorney for the City of Richmond*. In this case, a federal district court had upheld Virginia's law prohibiting private homosexual acts. By not hearing the appeal from the lower court, the Supreme Court affirmed the decision. The action produced considerable debate and suggests a dimension of public expectation generated by the right of privacy. Three judges wished to hear the appeal, indicating that they viewed it as within the tradition of constitutional privacy. Conceptual development on constitutional matters is thus evident in petitions for review which at least two or three justices wish to hear.

Subsequent denials of "cert" (where the Supreme Court declines to hear an appeal) are noteworthy. During the Supreme Court's 1978 term, an employee who had been dismissed by a nursing home because he was a homosexual was held to lack standing to challenge the dismissal of his case by the district court because there was not an adequate basis to satisfy the constitutional requirement that the government be involved (*Batt* v. *Marion Heights, Inc.*, 1979). Moreover, between 1980 and 1982, both the Navy and the Army were successful in their efforts to oust individual homosexuals from the service, and the Supreme Court denied review of these cases. Both instances rested on the issue of homosexual acts and not simple identification as homosexuals.

Although the United States Supreme Court has avoided the issue, gay rights has received judicial attention in the lower courts. In particular, there were two well-publicized cases in the mid-1970s, *Gaylord* v. *Tacoma School District* from the Supreme Court of Washington in 1977 and *Gish* v. *Board of Education of Paramus* from the Superior Court of the New Jersey Appellate Division in the same year. In *Gaylord*, the issue was the constitutionality of a school's decision to fire Mr. Gaylord for immorality because he was a known homosexual. Although it denied Gaylord's apeal, the Washington court did indicate that simple "immorality" as a ground for discharging a teacher would be unconstitutionally vague. But, citing church doctrine, the justices from the state of Washington found that homosexuality could be expected to affect a teacher's capacity to do his job. In *Gish*, a gay teacher refused to undergo a psychiatric exam that the school board had ordered him to take. The New Jersey court was unreceptive to constitutional arguments that relied on First and Fourteenth Amendment grounds. Here again, privacy protection proved to be negligible.

In a slightly less charged but certainly equally private sphere, that of heterosexual relations, the federal courts have been willing to intervene on occasion. One of the leading cases involved a teacher, Kathleen Sullivan, from South Dakota. In the early 1970s, she was fired because she was living with a male friend and the school authorities had determined that this would be a bad example for young people. In *Sullivan* v. *Meade Independent School District, No. 101* (1976), the judges of the Eighth Circuit considered the case in light of the privacy right. Even in 1976, with the right getting considerable attention, the judges did not believe that the privacy right would protect a teacher who violated the community's mores. Two years later, the Supreme Court refused to review a lower court decision sustaining the discharge of two public library employees for "living together in a state of open adultery" (*Hollenbaugh* v. *Carnegie Free Library*, 1978). Thus, although there is considerable commitment to lifestyle diversity on the part of the public, protection has not been forthcoming from contemporary judicial holdings on the reach of the Constitution.

The Pendulum of Privacy

The long struggle to establish a legal right like privacy is a stage in the interpretive process. Once a right is established, expectations and interests may coalesce around the right, or it may simply fall into disuse. Both sorts of ideological activity are part of judicial interpretation. Since privacy after *Griswold* was a claim that made constitutional sense, it generated expectations both on and off the Supreme Court. These expectations were based on interpretive possibilities, as well as successful outcomes. The opinions of the Court reveal consciousness of the expectations and, for the most part, in the case of privacy, a disinclination to give them authoritative standing.

Coming to Be and Passing Away. The early abortion movement saw the basis for a privacy claim at a time when privacy was being elevated to a constitutional right (Lader, 1966). Litigation strategies are based on the possibility of such expansions, although their outcome will be influenced by a variety of factors. Holdings subsequent to *Griswold* revealed that privacy had come to be within the tradition of constitutional law, and therefore a possible object of struggle. Once it became an object of conflict, a matter about which reasonable people could disagree, constitutional privacy claims would succeed or fail as a consequence of political circumstances. Thus, judicial politics takes place within a realm of possibilities.

Since the relevant feature of judicial discourse is possibilities, ideas that haven't found a place in the conceptual structure can't be the basis for institutional action. Once a sensible claim has emerged, however, it may be treated in a variety of ways. Its popularity may increase, or it may be ignored. Even cases not taken, like the Virginia Sodomy Statute in 1976, can show the expectations held by those in the attentive community. The refusal to consider this statute received as much attention as most majority decisions because it appeared to be such an obvious privacy issue. Privacy was exceptionally popular after it first was considered to be a constitutional right in 1973, but 10 years later, privacy claims, although still numerous, were beginning to be far less successful in gaining a majority of the Court.* A claim may make sense, but the justices can still choose whether or not to take further cases or to rest their decision on different grounds. Thus, the use made of a right is a function of the predispositions of those on the Court. Its status as a basis for sensible claims depends on the recognizability of a right, which is necessary for constitutional discourse. A justice who is hostile to a particular concept or the outcomes it implies can simply refuse to use it. Yet, the response produced by such denials may be just the thing to keep a concept in the judicial eye (*Doe* v. *Richmond*, 1976). That seems to be the implication of cases involving lifestyle issues like sexual preference and living arrangements.**

Structural Commentary. We have traced the shift in the foundations of constitutional privacy from a basis in what some have called Fourth Amendment "property" protections (*Mott and Mott*, 1981) to the more recent (and less precise) liberty standard of the Fourteenth Amendment. This sort of analysis looks beyond the doctrinal arguments to how the substance of a policy is intertwined with the outcome. In this way, the role of a concept like privacy in constitutional policy making becomes evident, as does the drift in constitutional moorings. Some examples of the drifting standard include *Hollenbaugh* v. *Carnegie Free Library* (1978), where the Supreme Court denied certiorari to an unmarried couple who had been fired for their "immorality." The Court's application of a minimal scrutiny standard here was sharply criticized by Justice Thurgood Marshall as being inadequate to protect personal privacy (*Kelley* v. *Johnson*, 1976).

The weakness of the general liberty interest in the face of governmental pressure is evident in an area related to the classic "right to be let alone" (*Mott and Mott*, 1981). The leading case is *Whalen* v. *Roe* (1977), where the Court was asked about the constitutionality of a New York statute requiring that names and addresses of those who received certain prescribed drugs be reported to the state. A three-judge district court in

---

* The Index to Legal Periodicals has 3 references to privacy in 1926; in the 1955-1958 volume, it has 44 references to a Right of Privacy; in the 1970-1973 volume, there are 150 articles on the right cited.

** Grand shifts of fashion are possible. The greatest was the demise of "liberty of contract," the doctrinal base for turn-of-the-century protection of business interests, which associated constitutional liberty with judicial activism.

New York had overturned the statute on invasion of privacy grounds. The Supreme Court reversed the decision, however, holding that the likelihood of improper use of the information was not very great. The case was relied on in *DuPont* v. *Finklea*, (1977) when a district court sitting in West Virginia was asked to rule whether DuPont, a chemical company, had to turn over medical records to the National Institute for Occupational Safety and Health (NIOSH). The company was claiming to speak for the privacy interests of its workers, but against government interests in health and safety this claim was not sufficient. The district court used *Whalen* to support the government's interest in the medical records, reiterating Justice John Paul Stevens's view that individual invasions of privacy would be minimal. Thus, constitutional privacy has failed where it was employed to limit the prerogatives of government.

During the period of constitutional attention to privacy, Congress passed the Privacy Act of 1974, which committed the nation to protections against dissemination of information. In the years that followed, there was some deference to the old "right to be let alone," at least in its constitutional manifestations. The protection of expression as connected to a political or associational right of privacy was discussed in *Buckley* v. *Valeo* (1976). The case was a challenge to the 1974 campaign finance law passed by Congress to provide for disclosure of private contributors, public assistance in financing campaigns, and limits on the amount that could be contributed and spent by the candidate. This was fundamentally a First Amendment case with a focus on expression, but in the treatment of the questions raised in the case, privacy was connected to the expression of political opinion. In *Brown* v. *Socialist Workers '74 Campaign Committee* (1982), an Ohio statute that required candidates for public office to disclose contributors and recipients of campaign funds was held invalid under the First Amendment when applied to minor political parties that had historically been objects of harassment. In such clashes, there is a difference between privacy as a constitutional right and as a statutory protection. Whereas the statutes protect a form connected to the right to be let alone, the Constitution, given its commitment to freedom of expression and the connection of that right to a constitutional privacy right, protects expression itself. Thus, it protects a more assertive, political right, rather than the statutory privacy limits on intrusion by the press. (See "Unprotected Expression," Chapter 2.)

The evidence points to a structure of constitutional privacy which is different from that of the common law right. Although the Constitution gave the right penetrating implications, it had a narrower scope than the related common law protection. And like all Fourteenth Amendment liberties, it was limited to state action (*Arrington* v. *New York Times Co.*,

1982, 1983). Associational privacy, on the other hand, was joined to the security of person and home found for it in the Fourth and Fifth Amendments, thereby giving the concept an intangible dimension that had particular relevance to lifestyle. Thus, as part of the possible conceptions, privacy became a key to judicial decisions because the cases were about the meaning of the constitutional privacy right.

Autonomy

There is respect for the citizen throughout the Constitution. We see it in the acknowledgment by the Founders that the authority of government comes from the governed. This respect is in the concept of a right and it is behind the first ten amendments to the Constitution. Respect is also the basis for a constitutional right to autonomous action. In the late nineteenth century, autonomy as freedom from limits came to be associated with economic rights and corporate power, but it is more than that. The autonomy that is part of constitutional liberty is a broad freedom that is distinguishable from freedom of expression. Freedom in the First Amendment is political; its root, as we have seen, is tolerance. Autonomy is about the freedom to act, to move, to go about in the world. Its root is respect, but its meaning runs closer to lack of restraint. Autonomy seems more expansive than the protection offered by constitutional privacy.

Such figures as Isaiah Berlin and C. B. Macpherson have debated this kind of liberty. Although the debate developed as political theory, it is akin to constitutional interpretation, and it helps give depth to legal thinking. Constitutional privacy looks like a variant of the negative freedom which is characteristic of the liberal state according to Berlin (1959). This liberty is the traditional shield for those who have things to be protected; it is epitomized by the right to be left alone. The framework itself has been subjected to criticism by Macpherson (1973), but it retains sufficient currency to be suggestive here. Negative liberty is liberty in liberalism—from John Locke to John Stuart Mill—and it is close to privacy. Although not precisely an opposite, positive freedom includes the right to travel, protection for one's citizenship, and the capacity to live fully without governmental interference into one's social life. The freedom examined in the section that follows, called autonomy, is of the expressive, positive sort.

Autonomy is a broad category and is drawn out of many rights that are explicitly recognized as part of due process, as in the criminal procedure protections or the First Amendment. Autonomy is also related to rights and expectations that are seldom referred to and that have, in some cases, minimal authority. This is the case with the Second

Amendment to the Constitution, which states, in very precise terms, that "the right of the people to keep and bear arms, shall not be infringed." Although the controversy over gun control is intense, the Second Amendment does not produce vast amounts of litigation. When cases do get to the courts, the outcomes have been much less generous than one might suspect based on the constitutional protection for this right. In *Quilici* v. *Morton Grove* (1983), for example, the Supreme Court let stand an appeals court ruling that a local ordinance, which banned private possession of pistols, did not violate the Constitution. This constitutional challenge to an ordinance that clearly infringes on the capacity to "bear arms" was turned down at every level of the federal judiciary.

The peculiar language of the document and tradition of constitutional interpretation require that we start with the words. Freedom is mentioned explicitly in the Constitution only as an aspect of the First Amendment. In this context, it has been associated with religious and political activity. These freedoms are perhaps more carefully elaborated than general due process rights, and certainly they are easier to document. Constitutional interpretation places the other positive freedoms in the due process clauses of the Fifth and Fourteenth Amendments. By this circumstance, these freedoms become part of liberty. The positive guarantee of autonomy outside of the First Amendment is part of due process protection for liberty. Along these same lines, autonomy is a frame by which we can better understand some of the values in the Constitution. Unlike the concepts of liberty and privacy, autonomy has not been a "term of art," or part of the artificial reason used in interpreting the Constitution. Autonomy draws on the doctrinal base of liberty, and by comparison with privacy, autonomy has not been "constructed," or introduced as a constitutional right. Autonomy is a lens through which one can view some of the activities that are protected as constitutional liberty under the due process clauses.

Mental Illness

Mental patients have had less than the full complement of constitutional rights, even less than juveniles. When accused of crimes, they have been excluded from society, often without the special protections of the criminal law. Yet, as in the juvenile justice system, major changes have been taking place in the application of constitutional standards to this area. The last chapter looked at procedural or specific due process guarantees as they affect institutionalized persons. Here we consider the fundamental interests associated with the more general due process guarantees. The application of the concept of liberty to institutionalized persons illustrates the constitutional protection of liberty in the realm of physical and emotional autonomy.

Legal Responsibility. The mentally ill and the mentally incompetent have been outside the ordinary legal process under the theory that criminal responsibility requires sanity. There is a right not to be convicted while incompetent, although there is the problem of distinguishing competence from incompetence. The English *M'Naghten* standard of 1843 based the capacity to stand trial on the ability to tell right from wrong. In 1895, the standard of "an irresistible impulse" was introduced as a basis for avoiding criminal responsibility (*Davis* v. *U.S.*). It was over half a century before a modern standard would develop, the first in the case of *Durham* v. *U.S.* (1954). Here the stipulation was that the accused ". . . is not criminally responsible if the unlawful act was the product of mental disease or mental defect." The *Durham* rule would have jurors make judgments about medical states rather than social judgments; it thus created quite a stir (Pritchett, 1984:234). The result was a proposal for change from the American Law Institute in 1962. This group of influential lawyers and legal scholars sought a middle ground between the older standards and *Durham*. The standard was to be that the accused was not responsible if, as a result of mental illness, he lacked the capacity to tell right from wrong or obey the law; this standard was upheld in the federal courts in 1970 (*Wade* v. *United States*).

In looking at the ability to stand trial, the Warren Court was concerned with adequate representation for an accused person. In *Dusky* v. *United States* (1960), the justices were unanimous in holding that competence to stand trial requires more than the standard that was used by the district judge—this standard being an orientation "to time and place and some recollection of events." Competence, they held, requires that an individual be able ". . . to consult with his lawyer with a reasonable degree of rational understanding" and an understanding of the proceedings against him. In 1975, the Supreme Court amplified the *Dusky* standard in a case where the defendant had been denied a competency hearing and brought to trial on the charge of raping his wife (*Drope* v. *Missouri*, 1975). The trial proceeded even after the defendant was hospitalized for shooting himself. The justices found that a defendant's constitutional right to a fair trial was violated if the court did not wait for a psychiatric exam before proceeding with a trial where there had been testimony indicating possible incompetence. The defendant's absence during the trial added to the finding of unconstitutionality.

A few years before, the justices had been even more sensitive to the punishment inflicted on the handicapped, who had been given less than the standard due process protections. In *Jackson* v. *Indiana* (1972), they held that Theon Jackson, an illiterate deaf-mute with the capacities of a preschool child, could not be committed indefinitely solely on account of his incapacity to proceed to trial. This case made an important contribution to the conception of liberty and the protection for autonomy in the Constitution. In *Jackson*, the ruling was that one who is mentally incompetent "cannot be held more than the reasonable period of time necessary to determine whether there is a substantial probability that he will attain that capacity (to stand trial) in the foreseeable future." Where this is not the case, the government is required to institute civil commitment proceedings or release the defendant. On this precedent, the justices showed a sensitivity to the denial of freedom where it was due to mental illness. Thus, in *McNeil* v. *Director* (1972), the Court authorized the release of a person who had been sentenced to five years' imprisonment, but who was instead confined for six years in a state mental institution.

An issue of constitutional liberty going well beyond the boundary between due process and the determination of competence is what happens to a person who has been acquitted by reason of insanity. In 1983, in *Jones* v. *United States*, Justice Lewis Powell addressed the issue for the majority in an opinion announced just a year after John W. Hinkley, Jr., had been declared "innocent by reason of insanity" for the attempted assassination of President Ronald Reagan. The *Jones* case arose out of a petty theft. The defendant had stolen a jacket from a department store in the District of Columbia. Judged competent to stand trial, the defendant agreed to plead guilty by reason of insanity and was committed to a mental hospital, as provided for by the District of Columbia criminal statute governing mental illness. After 50 days, he was given a hearing where he was found to be mentally ill and a danger to himself and others. Jones appealed this decision, as he would rather have been judged under the criminal law instead of being civilly committed. Civil commitment meant indefinite confinement, whereas criminal conviction held out the possibility of a faster release from confinement. His appeal was taken up by the Supreme Court. In the opinion, Justice Powell reaffirmed the view that "commitment for any purpose constitutes a significant deprivation of liberty that requires due process protection" (*Addington* v. *Texas*, 1979). But in reviewing the statute that allowed for indefinite commitment, Powell wrote that confinement of an "insanity acquittee" rests on "his continuing illness and dangerousness," not on punishment for the crime, and thus confinement should be determined on the basis of a civil commitment standard, even though it is less protective of individual rights. The issues of constitutional liberty raised by the case emerge from the juncture of general due process and mental illness. The outcome in *Jones* is easier to understand in the context of John Hinkley's acquittal the year before.

Punishment/Treatment. Extreme and unusual punishments stemming from the determination that an individual is mentally incompetent have occupied the justices at least since *Buck* v. *Bell*, in which Justice Oliver Wendell Holmes allowed Virginia to sterilize "mental defectives," in 1927. This was not the kind of outcome for which we like to remember the Yankee jurist, but Holmes made it worse by proceeding with excessive flourish to argue that, "The principle that sustains compulsory vaccination is broad enough to cover cutting the Fallopian tubes. . . . Three generations of imbeciles are enough." As Harold Spaeth (1977) indicated, World War II, with its concern about racism and the virtues of liberal democracy, put a lid on this kind of talk. In 1942, without mentioning the *Buck* case, the justices overruled an Oklahoma statute providing for the sterilization of felons who had been twice convicted of crimes involving moral turpitude (*Skinner* v. *Oklahoma*). The standard used was one of searching judicial inquiry when fundamental rights are involved. Application of the Constitution in the present moral climate diminishes the likelihood that sterilization will withstand such scrutiny.

Of particular relevance to the liberty issue was a Supreme Court decision in 1976 that allowed a state hospital to give tranquilizing drugs to a patient who had been committed involuntarily, despite the patient's religious objections to the use of drugs. Such action, it was decided, would incur no liability (*Winter* v. *Miller*, 1971). Responding to pressure from the lower federal courts, the justices took up the issue of involuntary treatment again in 1982. *Mills et al.* v. *Rogers et al.* (1982) was brought by former mental patients who had been forced to accept unwanted "anti-psychotic" drugs administered by the Boston State Hospital. The district court recognized constitutionally protected liberties guaranteeing the right of the patients to decide ". . . for themselves whether to undergo treatment with anti-psychotic drugs." The appeals court proposed a "substitute judgment" standard of whether the treatment would be accepted voluntarily if the patient were competent to make a choice. The United States Supreme Court sent the case back to the lower court in light of a decision by the Massachusetts Supreme Court (*Roe III*, 1981) involving the right of mentally incompetent patients to refuse treatment with anti-psychotic drugs. The decision was based on recognition of a protected liberty interest.

Involuntary commitment has also gotten a great deal of attention since the 1970s. The issue arises in part from the increased use of psychiatric therapy in America. The Burger Court took up the issue of involuntary commitment while attending to questions of personal liberty, considering such things as how involuntary commitment was to be regulated and the obligations it imposed on managers of mental institutions. The leading case was *O'Connor* v. *Donaldson* (1975). With its tragic fact situation and hopeful outcome, this case became part of the Court's gloss on the Constitution. Kenneth Donaldson had been civilly committed as a mental patient in Florida nearly 20 years previously. Throughout his confinement, he had demanded his release on the grounds that he wasn't dangerous to anyone, that he was not mentally ill, and that he wasn't getting any treatment. He finally sued in the district court, basing his claim on an unconstitutional deprivation of liberty. There were some important administrative liability questions in the case, but the relevant consideration here is that the Supreme Court, without dissent, held that the Constitution guaranteed individuals freedom from involuntary civil commitment unless they were dangerous or needed treatment. While disputing the existence of a right to treatment, Chief Justice Burger indicated that "... involuntary commitment to a mental hospital ... is a deprivation of liberty ..." requiring due process (specifically *Specht* v. *Patterson*, 1967:608). The justices required a legitimate state interest in commitment, and an end to confinement when that interest could no longer be demonstrated. The interest could be either the public welfare, as in the case of someone deemed dangerous (*Minnesota ex rel. Pearson* v. *Probate Court*, 1940), or that of a person unable to protect himself, a doctrine dating back to 1890 (*Mormon Church* v. *United States*) but expressed more recently in *Hawaii* v. *Standard Oil Co.* (1972). The implication of Chief Justice Burger's concurrence and of the majority opinion is that individual freedom can only be restrained by involuntary commitment if the patient is receiving treatment or is dangerous to himself or others.

The case of mentally retarded patients presents slightly different issues of responsibility for the institution and those administering civil commitment. In a case involving a retarded 35-year-old who could not talk and lacked the basic capacity to take care of himself, the Supreme Court faced some of these issues (*Youngberg* v. *Romeo*, 1982). The institutionalized man's mother had committed him to a Pennsylvania state institution, but she had become concerned about his treatment while he was in the institution, and she had filed a federal action asserting that he had a constitutional right to safe conditions of confinement, freedom from bodily restraint, and a constitutional right to minimally adequate habitation. Justice Powell acknowledged the first two claims immediately, but he seemed to agonize a bit over the third. He decided that since no amount of training would lead to freedom this issue was moot and did not have to be decided. The opinion in the case balanced the rights of the state against those of the individual.

On the process of commitment, the justices have "... balanced individual, family and social interests" (as certainly seems to be appropriate) in concluding that the constitutional protections for liberty do not require formal adversary hearings when parents try to commit their children to state mental institutions (*Parham* v. *J.R.*, 1979; Gunther, 1980: 633-635). Although it was not very sensitive to personal freedom, this decision is consistent with the bias in favor of parents, which traditionally has limited the autonomy of children. (For a discussion of statutory rights in this area see *Pennhurst State School* v. *Halderman*, 1981.)

Liberty, in the context of a mental hospital depends on public health legislation. States must provide for mental health before constitutional liberties are affected. This creates a statutory base, which results in some deference to the legislative process on issues of constitutional right. Such deference is neither absolute nor particularly unusual. There has always been judicial deference to the legislative process in the American tradition, with the Constitution operating as a framework to set basic requirements. In the realm of mental illness, the power of the Constitution has been as a source of rights and protector of the personal autonomy on which rights are based.

Freedom to Move

The freedom to speak and to think with minimal interference is one of the cornerstones of civil liberties. Freedom of expression is held dear by those who have struggled in behalf of civil liberties, and it expresses their intolerance of any who would officially dictate acceptable speech. The focus here is on a corollary freedom that has received less attention. This is the freedom to act, to do, to move; a right so basic that there has been relatively little litigation on the subject.

The freedom to move is basic to the structure of the American polity. Like property, it joins the individual of the political system with the commercial requirements for movement and exchange in the marketplace. For Blackstone, it was "integral to the concept of liberty" (Blackstone, 1859:985). From after the Civil War until the turn of the present century, the right had been associated with either interstate commerce (*Crandall* v. *Nevada*, 1868), or "privileges and immunities" (*Paul* v. *Virginia*, 1869; *Twining* v. *New Jersey*, 1908). In the interstate commerce case, the Supreme Court had unanimously declared unconstitutional a tax of one dollar on anyone leaving Nevada. (Since that time, Nevada has developed more seductive ways—like gambling—to keep people in the state.) Later in American history, it was asserted that the right to travel was so basic that there was no need to mention it. This was Zechariah Chafee's contention in a treatise he wrote on human rights in the original Constitution (Chafee, 1956:185). The explanation suggested by the Court was that a right to travel was implied by the nature of the union (*Shapiro* v. *Thompson*, 1969:629), perhaps emerging from its federal structure (*United States* v. *Guest*, 1966: LeClaire, 1981:991).

Well over half of the Bill of Rights contains due process protections that have a bearing on involuntary confinement. Traditionally associated with criminal procedure, provisions in the Fourth, Fifth, Sixth, and Eighth Amendments make it clear that the state cannot restrain individuals arbitrarily. Such guarantees as the Fourth Amendment's provision for arrest warrants, the indictment, double jeopardy, and due process guarantees of the Fifth Amendment, the stipulations about the nature of a trial provided for in the Sixth Amendment, and most dramatically, the bail provisions of the Eighth Amendment, monitor the loss of freedom. These are criminal procedure guarantees, and it should not be overlooked that they stem from a right to move freely in the world without fear of incarceration or other punishments that inevitably affect one's liberty. Yet, the truth is that the right is rarely talked about (Houseman, 1979). Consequently, it needs to be said here. The freedom to move is constitutionally guaranteed.

International Travel. Freedom to move has been associated with free expression. For example, the freedom to move is implicit in the right to peaceably assemble for political purposes. Other cases involving a right to travel have been associated with the political freedoms of the First Amendment. In the late 1950s and early 1960s, when the Supreme Court was considering the excesses of the Cold War, it decided cases such as *Kent* v. *Dulles* (1958). In this case, the Court decided that State Department regulations requiring applicants for a passport to take an oath that they were not members of the Communist party were authorized by statute. A few years later, in a related case, *Aptheker* v. *Secretary of State* (1964), a federal statute that made it a crime for members of Communist organizations to obtain a passport was held to be unconstitutional. The ground here was that the decision was too broad a restriction on the right to travel and was thus a denial of due process under the First Amendment. Freedom of movement in the Constitution is thus linked to political expression.

Another element of free expression has been the right to international travel unrestricted by political considerations. The Court's decisions circumscribe the right, pitting individual free expression against national security, as perceived by the State Department. This is inevitably an unfavorable balance. In *Zemel* v. *Rusk* (1965), the Warren Court, under the pen of Chief Justice Earl Warren, examined whether the Secretary of State could refuse to validate the passports of United States citizens for travel to Cuba. Arguing denial of an expression-based right, those who wanted to visit the communist island were unsuccessful before the Warren Court. Justices Douglas and Goldberg dissented on the grounds that the right to travel overseas, as well as at home, was part of the citizen's liberty under the Fifth Amendment. They noted that the freedom of movement has large social values because it is so closely associated with freedom of expression. Two years later (*U.S.* v. *Laub*, 1967), the Supreme Court decided that travel to restricted areas did not constitute a crime. Regulation of entry into the United States, on the other hand, while not entirely beyond the reach of the Fourteenth Amendment because the amendment applies to persons rather than merely to citizens, is essentially a political issue and the federal government has had quite a bit of latitude to set the conditions for entry into the country. Restrictions were greatest in the 1950s (*Shaughnessy* v. *U.S. ex rel. Mezei*, 1953). Although we expect the State Department to be less influenced by extreme paranoia today than in the 1950s, it still does regulate entry for political purposes (*Kleindienst* v. *Mandel*, 1972), and it has continued to try to influence international travel.

Travel cases have generally involved additional rights that were infringed when travel restrictions were introduced. In the late 1970s, the Secretary of Health, Education, and Welfare denied welfare benefits to a person who was outside the United States for a period of more than 30 consecutive days. This case went to the Supreme Court, and it was determined that the denial did not violate the right to travel (*Califano* v. *Aznavorian*, 1978). Usually, however, the issue in international travel is freedom of expression. This was the case in the celebrated litigation surrounding the revocation of Phillip Agee's passport by the Secretary of State. A former CIA employee who had his passport lifted on the judgment of the Secretary of State, Agee was considered a danger to national security. The former agent had been publishing information about CIA activities in an effort to discredit the undercover efforts of the agency. The State Department contended that Agee's disclosures were responsible for a variety of acts of violence against the CIA and its agents. As usual, the outcome (revocation was upheld) is less significant for indicating the structure of this constitutional right than is the assertion of the right in the international atmosphere of intelligence activities at a time when the CIA was reasserting its prerogatives. The right to travel was not treated lightly here (*Haig* v. *Agee*, 1981), although the opinion seems to have been a departure from prior rulings, with its suggestion that in the international sphere, travel under a United States passport is closer to a privilege than a right (Farber, 1981).

Domestic Moves. The more prosaic domestic travel cases are less closely linked to the First Amendment. However, they have strong economic dimensions. One such case was *Edwards* v. *California* (1941), which came out of the Depression of the 1930s. During this period of economic hardship, particularly in the East and Midwest, California passed a statute that made it a crime to knowingly bring into the Golden State ". . . any indigent person who is not a resident of the state." Justice James Byrnes, who served on the Supreme Court a very short time, was assigned to write the opinion of the Court. He asserted a fundamental principle of the American Constitution—that it established a market-place with freedom of movement and minimally obstructed commerce. Thus, the California restriction was held to be unconstitutional. Justice Douglas's concurrence, joined by Justices Black, Murphy, and Jackson, presented "the right to move freely from state to state . . . protected by the privileges and immunities clause of the Fourteenth Amendment against state interference." Although the ground was a matter in dispute, the freedom to move was described in traditional libertarian terms.

In *Shapiro* v. *Thompson* (1969), equal protection guarantees were used to safeguard the right to travel between states. By the interpretation current at the time, a "fundamental" liberty was the basis for claiming equal protection and due process violations. Here, concern about equal-ity and the standing of that right in the 1960s contributed to the freedom to move. In *Shapiro*, state and federal provisions refused welfare benefits to individuals who had resided for less than a year in the state administering the benefits. The justices viewed such requirements as depriving citizens of their constitutional freedom to travel ". . . through-out the length and breadth of our land." Subsequent cases involving travel raised related concerns. In *Memorial Hospital* v. *Maricopa County* (1974), a California county required a year of residence before an indigent could receive free non-emergency medical care. The Court viewed the requirement as a deprivation severely limiting the right to travel. However, in *Starns* v. *Malkerson* (1971), a state university regula-tion that reduced tuition after a year of living in the state was upheld as was a residency requirement for free schooling in Texas (*Martinez* v. *Bynum*, 1983). But in *Vlandis* v. *Kline* (1973), a requirement for out-of-state tuition based on the student's residence address at the time of initial registration had been struck down as creating a statutory presumption of nonresident status that could never be overcome. (See final section.) This was in violation of the Constitution.

Laurence Tribe's analysis of travel emphasizes the personal auton-omy and equal protection issues that have been associated with this right (Tribe, 1978). Cases that have gotten to the Supreme Court affirm the relevance of these concerns for constitutional protection of the freedom to move. The outcomes vary, however. In *McCarthy* v. *Philadel-phia Civil Service Commission* (1976), it was held that the right to travel does not prevent restricting municipal employment to city residents. In *Jones* v. *Helms* (1981), Georgia was allowed to increase the penalty for abandoning a child if the child abandoner left the state. On the other hand, Alaska was not allowed to have a preference for its own residents in hiring for work in its oil- and gas-related industries (*Hicklin* v. *Orbeck*, 1978). It has thus been the corollary rights that have determined the degree of freedom to move protected by the Constitution.

For all its familiarity in conventional discourse and social life, there has been some confusion over how the freedom to move or travel is to be constitutionally protected. This may be related to the close association with economic conditions which is evident in the leading cases. This is an area where the justices have moved cautiously. Similarily, in situations of clear material constraints, the appeal to the Constitution makes less sense. Where scarcity is believed to have limited choices, rights claims will be looked on less favorably. This was the case during the gasoline crisis of the early 1970s. Governors of the various states were telling individuals when they could fill up their gasoline tanks (generally on odd or even days) and with how much gas (not less than half a tank in Massachusetts). Yet, there were very few legal challenges, and no audible cries of constitutional violations. Here, the material constraints, the scarcity people faced, minimized the utility of a constitutional appeal. The freedom to move has not achieved the constitutional stature of the right to free expression because it is perhaps too closely tied to social and economic conditions. The constitutional right to travel has thus been underdeveloped, but it remains a widely held expectation.

Lifestyle Autonomy

Some protections derived from constitutional liberty challenge the distinction we have tried to draw between privacy and autonomy. Consequently, we will refer to them in much the same way. Whereas we considered reputation and sexual preference to be lifestyle privacy issues, here we consider appearance, living arrangements, and certain health care issues under the rubric of "lifestyle autonomy." In many of the autonomy cases, privacy is actually mentioned as a source of constitutional authority. This was true in a case about regulation of hair length on the police force, discussed below. In this case and in the others in the autonomy section, however, the claim differs from those of the privacy section. The assertion of liberty behind the claim is more positive, and it incorporates the general implications of protection for autonomous action to a greater extent than was the case in the privacy section. The somewhat fuzzy distinctions in this area are reflected in the classification scheme of "lifestyle autonomy" in order to show that issues of appearance, living arrangements, and health care are related to issues of reputation and sexual preference.

Appearance. Some claims in the 1970s reveal a great deal about expectations for constitutional liberty, even though they were not successful. The decisions checked expansion of the right by interpreting constitutional liberty to include only those specific areas already protected by constitutional privacy. By moving to greater abstractions, the Court has been able to minimize the broader implications of earlier cases associated with constitutional liberty. In *Kelley* v. *Johnson,* decided April 5, 1976, Justice William Rehnquist referred to claims against infringement on the "individual's freedom of choice with respect to certain basic matters of procreation, marriage, and family life" as having been given constitutional protection. But he denied the applicability of the constitutional challenge:

> ... whether the citizenry at large has some sort of "liberty" interest within the Fourteenth Amendment in matters of personal appearance is a question on which this Court's cases offer little, if any, guidance (*Kelley*, 1976:1444).

The matter at issue was the right of a police officer to determine the length of his hair. That privacy was involved in the case is evident both in the references to the same cases that established that right and in the dissent by Justice Thurgood Marshall, which tied personal appearance to "the right to be let alone" (*Kelley*, 1976:1448). While the decision rests on the special circumstances of the case, Justice Rehnquist's effort to avoid the privacy claim is evident. The tradition about concern for autonomy of the person brought the case before the Court, and while the interest in privacy may have had a bearing, the case is better understood in the context of constitutional liberty generally.

Appearance was the principal lifestyle issue of the 1960s and early 1970s. It received considerable attention in the courts during that period and for a few years after. In general, the judiciary offered support for institutional standards, as in *Kelley* and in a circuit court decision by Judge John Paul Stevens, who at that time was a justice of the Seventh Circuit. In the case of *Miller* v. *School District No. 167* (1974), Judge Stevens upheld the dismissal of a junior high school teacher because he had a beard and wore "faded levies," an appearance the justice viewed as presenting "such a risk" that it "warrants closer judicial scrutiny." Changes in less than a decade make such assertions of autonomy appear rather tame, yet individuals would still be advised not to rely on the robed arbiters of the law for a constitutional right to appear different.

Living Arrangements. The first refusal to expand protection of privacy following *Roe* v. *Wade* came in 1974 over a zoning ordinance directed at unrelated persons living together (*Village of Belle Terre* v. *Borass,* 1974). The controversy, which involved students sharing a house, was only slightly removed from the more traditional context of home, family, and sexual relations. The case was brought before the Court on the expectation that a village ordinance excluding nontraditional families violated a right protecting living arrangements. The expectation was a result of past developments in the interpretation of privacy, such as the 1969 obscenity case, *Stanley* v. *Georgia*, which limited prosecutions for possession of obscene materials in the home. That the court chose to hear the *Belle Terre* case is an indication that a number of justices were interested in considering expansion of constitutional liberty to this lifestyle area. Although the constitutional challenge to the ordinance was unsuccessful, the clash of constitutional values was evident in the opinions of the Court. Justice Douglas, writing for the majority, took the traditionally deferential stance toward legislation in what he considered an economic issue—zoning—and he decided against the unorthodox lifestyle position. Justice Marshall, on the other hand, saw the decision as to "... whether a person's 'intellectual and emotional' needs are best met by living with family, friends, professional associates or others" as falling "... within the ambit of the right to privacy protected by the Constitution." Although the claim was unsuccessful, the fact that it reached the Court and the level of controversy it generated showed that this was a reasonable constitutional argument, a product of the tradition of constitutional discourse.

A subsequent case, *Moore* v. *City of East Cleveland* (1977), moved along the course charted by *Belle Terre*. Here, the challenge was over a "single-family" zoning ordinance that defined "family" in the mythical terms of a "nuclear" unit. The case involved a grandmother, her son, and two grandchildren. The city had ordered the grandmother to expel one of the grandchildren from the home or move. Here, constitutional protection stemmed from the intrusive way the municipality defined family. The plurality traced judicial protection of marriage and family life back to the 1920s, when the court had guaranteed a family the right to send children to religious schools (*Pierce* v. *Society of Sisters*, 1925). While indicating that the family was not beyond regulation, it also stipulated that in this realm the justices had looked closely to determine whether the interests advanced by the government were important and whether they were served by the challenged regulation. Under this scrutiny, the ordinance did not survive. As Justice Powell wrote for a plurality, although it purported to have an aim of minimizing congestion in residential communities "... the ordinance permits any family consisting only of husband, wife, and unmarried children to live together, even if the family contains a half dozen licensed drivers, each with his or her own car." Paradoxically, he pointed out, an adult brother and sister who used public transportation could be prevented from living together.

Another area involving lifestyle choices and the appropriateness of legislative classifications, the right to marry, was taken up in the case of *Zablocki* v. *Redhail* (1978) and was resolved by an 8-1 majority in favor of Redhail. In this case, Roger Redhail was prevented from marrying under a Wisconsin statute that required a court order for anyone wishing to marry who had support obligations for a minor child. For the majority, Justice Marshall argued that because of the fundamental nature of the right to marry, the statute deserved careful scrutiny. Relying on the rights derived from constitutional liberty via the privacy route, the justices found protection of a right to marry, which became the basis for turning back the Wisconsin legislation, was unnecessarily intruding on interests protected by the Constitution.

In a child custody case that the Supreme Court refused to hear, the Kentucky Court of Appeals had given its approval to modification of custodial arrangements where the mother was a lesbian. Kentucky statutes provided for such a change if it was found that the custodial environment "may" endanger the "physical, mental, moral, or emotional health of a child." In the case that was denied review in 1980, a psychologist's opinion had been that the "custodial mother's lesbian lifestyle will cause her two and a half year old daughter possible embarrassment, internal conflicts, and difficulty in achieving heterosexual identity of her own." This was the basis for change to the custody of the father (*Stevenson* v. *Stevenson*, 1980). Thus, after a divorce, the family crucible is broken and with it claim for autonomous action beyond state interventions.

Health Care. Another controversial issue during the period brought terminally ill cancer patients into court against a government agency that monitors acceptable medical practice (*United States* v. *Rutherford*, 1979). The issue was federal legislation implemented by the Food and Drug Administration, which put the drug Laetrile beyond the reach of cancer patients who desired to use it. The constitutional privacy issue was not developed by the Supreme Court, but the federal district court for the western district of Oklahoma had found that Laetrile, in proper dosages, was nontoxic and effective and ordered the government to permit limited purchases of the drug by one of the plaintiffs. The lower court had been particularly receptive to the claims of terminally ill patients and recognized a limited right to the drug. The Supreme Court, however, acknowledged neither the special circumstances nor the particular reading of this liberty interest, and it reversed the lower court decision.

Having looked at lifestyle autonomy and having seen its effect on the right to live in a variety of ways without fear of losing one's job or reputation or being forced out of one's home, it is clear that the judicial responses have not been as favorable as civil liberties litigators might have hoped. This is an area where the liberalism of the Warren Court left some possibilities that simply were not used by the justices in the Burger Court.

Autonomy and Due Process

Liberty in the Constitution is a right associated with institutions and conditions that are often at the fringe of social life. In the context of mental illness, constitutional liberty was linked closely to due process protections, although there were other issues like treatment and fairness that also came up. Similarly, the lifestyle freedoms and the freedom to move involve procedural protections. Whether the libertarian issue is choosing one's roommates or preserving one's sanity, the protection that delineates the right is very often procedural. Here, we will consider some issues in which the autonomy preserved by constitutional liberty is intimately involved with the procedural guarantees. The section begins with juvenile justice, where a relatively recent shift in the procedural protections is returning a degree of autonomy to younger people. We conclude with a discussion of general presumptions about people, as made in statutes—such as whether a man can be as good a parent as a woman—which do not take into consideration individual facts. In this sense, we are back to the beginning of this chapter, since an element of autonomy and thus an aspect of constitutional liberty is freedom from classifications that do not adequately respect people.

Juvenile Justice. Juvenile justice is based on the idea that the state can better serve children if it acts like a parent rather than as the neutral authority it is expected to be when dealing with adults. Under the early twentieth century criminal justice "reforms," proceedings against juveniles would have a "civil" form. Although they would not be considered criminals, neither would children be entitled to bail, indictment, public or jury trials, the Fifth Amendment, or counsel. The movement was away from legal formality and toward recognition of conditions like childhood. The shift was from the liberal guarantees of due process to authority relations modeled on the family, with its informality and unquestioned authority.

The practices began to be reversed in the late 1960s, at least in part as a result of new suspicion in the Constitution toward the making of distinctions among groups (which will be taken up in Chapter 6). The due process revolution in this area was actually a counterrevolution that turned back an earlier reform. It came to the Supreme Court in the case of Gerald Francis Gault. Gault, who had been placed on probation for being with a friend who had stolen a purse, was sent to a juvenile jail after being caught making an obscene telephone call. He was to remain in the juvenile jail until he turned 21—a six-year period. Gault appealed on the grounds that he would not have received such a sentence if he had been an adult (*In re Gault*, 1967). The decision from the Supreme Court began with a review of the juvenile justice movement and, under the pen of Justice Abe Fortas, went on to argue that ". . . the condition of being a boy does not justify a kangaroo court." The justices held that Gault had been denied his liberty without due process and required that in the future there be notice of the charge, the right to appointed counsel, and the right to confront witnesses and remain silent. Three years later, they added the requirement of proof beyond a reasonable doubt for conviction (*In re Winship*, 1970). The intensity of the movement away from the practice of watered-down constitutional rights for juveniles diminished as the 1970s progressed. In occasional cases, however, the justices did review the treatment of juveniles with attention to the constitutional promise of protection for one's liberty. In 1983, for instance, the Supreme Court noted "probable jurisdiction" in a case where state statutes authorized pretrial detention of juveniles upon testimony that they might commit a crime (*Schall* v. *Martin*, 1983). The standard was that a person's youth ought not cause him to suffer more than if he were an adult. This recognition is also evident in the case of mental patients, where it goes beyond specific due process guarantees, and into concerns about treatment and the place of the patient in the community.

Statutory Presumptions. At the root of constitutional liberty is the same conception of the citizen we examined in the due process chapter. This conception incorporates a shared concern for humanity governing the treatment of each individual. This sensitivity to individuality is threatened by legislative classifications. Here, the justices of the Supreme Court have been critically attentive to burdens placed on people because they have a certain characteristic, like their race or their sex. This concern is associated with constitutional liberties because of the denial to individuals of the opportunity to rebut, that is, to act as autonomous individuals. As Professor Stanley Friedelbaum has pointed out, this concern about irrebuttable presumptions has ". . . served in the protection of substantive liberties" (*Friedelbaum*, 1976:93), by calling for an individual finding wherever the presumption on which legislation is based is not ". . . necessarily or universally true in fact, and when the State has reasonable alternative means of making the crucial determination" (*Vlandis* v. *Kline*, 1973:452). In *Vlandis* (1973), a Connecticut statute that classified individuals as permanent nonresidents for determining tuition status was declared unconstitutional. In *Stanley* v. *Illinois* (1972), the Court condemned, as violating due process, a state's assumption that unwed fathers are unfit to raise their children. In this case, the father had demonstated his concern for the welfare of his child (*Stanley*, 1972:651). Friedelbaum notes that the burden has been shifted to the state to justify its actions in particular cases. Although described as being in the tradition of substantive due process by its detractors and by some of its defenders, the notion of individual judgment is at the core of the traditional judicial action.

Unchallengable statutory presumptions are such an affront to traditional liberty that, if examined by the courts, they are generally held to be unreasonable. Laurence Tribe calls them statutory "rules of thumb" and he contrasts such presumptions with the rights of personhood and privacy in his discussion of *Cleveland Board of Education* v. *La Fleur* (1974). Here a school board required female faculty members to take unpaid maternity leaves whether the teacher's ability to teach was impaired by pregnancy or not. The Court held that this involved an "unwarranted conclusive presumption" that seriously burdens the exercise of protected constitutional liberty. Similarly, the district court in Delaware concluded that the fact that the director of a residence house at a state college had given birth to an illegitimate child was not enough to establish present or continuing immorality on the part of the director. The college and its officials, therefore, had acted unconstitutionally when they applied what the Court called an irrebuttable presumption of immorality and terminated the woman's employment contract (*Lewis* v. *Delaware State College*, 1978).

In a number of sex discrimination cases that were decided in the mid-1970s, the Court drew on its concern about irrebuttable presumptions to bring sex stereotyping and sex classifications under the authority of the Fifth Amendment when the Fourteenth Amendment did not apply to the situation. This "slight of hand" was possible in the midst of concern about discrimination against women and because of views that the concept of liberty should protect people from being treated as faceless elements in a mass society. Thus, in *Frontiero* v. *Richardson* (1973), the justices affirmed the right of a female member of the armed services to claim a spouse as dependent under the same requirements as for males. The claim was decided on the basis of the due process clause of the Fifth Amendment. The Court ruled that "While the Fifth has no equal protection clause, it forbids discrimination that is so unjustifiable as to be violative of due process" (*Frontiero*, 1973). The due process argument is based as much in a liberty interest protecting against such treatment as a protection against taking property. The problem with these classifications was that they did not take account of individual responsibility.

These are some of the implications of the belief that individuals should be allowed to stand or fall on the basis of their own conduct and not because they belong to a particular group or because of some generalizations about shared characteristics. It has been evident to many that a stronger basis for attacking segregation in America than constitutional equality might have been the violation of constitutional liberty that we have considered here. Thus, if liberty had been the standard, the states would have been accountable for limiting the free choice of blacks, first in transportation and later in schools and other places. No promise of "equality" (see Chapter Six) would have legitimized segregation in the face of such a deprivation of liberty.

The concept of liberty has a great deal of institutional significance. Added after the Civil War, liberty was the vehicle for the elevation of judicial power and the expansion of federal constitutional rights. Capitalists, Communists, women who did not want children and grandparents who did, those in institutions who wanted to get out and those who wanted in, they all have appealed for protection of their liberty. In the process, they revealed two kinds of protection—that of privacy with its deliberate reconstruction of the Constitution to articulate new social concerns, and that of autonomy, a residual category with roots reaching deep into the culture of politics and branches covering a range of circumstances. Our treatment of liberty began with a new interpretation of "substantive due process." The result has been a synthesis derived from the practices of constitutional rights.

We now turn to a discussion of property. Like liberty, property is a right to which other rights, such as due process and equality, are connected. And like liberty, constitutional property has been a political resource for various interests throughout American history. In the next chapter, we define what property is, how it has been based in "settled expectations," and how it has been protected by the courts.

Property   5

The Penn Central Transportation Company owns Grand Central Terminal, a magnificent Beaux Arts train station at 42nd Street and Park Avenue in New York City. Its historic qualities are appreciated by many. Under a city ordinance designating the train station a landmark, the transportation company is limited in what it can do with the building. The company challenged the ordinance as unconstitutionally taking its property. In another case, Laverne L. Logan, a shipping clerk at Zimmerman Brush Company in Illinois, was discharged after a short probationary period. He claimed that his physical handicap—one of his legs was shorter than the other—was not a lawful basis for losing his job. Logan demanded a hearing over deprivation, without due process, of his property interest in employment. Jean Loretto, who owned a five-story apartment building in Manhattan, also brought suit over her property. The building she owned had been strung with wire and silver boxes for cable television. These fixtures ran down the side of Loretto's apartment building and over to neighboring buildings. The state had authorized the wiring of apartments in the city by Teleprompter Manhattan CATV. Ms. Loretto called this a violation of her property rights. These three cases reflect the variety of contemporary questions associated with constitutional property, as well as what the constitutional right is.*

The property right, a traditional element of the liberal creed, has not been considered an "individual" liberty for many years. Modern ideas about civil liberties can be traced to the Supreme Court's 1937 shift away from protection of economic or property rights and toward political liberties such as constitutional freedom and due process. Yet, significant decisions have been made since that time and a contemporary property right is now emerging as a civil liberty. This contemporary

* In the Supreme Court, the claims brought by Logan and Loretto were successful; Penn Central's claim was not.

167

right is based on a shift from protection of corporations to protection of people with property and expectations of various kinds. The treatment in this chapter is historical because the foundations of constitutional property need to be firmly established in order to understand this right as a civil liberty. In fact, the treatment of property in the recent past makes it necessary to step back for a look at the right in the more distant past. Consequently, this chapter discusses early constitutional cases like those after the Revolution and in the period of industrial expansion, in order to free constitutional property from some contemporary misconceptions.

Property has always been a pivotal right guaranteeing respect and status to some individuals. This right is easily associated with the protection of wealth, particularly for those who have a lot of it. Recently, however, the protections stemming from property have been extended significantly. Consequently, property has been included in the present treatment of rights that are fundamental to American democracy and on which the authority of the government rests. This chapter begins with an introduction to some conceptual problems in understanding property rights. Since protection from property has covered everything from Georgia bottomland to the right to 10 days of a modern high school education, we show how the system of authority has covered each of these protections. The evolution of the right—that is, the changing notion of what is to be protected by constitutional property—will be presented to clarify the nature of this concept and the social context to which property is tied. Recent environmental issues are addressed through the distinction between the police power, which eliminated danger, and eminent domain, which produced new benefits. Finally, the chapter will cover how constitutional property protects statutory entitlements such as Social Security, an issue which demonstrates the contemporary relevance of this basic right.

The Concept of Property

Property, especially the private property right, is associated with individual possession and control. The conventional view emphasizes the autonomy that comes with property ownership. But examination of practices in the constitutional setting reveals that property rights holders depend on government for the right to their property. Government defines the range of action within which the property owner is autonomous. When we say that someone legally owns a piece of land, we do not mean that he can do anything he pleases with it. Various laws permit him to use it in some ways, and not others. Legal ownership allows the owner to call the police to eject others who are trying to take his land by force or enter it without his permission. Similarly, the power of "eminent domain" gives the government the authority to seize privately owned land if it is needed for a public purpose, such as building a highway. These dimensions of the right, which tell us what a property owner can and cannot expect, are governed by constitutional property.

A System of Authority

Property, as a right to possess and control, within limits, is of particular relevance to expanding state authority. For property is "... a system of authority ..." that, like any right, "depends on the promise of government" (Lindbloom, 1979:8; Commons, 1924:247). When the courts rule on property, the decision involves the power or range of action one may lawfully exercise in a particular situation. "Property" has come to be used, even in legal writing, not in the precise sense of this power, but to describe the subject of the right. Yet, it is more consistent with the his- tory of property and legally appropriate to say that these things are simply an indication or sign of the right.

Changing Issues. As a fundamental right, the concept of property is stable, although the issues, reflecting changes in the subjects of legal conflict, have undergone continuous alteration. Thus, Karl Renner found the concept of property to be relatively fixed, but he argued that changes in its social functions had altered its meaning. When European and American society consisted, or were thought to consist, largely of individual families, each living on a plot of land and growing their own food, it was easy to think of property in land as being secure possession of a thing. Each family owned its own land, and nobody was permitted to take someone else's property. When these societies developed indus- tries, however, property came to function differently. If you owned a factory and had the capital (money) to pay wages, then property no longer consisted of the right to be left alone on your land, but rather it was the power to get other people to work for you. Through this transformation of the social function of property, Renner proposed that the "peaceful enjoyment of one's own property has developed into draconian control of alien labor power" (Renner, 1949:101). Thus, a comprehensive, materialist treatment of property would require atten- tion to its social function. Authoritative holdings, handed down by the Supreme Court, however, affirm Renner's thesis about conceptual continuity.

Recent scholars have seen changes in the property concept itself. Morton Horwitz described a "transformation" of the concept which occurred when land came to be viewed "as a productive asset" (Horwitz,

1977); that is, there was a shift from vested rights in property—where priority and natural use held sway—to explicit utility calculations—where the social value of the property was what mattered. Horwitz revealed a change in the forms of property protected by the right. The shift from the more stable vested rights to support for development and economic growth parallels a shift from property as agricultural land to property as industry. The result, according to the analysis in this chapter, is a change in the status of competing claims, rather than in the meaning of the concept—that there are claims that are protected by government. Another approach emphasizing change is that of C. B. Macpherson, who argued that property evolved from the expected protection of social standing prior to the founding of the American Republic, through a period in which property meant things or commodities, to a contemporary return to what people believe belongs to them (Macpherson, 1973). Thus, standing before the law has been an important part of the concept of property in both the feudal and the welfare state (Macpherson, 1978; Maine, 1886; Commons, 1924; Reich, 1964, 1965).

The "New" Property. A challenge has been presented to conventional views of property by an idea known as the "new property" (Reich, 1964). The initial challenge here is to understand what is being talked about. The "old" property is private ownership of such things as land, a house, cars, or television sets. The "new" property deals with welfare checks, medical care, and other benefits and services from government. These benefits are often called "entitlements" because certain individuals are entitled to receive them from the government. Thus, a law that provides that the government pay a mother $50 a month for each of her children if the father is not present in the house and if family income is less than $7,000 per year, gives the mother of six children an entitlement to receive $300 from the government each month.

From a conventional perspective, the "new" property looks very different from the "old," that is, if we think of the old property as the possession of things. Getting food by paying money one has accumulated seems different from being entitled to food because a statute says the government should give it to you. But it is possession and the rights surrounding it that are most relevant to the meaning of property, not how something was acquired in the first place. Even the old property is not really the absolute possession of something. To say one owns something is really to say that the government by law has promised to use its power to keep other people from taking the thing away under certain circumstances specified in the law. Thus, homeowners *expect* that, as long as they make the mortgage payments, they can occupy their houses and they are entitled to get the police to help them get rid of a stranger who puts up a tent on their lawn. By property, we mean that certain persons have expectations or entitlements guaranteed by law. Homeowners expect to keep living in their houses so long as they are legally entitled to do so. Welfare recipients expect to keep getting welfare checks, so long as they are legally entitled to do so. Homes are "old" property. Welfare checks are "new" property. Both are property, in that someone has a right to them in the sense of an expectation. Both are determined by a structure of authority.

The meaning of property is in flux. On the one hand, public prerogatives over property in land have been expanding as a result of environmental regulations and a commitment to land use planning (Bosselman, 1973). On the other hand, extensive government obligations to holders of statutory entitlements have become the basis of a "new" property right (Reich, 1964). The old rights, while much less absolute than they appear to the public, are still more comprehensive than the new rights of the welfare state. The rights in statutory entitlements, though more substantial than they have been, are a shadow of those associated with land. In a social order where the individual is highly dependent on the state, the necessity for a broader, more equitable conception of property is becoming clearer, and during a period when commitment to public assistance is being questioned, it is essential to understand the legal foundation of property. The approach presented here is particularly attentive to different historical contexts. This is meant to amplify the relationship between interpretive parameters in the Constitution, material interests evident in the society, and the choices made by judicial authorities in the cases before them. These change over time.

Constitutional Protection

A basic tension in the meaning of property is that between private possession under the common law maxim of *salus populi*, which means that the possession is for the public good, and possession under a "vested" or absolute right; the former meaning acknowledges that the right is subject to policy considerations—what the government will acknowledge as possession in its statutes. The latter position comes from the myth of property attributed to John Locke and disseminated in America through the work of William Blackstone. This position treated property rights as elevated above community regulation, or "vested." This view was received in America while the Constitution was being written, and it is this absolute or fundamental property right that is the subject here. This is the property that is governed by the Constitution. In constitutional history, the "things" to which the right is applied

171

have changed, but the nature of the dominion, the relationship that is the essence of constitutional property, has not changed much at all. The political choices evident when a society protects slaveholding of course differ from those in a society where it is illegal. Yet, the manner in which the choices are protected can be the same in both instances. That is, slaves at one time and welfare benefits at another may fall under the guarantees of the Constitution. The special relation between the Constitution and that which is protected by the property right is the key to the analysis of property.

Mechanisms to protect economic interests can be found throughout the Constitution. The term "property," however, appears only in the due process and compensation clauses of the Fifth Amendment. Here we have the statement, ". . . nor shall private property be taken for public use without just compensation." The Bill of Rights represents the enlightenment theory of individual autonomy, and the Fifth Amendment picks up the Magna Carta's requirement for immediate payment on the public taking of provisions, reflecting the tension between the individual and the state.

The early Supreme Court protected a wide range of economic interests with concepts that were equally varied. In the nineteenth century, Chief Justice John Marshall developed protections for steamboat lines and college charters based on the Constitution's commerce and contract clauses. In the Jacksonian era, the promise of compensation was restricted to land. Due process protection of property gained significance after the Civil War, as property began to be valued for what it was worth in the market rather than how it could be used (Commons, 1924). This prepared the concept for the age of "finance capitalism" (Lerner, 1933:136-137), when the most valuable property, stocks and securities, had little actual utility. Although judicial attention turned away from economic matters after the New Deal court fight of 1937, this period of official rest for constitutional property was characterized by growth in protection for political liberties giving constitutional rights a more progressive caste.

The idea that property and liberty could be separated grew with the Industrial Revolution (Reich, 1964:772). Progressive reformers attacked property as representing power over others, rather than protection of the individual. The consequence was an attempt to transfer this power to the government, thereby removing it from the sphere of fundamental rights. This is evident in the post-1937 "double standard" emphasizing civil rather than economic liberties in the Constitution (Funston, 1978:199-206). Exclusion of property from treatises on civil liberties has been a result (Way, 1976; Abraham, 1982). While legal scholarship has taken note of the peculiarities of a double standard (Tribe, 1978;

Gunther, 1979), generally property is still not seen as a civil liberties issue. Despite economic implications of individual liberties such as equal protection or the right to counsel, property has not been among the legal rights guaranteed by the Supreme Court since the double standard was introduced in 1937.

After avoiding property rights for 40 years, the Supreme Court has recently demonstrated a fresh interest in the area. Contemporary holdings that individuals have a constitutionally protected right in licenses, franchises, and social welfare benefits (*Goldberg* v. *Kelly*, 1970; *Goss* v. *Lopez*, 1975) focus attention on the property right. The Court, having contributed to the authoritative meanings since the founding of the American Republic, provides a foundation (and a foil) for investigating the nature of legal property. Commentary and observations from other sectors add to our understanding, but judicial interpretation serves as a basis when describing the constitutional property right.

The Tradition:
Settled Expectations

In his treatise on constitutional law, Laurence Tribe considers a model of "settled expectations" to be one of the distinctive forms of constitutional adjudication. To Tribe, the model is composed of two "sets of restraints on government power," which vest rights in property and contract on the grounds "that certain settled expectations . . . should be secure against governmental disruption, at least without appropriate compensation" (Tribe, 1978:456). Protection for settled expectations is behind the Fifth Amendment promise that people will be protected and that they will be compensated for justified "takings" of their property by the government. In the Constitution, protection of property is a matter of guarantees of this sort, rather than possession of tangible things.

When the judges and justices of the federal bench adjudicate property rights they are dealing with official promises or expectations. Karl Marx put the situation in a characteristic way when he wrote that ". . . the railways do not 'actually' belong to the shareholders, but to the statutes" (as quoted in Edelman, 1979:40). Thus, it is the statutes that guarantee ownership and define shareholding. In the United States, a new government replaced the weak Articles of Confederation in order to establish a nation. This government used its authority to maintain traditional property relationships, many of which had existed under the Crown. Challenges that made their way to the Supreme Court, from the very early ones to the present, characteristically involved expectations that were inherent in the promises of the state (Tribe, 1978:456-473). On the other hand, the Court has only been minimally attentive to how property has been acquired. It is difficult to find any special sensitivity, much less preoccupation, with the Lockean notion that a person creates an interest in property through "The labor of his body and the work of his hands. . . ," as outlined in Locke's *Second Treatise*.

In order to understand the constraints of constitutional ideology, and the incremental contributions that characterize the Supreme Court's bouts with property, this section examines shifts in the things possessed in terms of settled expectations—the concept that allows them all to be considered property. At each period in American history, the Supreme Court has been confronted with different kinds of claims for the protections of the property right. These periods are described with reference to the legal distinctions that emerged from judicial interpretation of property. They reflect changes in social, political, and economic relations. From period to period, this chronology is conceptually continuous. The subject of the right moves from debts through grants to status and franchises. But each subject is related to the core concept of settled expectations.

Issues that reached the Supreme Court when the nation was forming reflected an unstable political environment. Thus, the first few decades brought problems involving government authority. The theory of property rights as expectations emerged from the early cases on title, debt, and offices. Later, commerce added new concepts, and the Constitution was called in to protect grants and monopolistic guarantees as obligations of government. The issue of expropriation, which is treated in the next section, also took its meaning from expectations protected by the Constitution. More recent property is clearly associated with entitlements from the state. Cases involving welfare benefits and unemployment compensation will be examined with the focus on the prospects for moderating a clash over the nature of government "largess."

Debts and Offices

Fears were expressed at the constitutional convention (Beard, 1913) and during ratification that the new federal government would take control away from the states in respect to economic matters such as ". . . legal tender laws, their legislation as to British debts and Loyalist properties and their state land grants and land titles" (Warren, 1922:190-191). These fears were generally borne out. In fact, these were the areas in which the national government first exerted its authority. Consequently, litigation bearing on these issues dominated the Supreme Court's early dockets. Most of these decisions were based on grounds other than the Constitution, such as treaties or statutes. The Supreme Court ruled on the disputes in order to indicate the authority that should be relied on, and not surprisingly, this was often that of the national government. Some of these are not strictly constitutional law cases, rather they are decisions of the nation's highest court on cases in which lower courts and other jurisdictions could not agree. Thus, these decisions point to law that is fundamental.

In one of their first opinions, *Georgia* v. *Brailsford* (1792), the Supreme Court justices addressed a debt due to a British subject. In this case, the Court discussed the state-backed guarantees that constituted possession. Relying on "the law of nations and the treaty of Peace," Chief Justice John Jay ruled that British debts could be revived after the war in spite of what the state of Georgia had legislated. Brailsford still had a right of action to recover ". . . the property which had never in fact or law been taken" (*Georgia* v. *Brailsford*, 1792:415). Although it might have been hard to collect the debt during the war, the "property" had not been transferred. Property was not a function of whether a debt could be collected but of legal right.

As it had been in the *Brailsford* case, state authority was exercised to protect individual interests in admiralty cases. These cases involved questions of possession and control arising on the "high seas." Like disputes over relations between the new states, these issues came first to the circuit courts, which at that time were conducted by Supreme Court justices riding in the hinterlands. The Supreme Court subsequently took some of them up, claiming national authority over these previously contentious areas. In early Supreme Court cases, the contest over property first required that the jurisdiction of the new courts be settled. Once that had been established, it was a small step to determining which of the parties had the best federal claim. As Sheldon Goldman has reminded us, the overriding issue from the ratification of the Constitution until the Civil War was ". . . the nature of the American Union" (Goldman, 1981:23), that is, the power of the national government relative to that of the states.

As early as 1796, protection of property by the Supreme Court in the interest of the new government began to employ a constitutional foundation. *Ware* v. *Hylton* (1796) was argued before the Court by John Marshall as attorney for the state of Virginia, just a few years before he was appointed Chief Justice. The issue in that case was the status of the treaties that ended the Revolutionary War when their provisions conflicted with the interests and sometimes explicit statutes in the states. The treaties were supposed to settle issues arising over the validity of prewar debts and wartime confiscation of property. *Ware* was the first exercise of Supreme Court review over the states—and attorney John Marshall lost the case. Although interpreting a treaty, the case involved constitutional authority, and it heralded a judicial propensity to preserve property in accord with settled expectations.

The Court turned to property in the form of disputed inheritance in *Calder* v. *Bull* (1798). Here, legislation that had changed the status of a will was challenged on property, *ex post facto*, and natural law grounds. The *ex post facto* claim was that the law changed the rules without warning. While the principle of compensation to individuals when their property was taken for public use was recognized in the late nineteenth century, it is said to have had little significance in the Federal Period after the Revolution (Horwitz, 1977:63). This period of constitutional property is often ignored; perhaps because it came before the age of contracts or because the status of statutory property was not yet clear. In *Calder*, however, there is evidence that compensation had such an impact. Justice Samuel Chase's opinion dismissed an *ex post facto* claim that the Constitution prohibited such statutory protection, holding that such protection ". . . was not considered, by the framers of the Constitution, as extending to prohibit the depriving a citizen even of a vested right to property. . . ." The discussion by Chase presents the property right as a guarantee from the State: ". . . the right of property . . . is conferred by society, is regulated by civil institution, and is always subject to the rules prescribed by positive law" (*Calder* v. *Bull*, 1798:394). These are clearly not simple Lockean conceptions. State power, not accumulation or labor, was the basis of property. For Chase, rights were ". . . the power to do certain actions; or to possess certain things, according to the law of the land" (*Calder* v. *Bull*, 1798:394). At a time when appeals to natural law were common, the Supreme Court established the authority of the state over property on the basis of "settled expectations" under law.

Along with the usual fare of common law and admiralty cases came a constitutional dispute that would become the most important one of this period. Although it is generally viewed for what it has to say about judicial review, *Marbury* v. *Madison* (1803) suggests some early considerations surrounding constitutional property. The case was a dispute over when an official appointee was entitled to that appointment. William Marbury brought to the Supreme Court his claim against James Madison, the secretary of state, because he had been promised a judgeship but had never gotten his letter of appointment from the secretary of state. The case is about which expectations are legitimate. Although the Chief Justice made a tactical retreat from the merits of this case, he noted in passing that the appointment was official when the government had made its decision, not when the letters of appointment were delivered. Marbury should have become a judge when the secretary of state signed the letters, not when they were delivered. The implication was that evidences of the office were the property of the office holder, whose appointment according to law makes the commission process complete. The significance of the property aspect of the holding was that it rested on official action, rather than on anything tangible. Marshall cited Lord Mansfield who believed that the power of the courts should be available "whenever there is a right to execute an office, perform a service, or exercise a franchise (more especially if it be a matter of public concern, or attended with profit)...." (*Marbury* v. *Madison*, 1803:168-169). The contribution of the decision is to the rights in expectation (which Chase had considered central to the "real" property right) as inherent in those powers dependent on "the law of the land."

Although the admiralty cases had a robust quality characteristic of a maritime wilderness, the subjects of property treated by the justices in this period are familiar. Only property in slaves is particularly unusual. As property, it would be as out of place in contemporary litigation as Social Security cases would have been in 1795. The new government protected property in slaves as it did property in land and debts. The ownership of persons, however, brought liberty and property into conflict. It was a volatile issue that evoked considerable scrutiny even in 1810. In that year, a Maryland law prohibiting the slave trade was held not to be able to grant freedom or deny property without an examination of the pertinent facts. Thus, the nature of the ownership is familiar even when the subject is foreign because of continuity in the meaning of the concept of property.

Property cases before the Court raised sovereignty issues because the relation between the nation and states was so often central to each case. Before the second decade of the nineteenth century was over, the outlines of a federal system had appeared. The Supreme Court contributed to the new system by adjudicating conflicts over ownership of property. *Martin* v. *Hunter's Lessee* (1816) considered a dispute involving Philip Martin who had inherited land in Virginia from Lord Fairfax. The problem was that Lord Fairfax's land had been confiscated during the Revolution and part of it had been sold to David Hunter after the war. Martin went to court to clear the land of Hunter's tenants. The issue was ownership or "title," and it rested on a conflict between two governments, one old and one new. The Supreme Court had actually heard the case three years earlier and had found that Virginia had violated the treaty of 1794 in dismissing Martin's claim. But the Virginia Supreme Court had refused to enforce the United States Supreme Court decision in the case, asserting its "co-equal" sovereignty with the federal government. When it came to the Supreme Court a second time, Republican Justice William Johnson feared that the case threatened "... the permanence of the American Union" (*Martin* v. *Hunter's Lessee*, 1816:363). The opinion was delivered by Justice Joseph Story, and it held that the authority of the Constitution of the United States came from the people and not from the "states in their sovereign capacities." Thus, the property right, according to the Supreme Court, rested in this case with Martin, the heir to a British lord, rather than with the tenant, an American who occupied the land under an agreement with Hunter, another American, who had purchased the land from his state government.

The rights claimed from 1795 to 1820, roughly the Federal Period, thus raised questions about the legitimacy of action by public officials. As might be expected for a new nation, they involved conflicts, in which the authority to resolve the conflict was itself in dispute. This is evident when one turns from the subjects of the disputes—land or money—to the system of authority that lurks behind the issues for the courts. Thus, in this period, the Supreme Court's efforts involved stabilizing federal authority by settling claims that had arisen in areas where the authority was unsettled. The most tangible aspect of *property* in these cases was likely to be a government document, such as a title or certificate, although sometimes such a document did not even exist. Governmental authority as a way of holding land or wealth was the subject of the cases. During the next period, the government would take a more active role in creating the property in the first place.

Contracts and Grants

From about the end of the Federal Period until mid-century, constitutional protection for property grew in importance. At that time, the form of constitutional property was "the obligations of contract" and adjudication during this period contributed to the evolution of the right. The Supreme Court initially directed its attention to expectations that were vested through state charters. Its decisions limited the range of legislative prerogatives and any rethinking lawmakers might have wished to engage in. Governmental obligations linked the earlier property cases to constitutional adjudication under the contract clause. The obligations of the states were refined during this period, with an increasing willingness to consider the expectations created by statute in the context of economic development.

The issue in *Fletcher* v. *Peck* (1810) was title to lands given under a state grant. The case arose out of a real estate deal in Alabama and Mississippi involving 35 million acres around the Yazoo River. The land was sold to speculators by the Georgia legislature in 1795. Many of the legislators appear to have been bribed to make the sale (Magrath, 1967). When voters found out, the legislators were replaced, and the grant was rescinded. A number of parcels of land, however, had already been sold to innocent buyers, and it was from this group that legal action for clear title surfaced. Chief Justice Marshall depicted the Constitution as protecting citizens ". . . from the effects of those sudden and strong passions to which men are exposed (*Fletcher* v. *Peck*, 1810:138; Beard, 1913). He saw these passions expressed in the contested legislation. The Court's holding was sensitive to the difficulty of those property owners who did not "bear the strain" of the earlier fraud. Because of this obligation, the Constitution limited the government's power to review its own actions. As with the *Calder* case, the property right was supported by prohibitions in the Constitution, such as protection against *ex post facto* laws and bills of attainder. This constitutional amalgamation amounted to protection of expectation where it has a legitimate basis.

By 1819, constitutional property under the contract clause was strong enough to guarantee the continued existence of a corporation (*Dartmouth College* v. *Woodward*, 1819) against legislative "attack," when the New Hampshire legislature wanted to make Dartmouth College a public institution. The constitutional provision against "impairing the obligations of contract" was the doctrinal basis; the result was a "pure" property with expectations based on the original grant from the legislature rather than possession of a tangible thing. (We remember the emotional stake of alumni like Daniel Webster as being a constitutionally protected interest.) Adjudication under the contract clause then guaranteed an intangible expectation, which was the essence of property. Soon after it sided with tradition at Dartmouth College, the justices of the Supreme Court preserved other traditional forms of property which were threatened by "contract impairments" resulting from legislative action. They declared a New York bankruptcy law unconstitutional in *Sturges* v. *Crowninshield*, 1819, since it weighed on property, and they invalidated legislation that had nullified rents in land by holding that ". . . a law which denies to the owner of land a remedy to recover the possession . . . [or] the profits . . . impairs his right to, and interest in, the property" (*Green* v. *Biddle*, 1823:75). The Court had suggested that profits would be protected as a facet of expectations. The Constitution had thus been used to moderate the effects of state intervention in debtor-creditor relations.

The subject of *Gibbons* v. *Ogden* (1824) was a monopoly, which was treated as property and which was a characteristic object of constitutional scrutiny during the period. Treatment of this and similar forms of property transformed the right from a static to an instrumental guarantee sensitive to development (Horwitz, 1973). The Supreme Court contributed to this trend in *Tyler* v. *Wilkinson* (1827). In spite of homage to the ideal of vested rights evident in the statement by Justice Joseph Story that "the fundamental maxims of a free government seem to require that the rights of personal liberty and private property should be held sacred" (*Wilkinson* v. *Leland*, 1829:657), the justices legitimated a state grant that would bridge a navigable creek despite the claim to prior property rights in the area under dispute (*Wilson* v. *Blackbird Creek Marsh Co.*, 1829). The Court's orientation to legislative prerogatives fostering economic expansion grew throughout the period. This was expressed in *Charles River Bridge* v. *Proprietors of Warren Bridge* (1837), where the rights on both sides were derived from legislative grants. The property issue involved the prerogatives of the state over property it had created, and there was greater deference to the new grant than to the older one. The opinion in this case rings with enthusiasm for expansion. It held that an established charter to operate a toll bridge did not preclude Massachusetts from granting a competing authorization for a free bridge. Chief Justice Roger B. Taney ruled that "Any ambiguity in the terms of the contract must operate . . . in favor of the public" (*Charles River Bridge* v. *Proprietors of Warren Bridge*, 1837:420). The winning party represented development, and a propertied interest derived from the state was triumphant, as it was bound to be, since it existed on both sides of the dispute.

Contract, the most adjudicated protection of property before the Civil War, was transitional. Choice of this standard may have resulted from the unavailability of Fifth Amendment protections for challenges to state statutes so characteristic of the period. Where change confronted tradition, the state was given an opportunity to enhance economic growth (Commons, 1924:6). There was marked insensitivity to old wealth, or even old statutory promises, as the building of new bridges and the licensing of new shipping lines showed (*Pennsylvania* v. *Wheeling and Belmont Bridge Co.*, 1856). There was also evolution in the period toward intangible interests. This emerged from the longstanding attention to the legal status of debts, titles, and offices that had occupied the Court from its inception. Thus, the developmental thrust in the country determined the outcomes of these disputes and made protected expectations contingent on their relationship to economic growth.

Status and Franchises

Slavery cast an influential shadow over property rights before the Civil War, and its jurisprudential legacy—the view of law that it spawned—would be influential for years after the conflict ceased. This was a period when questions of status and issues related to one's position in the community, as well as franchises to do business or practice a profession, reached the Supreme Court. During this period, the power of legislatures was generally consolidated, and the result was a constitutional property right that delineated the parameters within which legislative power could be exercised. Doctrinally, the protection of property shifted from contract to due process. Contract, which had been spelled out in terms of obligations, gave way in the attention of judges to discourse on what property was and what could be done with it. With inclusion of the Fourteenth Amendment's due process guarantees in the Constitution, the range of protection for property was as great as that in the contract clause (Article I, Sec. 10), both in the levels to which it was applicable and the relationships that could now be protected.

Changes in the use and application to which the constitutional protection for property would be put arose from lower levels in the legal hierarchy. This has often been the case with the emergence of new ideas, as was evident in the influence of the lower federal courts and judges like Learned Hand and Jerome Frank on constitutional freedoms of expression. With property, the New York Court of Appeals set the stage for the invalidation of legislation on constitutional grounds with its opinion in *Wynehamer* v. *New York* (1856). New York State had a due process clause guaranteeing the property right, and when the legislature passed a prohibition law forbidding the sale and storage of liquor in the state (Goldman, 1982: 181-182), Mr. Wynehamer claimed a constitutional right to his booze. The justices of New York's highest court upheld his claim. The use of due process in this instance did not rely on how the property was taken, and it did not make the issue a matter of procedure. The decision turned instead to the fact that property which had been legally possessed would have to be destroyed. This was an instance of due process being applied to the substance of the legislation rather than to the procedure. The holding was not immediately controlling in the Supreme Court, however. In the same year as the decision in *Wynehamer*, the Court protected a piece of property from expropriation because the process had not been "according to some settled source of judicial proceedings" (*Murray's Lessee* v. *Hoboken Land and Improvement Co.*, 1856). Although *Murray's Lessee* emphasized procedure, Justice Benjamin Curtis's opinion also drew on the more general protection for property, which derives from the phrase "by the law of the land" in the Magna Carta. Two years later, in *Dred Scott* v. *Sandford* (1857), a divided Court declared the Missouri Compromise—the act of Congress dividing the country into free and slave states—to be invalid because it deprived slaveholders of their property. Here, a broad reading of the property protection was similar to *Wynehamer*, but the interests at stake were dramatically different.

The war and the constitutional amendments that followed reversed the outcome of *Dred Scott*, but the decision in that case did suggest an extraordinary judicial confidence in constitutional property protection. The Constitution was held to supersede an act of Congress—the

Missouri Compromise—and the nation was not in a mood to accept that reading. Yet, there was another property issue raised by the case, which was given fuller treatment in a dissent to the decision. According to Justice Benjamin Curtis, the Missouri Compromise did not cause a constitutional property violation because "Slavery . . . is created only by municipal law. . . . The Constitution refers to slaves as 'persons held to service in one state, under the laws thereof. . . .' Nothing can more clearly describe a status created by municipal law" (*Dred Scott* v. *Sandford*, 1857:564-633). The choice as to what will be considered property is political, a matter for legislation. The Constitution here simply indicates what follows once property has been recognized. While before the war, blacks would be a commodity and a form of property, their status as citizens after the war would override claims of ownership. Thus, once state law had created a particular status or relationship, it could be protected by the Constitution. By the end of the period, this kind of property—status related to passing for white—was employed unsuccessfully to block the emergence of a segregated society in the postwar South. (See *Plessy* v. *Ferguson*, 1896 and Chapter 6 for details.)

The Civil War Amendments protected the former slaves' status as citizens. The disputes that initially arose under these amendments, however, dealt more with economic status. The *Slaughterhouse Cases* (1873) are included in discussions of civil liberties because they suggested how the judiciary would approach the Civil War Amendments. With reference to butchers in New Orleans who had been put out of business, the Supreme Court limited the application of due process protections to newly freed slaves—an interpretation that was shortlived. The case is important as it bears on property rights. It was brought by small butchers who could not work in New Orleans due to a monopoly granted by the State of Louisiana to the Crescent City Livestock Landing and Slaughterhouse Company. The state justified the monopoly as a health measure. The excluded butchers maintained that the state had taken their property without due process. The Supreme Court majority rejected this claim. The dissenters, however, as is sometimes the case, had a more forward-looking view, and they argued that property could be a means to wealth, as well as wealth itself. John R. Commons described the Court as divided between property as "use value" derived from tangible holdings, like land, and property as "exchange value," some status or franchise that enabled one to make a living (*Commons,* 1924:11). The majority had looked to the common law meaning with its attention to possession and use. The dissenters considered the right to conduct a business to be property. Justice Noah Swayne wrote that "Property is everything which has exchangeable value, and the right of property includes the power to dispose of it . . ." (*Slaughterhouse Cases,*

1873:124-130). Justice Joseph Bradley relied on customary arrangements in order to establish that "... a law which prohibits a large class of citizens from adopting a lawful employment, or from following a lawful employment previously adopted, does deprive them of liberty as well as property without due process of law" (*Slaughterhouse Cases,* 1873:111-124). Although it was of no benefit to the disgruntled butchers, the idea that "... their occupation is their property," emerged in the case, with the justices treating capacity or legal status to earn a living as a property matter. The right to earn a livelihood was thus articulated where state power transformed a free market into a regulated one.

As professional status and franchise became objects of property protection, they set new limits on the exercise of legislative power. In 1888, the right to practice medicine came under the constitutional umbrella (*Dent* v. *West Virgina,* 1888) and in 1897 "... the right to pursue a calling" (*Allgeyer* v. *Louisiana,* 1897:583) was included. In the later case, the issue was a statute that prohibited Louisiana businesses from buying insurance from out-of-state insurance companies unless they were licensed by Louisiana and had a representative residing in Louisiana upon whom process could be served. This statute was held in violation of the Fourteenth Amendment as a deprivation of the liberty "... to be free in the enjoyment of all [one's] faculties..." (*Allgeyer* v. *Louisiana,* 1897:583). Subsequent cases guaranteed the rights of various groups to earn a living. This included aliens (*Truax* v. *Raich,* 1915) from early on, as well as lawyers, to whom the guarantee was applied much later (*Schware* v. *Board of Bar Examiners,* 1957). The conjunction of liberty and property which took place after the Civil War was essential to the dramatic elevation of corporate prerogatives in subsequent years. The old deference to legislatures declined until well into the Depression of the 1930s, while *fin de siècle* adjudication spawned a new development—the calculation of property interests for which the government would have to offer compensation. The clarification of government prerogatives under the "police power" and the issues surrounding expropriation are the subjects considered in the next section.

Regulation and Expropriation

The constitutional promise of compensation when property is taken, or "expropriated," by the government developed with the regulatory state. It has roots in the American Revolution and emergency expropriation of "Loyalist" property during that war. But it developed slowly. Through most of the nineteenth century, the federal government was more actively disposing of property than acquiring it. The

Civil War expanded the government's power and laid the basis for its increased control over the economy. This period also left a legacy of constitutional limitations on government. Constitutional property restrained public authority on the grounds that "certain settled expectations ... should be secure against governmental disruption, at least without appropriate compensation" (Tribe, 1978:456). The consequence was clashes between the government and private interests. Determining when there was a lost expectation that required compensation sharpened the constitutional standard for protecting property rights. The property right amounted to a settled expectation that would be honored by the government.

While these developments depended on the Fourteenth Amendment, the leap in interpretation that brought down the greatest scorn on the property right was the acceptance, after the Civil War, of corporations as persons under the Fourteenth Amendment to the Constitution. Some federal willingness to take steps in this direction had been evident before the war, and by 1871, Congress had included corporations in legislative use of the term "persons" (Goldman, 1982:184). In 1886, the Supreme Court accepted the argument that those who drafted the Fourteenth Amendment had intended to include corporations in its protections of persons from deprivation of life, liberty, or property. Although the validity of this argument has been challenged and the Court's insight questioned, there is no doubt that this view has become an accepted constitutional convention. The doctrine that corporations were covered by the Fourteenth Amendment was zealously employed around the turn of the century to protect corporations from public regulation, and although the Court has retreated from that position, constitutional property still carries the stain of this arrogant use.

The constitutional property right began to be associated with a distinction between legitimate exercises of the police power, or "policing," and expropriation for which compensation was required, or "taking," when the federal government became involved in expropriating property and federal courts took on the task of monitoring state economic regulations. Under the police power, the government does not acquire a property value, at least it is not supposed to. In the case of the fruits of a prohibition or a drug arrest, for instance, the intoxicating contraband is supposed to be destroyed or used as evidence. It is not supposed to be consumed or exploited. Expropriation, on the other hand, is associated with "taking." The prevailing explanation of the government's power in this area holds that eminent domain "takes property because it is useful to the public. . . ," while the police power "regulates the use of, or impairs rights in, property to prevent detriment to public interst . . ." (*Corpus Juris Secundum*, 29A:178). Policing is primarily aimed at eliminating danger, as well as contributing to the general welfare, as might be the case with closing down an urban stockyard. And conversely, eminent domain is supposed to produce some new benefit, although it very often also serves to eliminate a danger, such as by straightening a dangerous curve in the road. The distinction, however fuzzy, is part of the structure of constitutional property, and it will be used here to further elaborate this fundamental right.

The Police Power

In *Mugler* v. *Kansas* (1887), a state law that prohibited the production or sale of alcoholic beverages was upheld by the Supreme Court because it had a "real or substantial relation" to interests that the state could serve. From that point until the present, provision was made for compensation where an exercise of legislative power went beyond the bounds of the "policing" standard. Justice John Marshall Harlan's opinion in *Mugler* set the framework for compensation law in the constitutional setting (Sax, 1971). His analysis begins with the observation ". . . that all property in this country is held under the implied obligation that the owner's use of it shall not be injurious to the community" (*Mugler* v. *Kansas*, 1887:665). Harlan required a real or substantial relation between the objects claimed for legislation and the laws themselves. The result was that an exercise of the police power did not cost the government anything, while eminent domain had its price. With this development, property became tied to the state's obligation to provide constitutional protection, including compensation. Not only the value of property, but whether something, like liquor, could be held as property was a matter regulated by the Constitution.

Justice Harlan argued that when regulation prevented injurious uses, the owner's interest in those uses was not constitutionally protected property, and it would not be considered "taken" (*Mugler* v. *Kansas*, 1887). Harlan distinguished between the government as proprietor and prohibitor. He also looked at how the property was used— whether the use was innocent or noxious. This was generally a satisfactory framework for Harlan's time. In the twentieth century, however, as the scope and amount of governmental regulation grew, Justice Oliver Wendell Holmes supplied a broader approach to cover such things as zoning, business legislation, and conservation action. Holmes shifted the framework from a qualitative distinction between takings and police power to a difference in degree, and he introduced principles of valuation. The aim was to balance the interests of the property owner with those of society. In *Hudson County Water Co.* v. *McCarter* (1908), Holmes stated that destroying the *value* of property went beyond the police power. This established that community interest in abating nuisances would have to be balanced against the (new) right of property owners to retain the value of their property.

The police power was great enough in the nineteenth century to encompass many regulations that would later be considered unconstitutional because the category "noxious use" was then much broader than it would become in time. Laws specifying maximum length for wharves and prohibiting land from being used as a cemetery were considered lawful acts on behalf of the community. Even the right to remove stones from one's own land was challenged successfully in the nineteenth century when a landowner planned to use "his" beach as a quarry. It was held that "protection and preservation of beaches . . . is obviously of great public importance." Massachusetts Chief Justice Shaw felt that the right to determine what was necessary for this sort of land lay exclusively with the legislature (Scheiber, 1982:308).

Policing is still the standard for regulatory activity, and the property right is still a function of the standards for government regulation. Most cases dealing with property and economic rights are decided directly on the statutes, and it has been rare in the recent past for a regulatory statute to be superseded by the constitutional protection. For instance, in a modern version of the famous "filled milk case" (*Nebbia* v. *New York*, 1934)—where regulation of processed milk was upheld as a legitimate public health function—the Supreme Court in 1981 held that Minnesota could ban sale of milk in plastic nonreturnable containers (*State of Minnesota* v. *Cloverleaf Creamery Co.*, 1981). This environmental regulation had been passed to cut down on the amount of non-biodegradable trash that was accumulating. Milk producers invoked the equal protection and commerce clauses for relief. They were successful in the Minnesota Supreme Court and nearly carried the day in the United States Supreme Court, but the majority denied constitutional protection for the regulated property and stuck to its historical deference to state legislation in the economic sphere.

The thrust of the clause in the Constitution giving Congress the power to regulate commerce "among the several states" has set the regulating framework. Although colored by its association with antisocial corporate prerogatives, regulation is part of the framework for property rights. In 1981, Justice Lewis Powell, writing for the majority in a commerce case, indicated that the Constitution still required some aspects of trade to remain free from interference by the states, even where Congress has not legislated (*Kassell* v. *Consolidated Freightways*, 1981). The case involved the ongoing battle between states and the federal government over who should determine the kind of trucks permitted on the highways, with the Court deciding against Iowa.

Taking by Eminent Domain

The conditions under which private property can be taken by the government for public use—taking by eminent domain—define the constitutional right in this important area of control over one's land and resources. The courts have spent two centuries deciding what is property under the Fifth Amendment. While the citizen may have certain desires or expectations concerning a piece of land, these are not property rights unless they are recognized by the government. There is a tension between the everyday idea of property as something protected by the government and this legal reality. There are many bases to a property claim that the government must recognize, and they all amount to an interest that is sanctioned by the law—for example, a contract or a debt. The official beginning was noted by Justice William Strong when the government expropriated land for postal sites in 1875: ". . . this power of the Federal government has not heretofore been exercised adversely" (*Kohl v. United States*, 1876). In that case, Justice Stephen Field wanted to keep the government out of the expropriation business. But only a few years later, the Court found eminent domain to be an "attribute of sovereignty" with an illustrious heritage (*Boom v. Patterson*, 1879).

Traditionally, unless actual possession had clearly changed, one could not be certain one's property had been "taken." Through the first half of the nineteenth century, the predominant doctrine "no taking without a touching" required actual transfer of possession. The expropriation cases that resulted were old-fashioned in their requirement of nearly physical deprivation, as in the taking of title or possession of land. In *Munn v. Illinois* (1877), for instance, the Court ruled that loss of revenues did not amount to expropriation. In this and other cases, governmental authority held sway.

Public Use. The requirement that property only be taken for public use is indirectly stated in the Constitution and has been diluted over the years. The phrase in the Constitution is "nor shall private property be taken for public use, without just compensation." It has been interpreted to mean public use is a requirement for constitutional takings. The phrase might have been "nor shall private property be taken except for the public use and upon payment of just compensation." However persuasive this may be, this interpretation has been consistently rejected in the courts. Eminent domain is thus a public power grounded in the public interest. The issue of public use links general philosophical principles and American custom. In the early nineteenth century, with limited need for expropriation, eminent domain presented no problem to builders of mills, private roads, and the like. The rise of railroads, however, with their claim to public benefit and their monopolistic pricing, made eminent domain practices an important issue. In this form, the issue has continued, with many other business enterprises making a claim to public benefit.

There are two views on the nature of "public use." One holds that, in order for something to be a public use, it must be used by "the public." This would include such things as schools, parks, and libraries. It is a position held by courts most inclined to protect private property from state power. A broader view construes "public use" as "public benefit," and it allows for all sorts of justification for governmental actions short of public use, such as raising employment or providing decent housing. This view has become more common, and it does not require that members of the public be entitled to the direct use of the property. Private corporations often act as surrogates for the government enterprise following eminent domain where something is to be built on a piece of land. Though private benefit is derived from these projects, courts have often allowed them to be deemed public, according to the view that a use is not private merely because part or even the entire project is financed privately and there has not been a requirement that all benefits go to the public. This is an area where economic influences have fashioned the rules of the game to their own advantage.

Intangible Interests. The exercise of federal power by the grant of authority under "eminent domain" resulted in new conceptions of protected property. The focus was not only on physical property and title but also on the *value* of the property. In *Pumpelly* v. *Green Bay Co.* (1871), the Court ruled that flooding land for a dam was a taking, whether title passed or not. As time went on, the justices became increasingly interested in the loss of profits and other values that had not been considered compensable. Property was expanding from the thing lawfully possessed to the expectation of return. The idea that property is something to be exchanged, something with a market value, is evident in the "Minnesota Rate Case" (*Chicago, Milwaukee and St. Paul Railway Co.* v. *Minnesota*, 1890), which has been described as the first use by the Supreme Court of "substantive due process" to invalidate a state law (Goldman, 1981:214). The law had established a commission to set railroad rates, and the property issue arose with the impact of the rates on profits. The legislation was struck down as an unconstitutional infringement. The emphasis on intangibles developed with government regulation of corporate activities, and property began to reflect a commitment to "going concerns." John R. Commons associated this expansion of the property idea with the federal government's interest in enlarging its tax base to include revenues as taxable property (Commons, 1924:182). Thus, in 1893, a franchise to collect tolls was protected by the Supreme Court from uncompensated takings on the ground that it was

". . . as much a vested right . . . as the ownership of tangible property" (*Monongahela Navigation Co. v. U.S.*, 1893). According to Laurence Tribe, the compensation requirement ensures a public benefit since it holds that when regulation goes "too far" compensation is required (Tribe, 1978:457-459).

In 1922, *Pennsylvania Coal Co. v. Mahon* changed the face of takings law. The Pennsylvania legislature had passed an act outlawing the mining of coal wherever it would "endanger." The Mahons, whose home was threatened by subsurface mining, obtained an injunction against the coal company under the act. When the case reached the Supreme Court, Justice Oliver Wendell Holmes argued that the act exceeded the police power, due to the loss of mineral rights. He stated, "The general rule at least is, that while property may be regulated to a certain extent, if regulation goes too far it will be recognized as a taking." Property was no longer just the land; it had become the right to make money from it. In holding for the mining company, Holmes bypassed contract considerations that might have stemmed from the mining easement on the Mahons' land, and he relied instead on the compensation clause. He described property as a "bundle of rights," a notion that he derived from the common law. This formulation calibrated the balance Harlan had struck between takings and the police power. Holmes indicated his belief that there was a ". . . danger of forgetting that a strong public desire to improve the public condition is not enough to warrant achieving the desire by a shorter cut than the constitutional way of paying for the change" (*Penn. Coal Co. v. Mahon*, 1922:416).*

This concept of a "bundle" provided the bridge for a movement away from property as things and toward property as revenues (Macpherson, 1973:127-128). Thus, in the Court's more recent treatment of private property issues, Justice Harry Blackmun addressed Fifth and Fourteenth Amendment protections raised in a Florida case where a county clerk claimed the interest on some money he was holding (*Webb's Fab. Pharmacies, Inc. v. Beckwith*, 1980) while the principle was being paid to a group of creditors who had "a state-created property right to their respective portions of the fund." The Court upheld the property right against the clerk's claim and what would have amounted to "a forced contribution to general governmental revenues." (See also *United States v. Ptasynski*, 1983.)

---

* Sixty years later, Justice Thurgood Marshall, confronting a "permanent physical occupation" of property, distinguished the situation from that in *Mahon* with deference to Holmes's formulation. When it permits an occupation, ". . . the government does not simply take a single 'strand' from the 'bundle' of property rights: it chops through the bundle, taking a slice of every strand" (*Loretto v. Teleprompter Manhattan CATV*, 1982).

Just Compensation

Generally, any right or interest that has a "value" is considered property (*United States* v. *Petty Motor Co.*, 1945). Suspicion of government and fear that its power might be exercised arbitrarily, as opposed to the "fair" impersonal workings of the market, has meant that the government is treated as simply another actor in the market when compensation for a taking is figured. The guide is "fairness." While the commentators struggle to devise a principle that can explain all the decisions, thereby making "sense" of them, the judges have shown a preference for a simple assessment of which expectations are valid (Ackerman, 1977). In practice, the conventions of the market and the tools of the economist have played a large part in the determination.

Market Value. Compensation is measured by the loss on the part of the owner, rather than by what the taker has gained. The concern stems from individual rights, rather than from public interests. The owner is to be restored to the same pecuniary condition as before the taking, *but not a better one.* This is a protection that the public not be "taken" (*United States* v. *Virginia Electric and Power Co.*, 1956). When there has been dissatisfaction with existing compensation awards—where they seem too high—the issue is usually framed as one of giving more than the "just" amount. The possibility of taxpayer challenges to such practices would be on grounds that the expenditures are not for "the public purpose" or the "general welfare."

The government has contended that it has only a minimal obligation to compensate property owners according to possible gains in the market. In 1924, the Court held that business losses caused by condemnation would not be compensated (*Mitchell* v. *United States*, 1924). A year later, it held that gains due to public improvements could be balanced against damages where compensation was at issue (*United States* v. *River Rouge Improvement Co.*, 1925). This stance continued for the next 20 years. Consequently, compensable interests in lost opportunities were limited. The Court refused to compensate on the basis of an expectation that a lease would be renewed. Nonetheless, the justices heard arguments in all the cases, indicating that they took them seriously. The government had taken the upper hand when compensation was held up by regulatory interests, due perhaps to the exceptional fact of "limits" that has always characterized private prerogatives over land. This was the basis from which Justice Robert Jackson asserted that "Rights, property or otherwise, which are absolute against all the world are certainly rare" (*United States* v. *Willow River Power Co.*, 1944).

Once compensation was required under the Fifth Amendment when there was something less than a transfer of possession, the Court began its clarification in earnest. One standard was "equitable principles of fairness" (*United States* v. *Commodities Trading Corp.*, 1950), a formula announced by Justice Hugo Black in a case where the War Department had requisitioned a quantity of black pepper at a price below market value. Justice Black held that the provider was not entitled to a value based on speculation. In the words of Justice Frankfurter, in the pepper case, ". . . just compensation . . . has a way of attracting far flung contentions" (*U.S.* v. *Commodities Trading Corp.*, 1950:133). While value in property as a function of an expected loss could be held compensable (*Almota* v. *United States*, 1973), policing such as open housing statutes did not demand compensation (*Jones* v. *Mayer*, 1968). The key, under the Constitution, came to be expectations that were consistent with governmental interest in the public welfare. Thus, while the Constitution does require that losses "be borne as part of the common lot," it does not protect all profits that "might be realized in the distant future" (*U.S.* v. *Commodities Trading Corp.*, 1950).

What would otherwise be merely a footnote in the constitutional development of compensation law takes on greater significance here because it is an example of the ongoing significance of the valuation issue. In the case of *U.S.* v. *564.54 Acres of Land, More or Less* (1979), the federal government began expropriation proceedings against land owned by a Lutheran summer camp on the Delaware River. The government was building a public recreation project and offered market value for the land, about $500,000, but the regional Synod of the Lutheran Church turned Uncle Sam down. The church elders wanted $5.8 million, the cost for developing new facilities elsewhere. Recognizing that traditionally the Supreme Court had tried to put the owner of condemned property "in as good a position pecuniarily as if his property had not been taken" (*Olson* v. *United States*, 1934), the Court in this case, under Justice Thurgood Marshall's opinion, stuck with the market value offer, although in the opinion it is evident that the market value amount left out some compelling considerations, such as the public welfare benefits of a nonprofit summer camp and the nontransferable values that were part of the camp's unique situation.

Public Welfare. A demystification of property rights sought by environmental groups like the Sierra Club and the Audubon Society touches on the compensation issue. Environmentalists argue that land use should be reviewed under the standards applied to other governmental regulations (Bosselman et al., 1973:246). Holmes's formulation is their target because the compensation requirement derived from his "bundle of rights" benefits propertied interests by limiting the capacity of the state to regulate. The environmentalists would eliminate the calculation of property loss, substituting instead a due process standard holding governmental regulations invalid only if they fail to bear a reasonable relationship to a valid public purpose. The result, if due process rather than the bundle of rights standard were applied to property, would be a shift to the purpose and effect of the regulation. Influential environmental lawyers like Fred Bosselman would have the Court reassess its tradition of balancing loss in the value of land against public benefit and would have the Court declare that where legitimate public purposes are being served, a "mere loss in land value will never be justification for invalidating the regulation" (Bosselman et al., 1973:253). Although this argument does not attack the taking provisions directly, it suggests that expected profit should not stand in the way of public purposes.

The standard proposed by the environmentalists has not taken hold. Even Bosselman and his colleagues generally concede that if there is an actual appropriation of land for public use, such as for a park, highway, or reservoir, it must be accompanied by compensation. That is, while the decision as to whether or not to expropriate under public authority might well be disputed—especially according to the tenets of market choice theories—where there is an actual appropriation of value by the government, the expectation of compensation is widespread. The dispute involves the manner in which that loss is to be calculated, and market expectations remain the yardstick in this clash between property rights and regulation.

Grounded in the relationship between individuals and the state, questions of compensation involve weighing expectations. The relationship is the structural dimension in the Constitution that triggers the "just compensation" provision when private control and use is diminished. *Penn Central Transportation Co.* v. *New York City* (1978), mentioned at the beginning of the chapter, indicates how much the expectation standard has matured under the compensation rubric. What Penn Central Transportation Corporation could do with Grand Central Station was the center of controversy. The issue was whether New York's restrictions on the development of historic landmarks, as applied to the railroad terminal, constituted a "taking" in violation of the Fifth and Fourteenth Amendments. Justice William Brennan, writing for the majority, declined to develop a formula for determining when "economic injuries caused by public action must be compensated by the Government." He dismissed the corporation's challenge to the New York statute since there was no interference with "interests . . . sufficiently bound up with the reasonable expectation of the claimant to constitute 'property' for Fifth Amendment purposes." Conversely, "distinct investment backed expectations" are the key in determining whether state action constitutes a "taking." The corporation would have been able to claim a taking if it could have shown deprivation of a reasonable expectation. Similarly, a holding by the California Supreme Court that its state constitution protected picketing in a shopping center was not a denial of ownership rights under the Fifth Amendment according to the Supreme Court (*Pruneyard Shopping Center* v. *Robins*, 1980).

Property came under the compensation rubric after the regulatory power of the state had been established. Around the turn of the century, the issue of whether compensation was due to a property owner superseded the older public use requirement, and fair market value became the standard for determining the cost of a taking. With the "bundle of rights" metaphor, the Constitution became a means for evaluating a wider variety of interests in property. The result was the standard of legitimate or settled expectations delineating the prerogatives of private ownership. A reasonable profit became a protected interest under the constitutional standard of settled expectations. This move from public discourse on the value of particular takings to use of the market to protect settled expectations not only allowed a much broader definition of the expectations that would be protected as constitutional property, but it meant that the discourse within which these public benefits and private costs were calculated would be an economic one. Thus, in this area, as in others relating to the Constitution, other professionals vie with lawyers for authority in constitutional interpretation. We now turn to a discussion of statutory entitlements as protected property.

Statutory Entitlements

Reaching back to *Marbury* v. *Madison* (1803) and further, the Court recognized that actions by the government can create expectations for people—for example, that they will have a job, or be able to build a house. The government had to acknowledge certain obligations as a result of the expectations it had created. The expectations that one can depend on amount to property. Where the Constitution stands behind an expectation, we have called that expectation constitutional property. The Court acknowledged that "Property . . . may be construed to include obligations, rights, and other intangibles as well as personal things" (*Fidelity and Deposit Co. of Maryland* v. *Arenz*, 1933). The rise of the welfare state has been crucial to the "newer forms of property" (Oakes, 1981). The concept, which offers constitutional protection, is rooted in the structure of the modern state itself, which is the basis of legal authority, and as such, it has endured. Given the established property right to intangibles, the thing that is "new" about property to which people are entitled by statute is the grant itself, not that it is a form of property. This, like other expectations, is an obligation that has been taken on by government.

Rights v. Privileges

While the Supreme Court has consistently recognized that ". . . due process requirements are implicated" whenever government deprives an individual of common law possession or use of "real or personal 'property' " (Tribe, 1978:509), it has distinguished these protected areas in varying degrees from the entitlements to licenses, goods, or services provided by government. The distinction between individual "rights" surrounding the old property and "privileges" adhering in government largess can be traced to an opinion by Oliver Wendell Holmes when he served as a jurist in Massachusetts. In *McAuliffe* v. *Mayor of New Bedford* (1892), Holmes held that "The Petitioner may have a constitutional right to talk politics, but he has no constitutional right to be a policeman." This distinction made protections a function of government prerogatives over employment. Constitutional protection for property was not applicable where a benefit or expectation was the result of government largess. Consequently, there were minimal constraints on revocation of government benefits (Tribe, 1978:510). The distinction between some forms of property and others, between rights and privileges, that made this possible, began to break down by the mid-twentieth century (Van Alstyne, 1968).

Welfare Benefits. Reflecting increased regulation and new governmental responsibility, property provided the basis for a growing number of claims by the middle of the twentieth century. Initial arguments for the application of constitutional property to benefits were made with reference to Social Security, since this was viewed as an insurance program. Although the Social Security Act had been held constitutional in 1937, it was not until 1960 in *Flemming* v. *Nestor* that the justices addressed the status of benefits. The appeal in *Flemming* was unsuccessful, with the Court holding that benefits could be denied to a family following their deportation. But the fact that the challenge reached the Supreme Court indicates that the claim made some sense to the justices. In the area of government employment, where the first challenges had appeared in the nineteenth century, interests that had been treated as privileges were beginning to be treated as rights. While supportive holdings would not come for another 10 years, the 1960s brought increasing sensitivity to obligations and to the expectations arising from public assistance programs. In 1961, the Court held that when benefits were taken away there had to be an unusually important government need to outweigh the right to a prior hearing (*Cafeteria and Restaurant Workers Union* v. *McElroy*, 1961). A few years later, Charles Reich championed the idea that statutory entitlements were "the New property" (Reich, 1964). Arguing that the welfare state had altered the status of individuals, Reich suggested that statutory entitlements should be recognized as having new significance. Reich felt that benefits like unemployment compensation, public assistance, and old age insurance urgently "need the concept of right." Basing his claim on the social origin of property, Reich described distribution from government as "part of the individual's rightful share in the commonwealth" (Reich, 1964:786; Van Alstyne, 1977). The "new" right would replace the tradition of minimal protection in cases of suspension and revocation of a benefit, with a presumption favoring continuation of the benefit. Protection would not, however, establish any general right to such a benefit prior to its being granted by the state.

The case where statutory entitlements were officially recognized as property was *Goldberg* v. *Kelly* in 1970. It pitted New York City and state welfare authorities against beneficiaries who had been terminated or cut off without a chance to respond. In one case, the termination came because the Department of Social Services said a recipient refused to accept counseling and rehabilitation for drug addiction, while he argued that he did not use drugs. In the Supreme Court, Justice William Brennan noted that "It may be realistic today to regard welfare entitlements as more like 'property' than a 'gratuity.' Much of the wealth in this country takes the form of rights which do not fall within traditional common law concepts of property" (*Goldberg* v. *Kelly*, 1970:262). Brennan based his position on similar rights relating to unemployment compensation, tax exemption, and public employment. Property in statutory entitlements had gone beyond "mere" intelligibility and had become authoritative.

Employment Security. Entitlement as property was amplified soon after *Goldberg* as an interest in continued employment at a Texas college derived from an "understanding fostered by the college administration" (*Perry* v. *Sindermann*, 1972:600; *Board of Regents* v. *Roth*, 1972). Here, Justice Potter Stewart acknowledged that tenure brought property rights with it, holding that "property denotes a broad range of interests that are secured by 'existing rules or understandings'" and that "a person's interest in a benefit is a 'property' interest for due process purposes if there are such rules or mutually explicit understandings that support his claim of entitlement to the benefits" (*Board of Regents* v. *Roth*, 1972:601).

Subsequent opinions emphasized that "Property interests are not created by the Constitution; rather ... by existing rules or understandings that stem from an independent source such as state law. . ." (*Bishop* v. *Wood*, 1976:341; *Leis* v. *Flynt*, 1979). In *Goss* v. *Lopez* (1975), the Court found such property interests to have been present when high school students were suspended from their classes without a hearing. Justice White's opinion is linked to property by his finding that "appellees plainly had legitimate claims of entitlement to a public education" (*Goss* v. *Lopez*, 1975:573). The deprivation was held to be substantial, and concern that the holding would damage the educational process was superseded by the importance of the entitlement. This was a dramatic example of judicial perception that the nature of the property interest determined the extent of the due process required. The decision reflected the old "bundle of rights" scale suggested by Holmes, in which due process was treated as a "variable." This had been the standard to a degree, although there was also the understanding that the Constitution set minimum requirements for judicial proceedings (*Murray's Lessee* v. *Hoboken Land and Improvement Co.*, 1856). In the case of statutory entitlements, there has been an inclination to see legislation creating an entitlement as stipulating how much due process is appropriate. This would have been unlikely in the case of regulatory provisions or expropriation of land. Yet, cases dealing with more traditional expectations have simply not always acknowledged the extent to which land and material things, such as property, are dependent on the authority of governments.

A case where the Supreme Court considered the relationship between "the bitter and the sweet" in entitlements law (*Arnett* v. *Kennedy*, 1974; Lockart et al., 1981:252-259) demonstrates the constitutional limits on legislative prerogatives over this form of property. The case was an appeal by a federal employee who had been fired for accusing his boss of bribery. It arose after a few years of heated debate over the appropriate procedural guarantees to be accorded to property of different forms. The justices found themselves looking at a federal law that denied employees any right to a hearing until after they had been dismissed. In a plurality opinion, Justice Rehnquist and Chief Justice Burger seemed willing to allow the legislature to place conditions on the entitlement in its civil service statute in the form of limited procedural protections. Their position stemmed from the perception that due process could vary in entitlement cases. The justices passed the decision on to legislative bodies *for final determination* because the legislatures had created the entitlement.

Commentators appear torn over the legislative capacity to set procedural limits on statutory entitlements (Tribe, 1978:522-543). It may be that they still find it hard to see that entitlements are property and refuse to acknowledge the consequences for due process. Due process follows from the expectation that is property. If one takes the police power as a limit on statutory entitlements, as it is with all kinds of expectations, the puzzle may be a little easier to solve. Whether a property right exists depends on police power considerations or issues of more general public welfare. If it must be taken, property has been protected in the Constitution by due process and compensation requirements. Yet, there is a longstanding tension here. The tradition has been that legislatures are best equipped to handle the distribution and redistribution of wealth (Michelman, 1979). That may be true, and it is an accurate reflection of the constitutional tradition, which maintains that there should be deference to legislatures as they fill in the details on matters of public policy.

The Right Established. Although the adjudication of expectations was less successful during the mid-1970s (Friedelbaum, 1976:97), there was recognition that expectations constituted property. The justices allowed termination of federal disability benefits without a hearing beforehand, for instance, while acknowledging that their decisions had accorded benefits provided by the government a "statutorily created property interest protected by the Fifth Amendment" (*Matthews* v. *Eldridge*, 1976:334). Other failed litigation that recognized the right included a foster family desiring to remain intact (*Smith* v. *Organization of Foster Families*, 1977); a state prisoner being transferred (*Meachum* v. *Fano*, 1976); and a medical student who claimed to have been unjustly dismissed from school (*Board of Curators of the University of Missouri* v. *Horowitz*, 1978). In the latter case, Justice Rehnquist spoke of Ms. Horowitz's interest in her seat at the medical school as a challenge presented by the property right. She would have to show, however, that her interest was ". . . recognized by Missouri state law" in order to claim a constitutional deprivation. In this case, a deprivation of liberty seemed to the claimant to be the stronger basis for invoking due process guarantees. Not all appeals in this area and at this time, however, were unsuccessful. In *Memphis Light, Gas and Water Division* v. *Craft* (1978), the utility company had claimed an absolute right to discontinue service when bills had not been paid. The Supreme Court, however, recognized an exception when the bill was the subject of a ". . . bona fide dispute." The company would be liable for damages if the dispute turned out to be legitimate. Here, state protection against termination, except for cause, amounted to a property interest the Court was willing to recognize.

Seven years later, after Justice Potter Stewart had been replaced by Justice Sandra O'Connor on the Supreme Court, the Court upheld a job-related property interest associated with the rights of the handicapped. In *Logan* v. *Zimmerman Brush Co.* (1982), mentioned at the beginning of

197

this chapter, Justice Harry Blackmun boldly restated the definition of property as "... an individual entitlement grounded in state law" (*Logan v. Zimmerman Brush Co.*, 1982:4250) and ruled in favor of a shipping clerk with a short leg who claimed that he "... had been unlawfully terminated because of his physical handicap" (*Logan v. Zimmerman Brush Co.*, 1982:4248). The protected property was a species Blackmun traced back to *Mullane v. Central Hanover Bank and Trust Co.* (1950)—a "cause of action." In this case, the "cause" (or course) of action was provided by the Fair Employment Practices Act, and Logan was not to be denied access to these protections. Although it is probably too much to say that the opinion reveals a new enthusiasm for protection of modern, less tangible forms of property, at the very least it is clear that there is now a different attitude toward entitlements and expectations from those expressed by the Supreme Court 150 years ago when it described the poor as a "moral pestilence" (*City of New York v. Miln*, 1837).

There has been a reaction to these developments in the concept of property, however. On the Court, Justices Powell and Rehnquist dissented from the majority opinion in *Logan*. Off the Court, commentary has ranged from caution against reliance on "legal contrivances" to produce social change (McCann, 1983) to concern that the real gains from a revival of property rights will be in the sphere of the old and not the new property (Van Alstyne, 1980b). The history of civil liberties indicates that the rise of protection for statutory entitlements came at a time of diminished concern for more marketable forms of property. But this need not necessarily mean that attention to the older forms of property would be at the expense of the poor, as was evident in 1983 when the Supreme Court found that the Mennonite Board of Missions had not been given adequate notice about the sale—for nonpayment of taxes—of property it held in Elkhart, Indiana (*Mennonite Board of Missions v. Adams*, 1983). Here, sensitivity to due process rights seems to have been as important in the case as the right to property itself.

At an ideological level, legal commentary has, for some time, looked to civil libertarian gains to enhance protection of traditional forms of property. This is evident in a plea by constitutional authority Gerald Gunther that the status of civil right be returned to old-fashioned property. Gunther denied the dichotomy between property and noneconomic rights (Gunther, 1980), seeking support in Justice Potter Stewart's observation that "Property does not have rights, people have rights" (*Lynch v. Household Finance Corp.*, 1972). Stewart's comment in *Lynch* had come in the context of an effort to enhance the constitutional protections for home or savings accounts by associating them with "established" rights to travel and to the continuation of welfare benefits. Ten years after *Lynch*, there was evidence of the influence of civil libertarian gains on constitutional property in *Loretto* v. *Teleprompter Manhattan CATV Corp.* (1982), mentioned at the beginning of the chapter. In this case, a "taking" claim arose over a New York statute which provided that a landlord must permit a cable television company to install its equipment in her building. In holding that the regulation amounted to a taking of property under the Constitution, Justice Thurgood Mashall emphasized the personal aspects of ownership and the use-value of property when he said ". . . an owner suffers a special kind of injury when a *stranger* directly invades and occupies the owner's property." The concern here was for a very old right in the face of state support of a new technology and its corporate purveyors. This sensitivity is a consequence of the nature of property in the Constitution.

Compensation

Even at its height, however, constitutional protection for entitlements fell short of traditional protections for property. A major difference in treatment of the new property has been evident since *Goldberg* v. *Kelly* (1970), with the exclusive focus being on due process protection. The due process standard for the new property provides only part of the constitutional protection accorded under the *compensation* clause. Charles Reich suggested that compensation might be applicable to the new property (Reich, 1964:785), but the idea does not seem to have been taken seriously. "Taking" is the expression in constitutional law "for any sort of publicly inflicted private injury to property." A key consideration is whether an "injury" requires compensation or whether the only requirement is that it be carried out according to due process (Michelman, 1967:1165). Without compensation, entitlements are minimally protected. Were statutory entitlement cases to treat the revocation of government largess as a "taking," then a right on a par with that accorded to accumulated wealth would exist.

Protection of Entitlements. Compensation is symbolic of the higher status accorded to property when the right is associated with the market. Although property rights depend on the state and so are not simply a function of the market, this sensitivity has meant that individual interests accorded such protection have fared better than those without it, especially when they are set against the public welfare. This was clearly the case in *U.S. Trust Co. of New York* v. *New Jersey* (1977), where the Supreme Court struck down legislation because it impaired the claims of bondholders.

Although it is a limited protection, due process is certainly preferable to no protection at all. Fearing the loss of recent gains, students of fundamental rights generally stick to procedural protection, rather than pushing for compensation (Tribe, 1978:543). Recent judicial treatment, like that prior to 1937, is indeed sobering. Before the civil rights revolution, the justices had read the property of settled expectations narrowly in favor of the constitutional "liberty of contract." This reading was used in behalf of corporate interests against government efforts to regulate business. As recently as 1978, in *Allied Structural Steel* v. *Spannaus*, the justices invalidated a Minnesota statute designed to protect workers' pensions. This appeared to be a return to the old contract model of *Lochner* v. *New York* (1905), where rights in legislatively mandated entitlement schemes were diminished by judicial review of legislation (Tribe, 1979). This history continues to cloud the future of the new property.

Recognizing the limited nature of protection for entitlements in the past is a step toward more equitable property rights appropriate to the modern state. The central issue is whether a procedurally fair withdrawal of a benefit requires compensation in the same manner as when land or profits are taken. While both profit and personal security are properties in the modern state, they are not yet considered property in the same sense. Rights associated with the old property promise a "decent return"on investment. In *Penn Central Transportation Co.* v. *New York City*, for instance, the decision rested on the profit it was reasonable for the company to expect. The Court's attention was to the legitimate expectation of return on corporate property. The holding was that the transportation company was not prevented from making substantial profits on its building. If it had interfered with those expected profits, however, New York City would have been required to compensate the transportation company. This protection of the future benefits to be derived from property (Tribe, 1978) actually protects the old property over and above the strict compensation requirements. In the case of benefits derived from entitlements, however, the right holder's expectations are undervalued. Even after recent developments, the right lacks a compensation provision that would give statutory property such as entitlements a status comparable to other forms of property.

The traditional argument for compensation is that it distributes the burdens resulting from public action. Property owners whose back yards are needed for a subway station are not expected to make an extraordinary personal sacrifice for the common good. Although they can be forced to part with their land, they must be compensated. Welfare recipients with a legitimate expectation of benefits, who are very likely to be raising families on those expected benefits, could also lose the benefits due to programmatic changes; thus, they too ought to be compensated for the loss of property, which in this case, are lost welfare benefits. Bruce Ackerman (1977) has suggested that protections for holders of statutory entitlements, however, have been absent due to the traditional conception of property as "private wealth." But forms of property protected by the Constitution have never been defined in this way; property is a matter of expectations rather than private possession. Nonetheless, some statutory entitlements have not yet been treated as property in the full sense.

The transformation of entitlements into property remains incomplete. The old property retains the taking provision and the requirement for compensation. But with respect to the new property, the issues have been the conditions under which entitlement can be revoked, and not the possibility of compensation. In the traditional property calculation protecting the individual from the state, justice has substance. Where the expectations resting in public entitlements are altered, however, justice remains procedural at best.

Legitimate Expectations. Resistance to government policies that lead to severe deprivation and unfair takings, the tension caused by the threat of a taking, and the general demand for equitable treatment have a bearing on the compensation question from a utilitarian or policy perspective. With these considerations in mind, the principle of protecting a property interest through compensation becomes a matter of good policy. Since compensating an owner might lessen resistance and discontent caused by the threat of loss, the utilitarian perspective suggests that compensation might serve as an agent or tool of social change. In addition, some entitlements like Aid to Families with Dependent Children entail a commitment to right holders and an expectation bound up with family life in the most intimate way. Thus a requirement of compensation might mean that changes in policy would be applied only to prospective recipients and not to those already receiving benefits, as their expectations would already have been settled (Ackerman, 1977:54-56). If such protection were not possible, however, it could instead lead to a more serious calculation of personal loss through consideration of compensation costs.

The principle of compensation has been met with the apprehension that raising statutory entitlements to the level of property would bind legislators and policy makers to the status quo. David Grais, in an influential article on entitlements, put it this way, "If statutory entitlements and rights are equated . . . statutes that create entitlements to the continuation of a benefit also create rights to the continuation of a benefit, thereby making the benefit irrevocable" (Grais, 1977:709). But this response fundamentally misunderstands the nature of the constitutional property protection and the compensation provision. The history of compensation in the constitutional context is a history of the costs of interfering with a property right. In a case decided by the Supreme Court in 1983, *Boston Firefighters Union* v. *Boston NAACP*, minority firefighters had sought protection from layoffs that were being conducted in terms of strict seniority. The seniority provision was a statutory guarantee won by the union from the state and existing as a promise that defined job security. In a suit brought by the NAACP, the district court had modified the seniority system to prohibit reduction of minorities in the fire department. The court of appeals considered the "conflict between a statutorily established seniority system mandating layoffs on a last hired, first fired basis" and the court order that insulated a percentage of minorities from such layoffs. Given the context of racial discrimination, the court of appeals viewed the issue as a case of two competing rights. In this context, they held in favor of the minority firefighters, but with serious concern about the abrogation of a statutory employment interest held by senior firefighters. Subsequent to the decision, however, the state of Massachusetts came up with enough money to stop the layoffs, and the Supreme Court declared the case moot.

Though it is reasonable to fear vested interests that hobble the democratic process, rights define the nature of American democracy and settled expectations are a basis for allegiance in a political system. Once the implications of full property status are recognized, concern about irrevocability ought to diminish. Statutory entitlements, like contracts, create an obligation on the part of the grantor, supporting the right held by the grantee. Rather than tying the hands of policy makers, attaching the compensation provision to statutory entitlements would simply stipulate how policy is to be made and would honor the fact that in the welfare state certain expectations are property.

In this regard, it is crucial to recognize the role that expectations have in the creation of a property right. Federal courts have found property interests derived simply from expectations in cases where there is not even a statutory grant. In such a case, the Seventh Circuit Court in Chicago held that the Fifth Amendment entitled tenants to compensation for being displaced from their homes when inspectors determined that the homes violated the city's housing code (*Devines* v. *Maier*, 1981). Although welfare benefits and the expectations of tenants sound like an odd kind of property in ordinary language, these phenomena are more closely linked to conventional possession than some aspects of the old property (for example, "subsurface rights" or a desired rate of profit). There is neither history nor justice behind an argument that the expected profit in a case like *Penn Central* is more like constitutional property than the expected benefits (that is, food and shelter) of a welfare mother.

In the entitlement case, where property takes the form of public support payments, the compensation issue would arise if benefits were to be discontinued. If the expectation of a particular grant extended for a fixed period, like Social Security survivors' benefits to children until they are age 18, then it is hard to see how a cutoff prior to that time for children receiving benefits could not be considered a violation of settled expectations. Presumably, compensation would only become an issue after procedural fairness had been satisfied. For example, imagine a case where a recipient of Aid to Families with Dependent Children received a $50 allocation for each of five children. Should the state wish to cut payments back to allocations for only three children due to budgetary stringency, the property claim might simply limit the cutback to future recipients of these benefits.

There are programs, such as student financial aid, where grants are made contingent on future allocations. While the uncertainty costs in such policies are severe, the lack of legally binding expectations provides less support for these recipients to claim a property right to a given level of financial support. We can also consider the case of the tenured professor faced with job threatening "retrenchment" policies. Here, the property right to continued employment suggests that the compensation provision would affect administrative goals. An alternative solution to tight budgets might be to force cuts in other areas, such as maintenance and plant operation. Such cuts would, of course, diminish the value of continued employment (since most people don't like working in a building without heat or light), and this would in turn affect the cost of compensation. In practice, however, as provision for such retrenchment, many universities are explicitly lowering the level of expectations by inserting retrenchment provisions in employment contracts. Thus, the political tradition makes creating particular expectations matters of policy, but there is constitutional protection where legitimate expectations are at issue.

These are some of the implications of the compensation requirement for constitutional property. The actual holdings are not the determining factors, however. For example, it is notable that the conservative wing on the Supreme Court believes that legislatures may establish how much process is due for any specific entitlement as part of creating the entitlement. Justice Rehnquist's position appears to be that when property is created by statute, the statute maker is free to create precisely as much property as he wants. This view would hold that the legislature could pass a law that says you are entitled to a welfare check until the head of the welfare agency, for any reason or even no reason, decided to cut you off. This position, although it has a perverse logic to it, is flawed, for the legislative process is covered not only by the property right but also by such guarantees as that of equal protection and due process generally. Even if such a statute did not violate any right to property, it would violate other constitutional rights. Thus, the constitutional tradition has meant that once the legislature creates an entitlement, the Constitution, not the legislature, determines the minimum procedural protection that satisfies the Fifth Amendment.

The meaning of the property right is shifting. It has been undercut where it represents a barrier against government regulation and elevated where government is the source of an expectation. In this regard, our rights are subject to some social context, tradition of interpretation, or similar expectation. Given that property rights delineate the most fundamental legal possibilities, however, it is also important to show the inequities that exist in the property right, even inequities that are part of the new property. But we need not abandon the tradition in order to make it more consistent. If the promise of property for those less well off can be balanced with the advantages to the powerful, property might again be associated with civil liberty. Government ultimately ensures the old, as well as the new property. Individuals acquire the capacity to exclude, and not to be excluded, in the name of the general welfare. The Constitution guarantees this protection. In recognizing entitlements as more than mere privilege, the interpretation of the Constitution has moved toward greater equity in the right of property. Yet, if such benefits are to be considered property, just compensation would go some distance toward making it real property.

Conclusion

Constitutional decisions have to be intelligible, they have to make sense. This is particularly evident with as basic a right as the right to property. The outcome of a case is bound to disappoint someone, but generally there is an intelligible argument on either side. This was true of *Dred Scott* v. *Sandford* (1857), although blacks were denied rights of citizenship later placed in the Constitution, and it was true of *Arnett* v. *Kennedy* (1974), where employees dismissed from federal service were denied hearings prior to being let go, although Justice Rehnquist's opinion for a plurality was joined by only two of his colleagues.

Appeals are framed in terms of a tradition, which in the case of property amounts to settled or legitimate expectations. This is constitutional property. It has taken the form of title, contract, grant, compensable interest, and statutory entitlement. It has been protected under the contract, commerce, and due process clauses of the Constitution. The constitutional protection of property holds the State accountable for arbitrary action, and it limits the exercise of State power to the extent that this power clashes with legitimate expectations. In this form, property is a fundamental right that we can again associate with civil liberties.

In the next chapter, we turn to equality. We discuss interpretation of the equal protection clause of the Fourteenth Amendment and its application to both racial and sexual issues. We also explore "pure concepts" and the implications of these concepts for the meaning of constitutional equality.

Equality | 6

The Constitution requires that no state "deny to any person . . . the equal protection of the laws." Battles over how to interpret this provision have been as ugly as any in constitutional law. Yet, they have also held out the promise of social justice. Interracial marriage, busing for school desegregation, and male-only draft registration are some of the more contentious issues governed by equality in the Constitution. Pitched battles have also developed over issues of a more mundane nature, such as height requirements for jobs on the police force and want ads categorized on the basis of sex. These issues have been far more troublesome when they have raised questions under the rubric of constitutional equality.

The right to equality was introduced into the Constitution during the Civil War, and the subjects handled under this right reflect the concerns and puzzles of the period after the war. They are products of historical forces. But constitutional interpretation in this area has also had its own influence on the political agenda and set important standards for how people should be treated. The impact of concepts derived from this part of the Constitution has been to limit the meaning of equality and this was particularly evident in the failure of the Equal Rights Amendment, an issue with which this chapter concludes.

We begin with a discussion of what constitutional equality is, and then proceed to the "separate but equal" doctrine, exploring how the perverse logic of that formulation influenced the holding in *Brown* v. *Board of Education* (1954). One aspect of the holding, and an ongoing focus in the chapter, is colorblindness, a "pure concept" that sets the tone for constitutional equality. Emerging from racial discrimination, the concept is examined as it reaches into other policy areas like sexual discrimination. Because equality has developed in this way and because it has been in the forefront of constitutional controversies, it is a fine example of how legal ideology functions.

Constitutional Equality _____

This introduction to the concept of equality in the Constitution distinguishes "constitutional equality" from what it conventionally means to be equal. What the justices and lawyers have extrapolated from the constitutional text is related to ordinary ideas but has its own distinct limitations. According to this tradition, lines drawn on the basis of race and criteria like it are suspect while gross inequalities of condition in America seem beyond "constitutional" reproach.

To say that one thing is equal to another, there must be a basis for comparison. One can't equate different kinds of things—whether they be gold and tomatoes or segregated schools and integrated schools—without a basis for comparison. With gold and tomatoes, weight might limit the comparison so that equality can be determined. The basis for comparison in constitutional law is also selective. Schools can be evaluated in terms of the quality of an education or according to any number of other considerations. In constitutional law the aspect of a thing that is the basis for comparison will influence the meaning of the right.

In discussing constitutional equality, we can distinguish between a political, a social, and a material basis for the comparison. This distinction ranges from the most elemental physical considerations, through those of social life, to the ideological sphere of our political institutions. Action by the government can affect any of these spheres; hence, the constitutional right can have a variety of consequences and meanings.

Material equality covers such things as the *quality* of our shelter, transportation, or food. It incorporates these things in the most elemental or basic sense, such as how warm the shelter keeps us or how fast our transportation gets us where we want to go. Schools might be considered materially equal if they were the same distance from a child's house or if they had essentially the same physical structure or number of books in the library. Each of these aspects of a school would, of course, have consequences that went beyond the material, but that would not deny a value to this distinction.

Social equality has to do with how we are treated and with status; it is evident in the *value* we place on different kinds of shelter or transportation. Each of these things serves elemental functions and reflects a place in the social order. Social equality, then, does not directly refer to such things as the seats upon which we travel but rather to the difference in status between cloth and leather, or between the front and the back of the bus. This sphere, like the material, has significance for each of the other spheres.

Political equality refers to equality in the area of citizenship, such as the right to vote or hold public office. Because judges operate from the political sphere—understood in a very broad sense of the term—they are more comfortable articulating standards of equality for this sphere. Thus, many constitutional decisions were limited to equality in the political sphere. Political equality is not the highest form of equality, but it is the most rarefied because of its distance from the basic facts of life. It can seem separate while at the same time it is highly influenced by material and social considerations.

Highlighting these aspects of equality allows judicial positions to be mapped more clearly. As the basis for comparison, material, social, and political considerations may be incorporated at any point in an assessment of equality. The point of the assessment will also have an impact. There is a difference, for instance, between equal treatment and equality of result. Equal treatment generally applies the requirement of equality to an ongoing process. It requires that things be equal from the start. Equality of result looks to the finish and is not satisfied unless there is equality at that point. In the case of voting, for instance, equality of treatment from a political perspective might require the same registration requirement, whether for a test or a poll tax. Thus, a poll tax that required a fee for voting would not violate the principle of equal treatment; but a poll tax that prevented people from voting because they could not afford the tax would have an unequal result. Often equality of result requires that social or material barriers be taken into account (Clune, 1975; Tribe, 1978:997). And, in some cases, like providing absentee ballots for the disabled, equality of treatment conflicts with equality of result. The handicapped are treated differently in order to guarantee that they will be able to vote.

The difference between result and treatment is the point at which the comparison or determination of equality is made. This choice is a matter of political persuasion and it reflects political attitudes and interests. But again the bases of comparison will be relevant. Those who favor limiting the promise of equality to treatment have tended to confine its application to the political sphere where variables like social and material conditions are more easily disregarded. But this is not always true. Sometimes, as in cases coming under the "separate but equal doctrine," political and material equality were the standards used to deny social equality. We move now from this conceptual background to a discussion of the historical basis for this constitutional right.

Race and Equal Protection

The promise of equality was not part of the original Constitution. It was not even a dominant principle of the American Revolution (as it would be for the French Revolution only a few years later). Although a kind of equality was mentioned prominently in the Declaration of Independence, equality was not considered an "inalienable right." Later, in drafting the Constitution, compromises were made that offend contemporary notions of human equality, like the decision to count slaves when determining a state's representation in Congress, without counting them as citizens. The decision not to include equality as a founding principle was partly due to the unresolved status of the black population. Equality continued to be associated with the status of black Americans through the nineteenth and into the twentieth century; thus, it served as an important tool in the struggle for racial justice. But the limits on the constitutional meaning of the concept have much wider social significance, and these limits ultimately help us to understand a range of persistent inequalities.

The Civil War Amendments

Equality in the Constitution dates from the Civil War, which may be viewed as the American struggle for equality. The first result of this conflict that had a bearing on equality was the emancipation of the slaves. This was part of the war effort and was meant as an inducement for slaves to leave their masters and join the Union army. Emancipation was followed by a series of constitutional amendments: the Thirteenth, Fourteenth, and Fifteenth Amendments, which attempted to institution-alize the new status of the former slaves. The Thirteenth Amendment abolished slavery; the Fifteenth Amendment guaranteed voting rights;* and the Fourteenth Amendment, the cornerstone of constitutional equality and nationalization of the Constitution, provided that no state shall ". . . deny to any person within its jurisdiction the equal protection of the laws."

The amendments demonstrated a commitment to building a new society in the South. There were other efforts indicative of the period, such as the founding of Howard University in Washington, D.C., the election of blacks to Congress from the South, and widespread support of what we would call affirmative action today. In 1873, in the *Slaughterhouse Cases*, the Supreme Court affirmed that the purpose of the new amendments was to protect the rights of the newly freed slaves, but it limited the protection of "privileges and immunities" to those

---

* The Fifteenth Amendment, although overshadowed in this presentation of constitutional equality by the Fourteenth Amendment, deserves at least a nod of acknowledgment. Its history provides an interesting parallel, particularly the case of *Giles* v. *Harris* (1903) compared with *Plessy* v. *Ferguson* (1896). It is from the Fifteenth Amendment that Section 1983, which covers an entire volume of the U.S. Code, gets its authority to protect voting rights.

provided by the states. This decision marked the end of a brief period after the Civil War during which "equal protection" was understood as a promise of justice for former slaves. The change was dramatic. Black voter registration in South Carolina, for instance, decreased from 182,000 in 1876 to 91,000 in 1884. There were similar drops throughout the South. This change, and what followed, has blotted the positive aspects of Reconstruction from the national consciousness. Yet, the record indicates that equality made its debut in the honor roll of rights as a response to a specific historical circumstance that demanded attention.

Inclusion of the idea of equality in the Constitution gave judicial opinion on the meaning of equality, and on the efforts to eradicate the vestiges of slavery, new significance. Initially, decisions in this area are best understood in terms of judicial sensitivity to commercial interests, particularly state legislation of any kind that interfered with the establishment of "multi-state business structures" (Tribe, 1978:338), including such things as transportation systems and trading arrangements that went across state lines. Under this rubric, the justices upheld an award to a black woman who had been removed from a railroad car reserved for "white ladies" (*Washington A & GR Co.* v. *Brown*, 1873). In *Hall* v. *DeCuir* (1878), the commerce clause in the Constitution was interpreted as prohibiting Louisiana from applying a civil rights anti-discrimination statute to steamboats in interstate commerce. Justice Nathan Clifford offered his views on the advantages of separating the races in his concurring opinion; but free enterprise and the protection of a national market were the basis for the decision. Finally, in the *Civil Rights Cases* (1883), the Supreme Court ruled that two sections of the Civil Rights Act of 1875 were unconstitutional. The decision can be viewed in terms of judicial sensitivity to commercial interests, but it also established the "state action doctrine." To best understand this concept, we next explain the Court's interpretation of the Fourteenth Amendment, and then go on to explain the specific doctrinal evolution that has produced the contemporary meaning of constitutional equality, covering in turn the concepts of separate but equal, and colorblindness.

State Action Doctrine

The Civil Rights Act of 1875 was passed by Congress in an attempt to provide free black men and women in the South with equal access to public accommodations. This act made it illegal for private individuals to interfere with blacks who wanted food or lodging. In the view of the Supreme Court, the act ran afoul of the Fourteenth Amendment, which the Court said did not apply to private discrimination. Consequently, the Court interpreted the Fourteenth Amendment to mean that Congress could only regulate discrimination by governments. Laurence Tribe has pointed out that this reading of the Fourteenth Amendment was "plainly wrong" (Tribe, 1978:1153) because the Civil War Amendments themselves were the kind of legislation that the Court was holding unconstitutional. These amendments guaranteed not only common law rights of citizenship but freedom from servitude as well. Nevertheless, both limitations endured for nearly 100 years.

Thus, the state action doctrine established equality as a right directed against some form of government action. There is no constitutional remedy for the many forms of discrimination engaged in by one's putative friends and neighbors—from a social invitation to the more general preferences that influence human choices in those parts of our lives where the government has not become involved. But the exact extent to which, under the Constitution, the government is considered involved is much less clear. We present a number of cases here because it is in the constitutional promise of equality that the state action doctrine has its most far-reaching implications.

The most obvious avenue of involvement on the part of the state comes when government at some level or another actually becomes implicated in the management of a public accommodation. This was true in *Burton* v. *Wilmington Parking Authority* (1961). In that case, a parking facility owned and operated by a state agency leased some of its space to a restaurant that refused to serve blacks. The Court considered public ownership of the building to be sufficient state involvement to satisfy the constitutional requirement, and so the justices held that the restaurant was required to serve blacks. This sort of entanglement is even more obvious where the discriminatory agency is a subsidiary of the state government, such as a state university or a local public school. These subsidiaries are counted as if they were the state itself for the purpose of the Fourteenth Amendment's state action requirement.

In the most far-reaching and common kind of situation, the state's function as sovereign implicates as state action a wide variety of activities that might otherwise be treated as private. From *Shelley* v. *Kraemer* (1948), involving a private real estate agreement that would have had to be enforced by the state to be of any use, to *Griffin* v. *Maryland* (1964), where an amusement park that denied admission to blacks was held accountable for its discrimination because it had in its employ an off-duty sheriff who used the authority of his public office in guarding the park, the mantle of state authority has been what really defines any number of otherwise private situations. These cases remind us of the extent to which the government, either explicitly by a uniform or a robe, or implicitly in the authority it gives to law, constitutes our social world.

Finally, there are cases that go beyond the authority legitimately exercised by the government, but which have often been considered under the state action provision. In these cases, the state is more directly involved, but the action itself is illegal or outside the very authority that governs the situation. For example, in *Screws* v. *United States* (1945), a black prisoner was beaten to death by sheriffs in Baker County, Georgia. The response from the state, in support of its "law enforcement officers" was that the offending officer had exceeded his authority and thus did not bring the state into the situation. The majority on the Supreme Court rejected that contention, but the issue of state responsibility for irresponsible action on the part of those it employs continues to come up. Another version of questionable actions involves inaction. Such a case came to the Court in 1971 and involved the city of Jackson, Mississippi. The city had closed its swimming pools rather than follow orders to integrate them. The justices were split 5-4 over the issue. Although the outcome allowed the pools to be closed (due to the lack of an affirmative constitutional duty to operate swimming pools), the case is an instance where, even by not doing something, a government can be subject to constitutional limitations under the state action doctrine according to at least some of the Supreme Court justices.

The limitation on the capacity of Congress to implement Fourteenth Amendment protection lasted until the expansive jurisprudence of the Warren Court in the 1960s. During this period, the range of congressional action was expanded in *Katzenbach* v. *Morgan* (1966), where the Supreme Court upheld congressional legislation nullifying New York State's test for English literacy. The Court did this on the basis that the legislation came under congressional authority to "secure the guarantees of the Fourteenth Amendment." At present, Congress and the executive branch of government have become the major sources of enforcement against discrimination. In the early 1980s, for example, the Internal Revenue Service denied tax-exempt status to Bob Jones University and other religious schools because their religiously based admissions policies were racially discriminatory (*Bob Jones University* v. *U.S.*, 1983). Cases arising from these decisions and already discussed in Chapter 2 in terms of the limits to religious tolerance—which got the institutions a hearing—affirm the reach of administrative authority over racial discrimination.

Separate but Equal

The aspiration for equality put into the Constitution as the Civil War Amendments—and undercut by concepts like state action doctrine—was also limited by the emerging practice of "Jim Crow," the name given to the segregationist social policy legislated in the South.

It was against these institutions that the equal protection challenges were brought. The Court took up the first of the laws requiring separation of the races in *Louisville, New Orleans and Texas Railway Co.* v. *Mississippi* (1890), not long after it had decided the *Civil Rights Cases.* The challenge was again brought by business interests, this time against the state of Mississippi, which segregated the races in public transportation. The issue was viewed by the Court in terms of the constitutional provisions for interstate commerce, as earlier cases had also been viewed, but in this case the justices allowed the statute to stand because they did not view segregation as producing a "burden" on interstate commerce. Thus, by the 1890s, business interests, successful up to that time in resisting regulation for purposes of segregation *or* the promotion of social equality, had begun to lose out to those who were re-establishing domination of the white race over the black race in the South. This was the context for the opinion that was most responsible for legitimizing Jim Crow legislation in the Constitution and setting the conceptual parameters for debate on equality: *Plessy* v. *Ferguson* (1896).

Jim Crow in the Constitution. *Plessy* v. *Ferguson* (1896) was planned as a challenge to the racist institutions being built in the South after 1877. The case was brought by a diverse coalition of black and business interests who approached the issue from very different perspectives. In this case, the advocates realized the need to use the Thirteenth and Fourteenth Amendments in their appeal and to build on the tradition under which they had been most broadly interpreted—that of economic rights and laissez faire. Albion W. Tourgee, the lawyer for Homer Plessy, believed that a successful constitutional challenge was most likely to come from an assault on the administration of segregation by representing a "colored" defendant whose skin appeared to be white. (Plessy was chosen because he fit this description.) The argument in *Plessy* would be that there was protection in the due process clause for those who could "pass for white." This, the lawyers thought, might appeal to a conservative Supreme Court. The victory, although it would be limited, would make Jim Crow difficult to administer. This challenge was appealing to the railroads for whom the new legislation was an economic burden. The New Orleans *Crusader*, a newspaper, and civil rights organizations behind the suit received considerable flack from members of the black community who considered Homer Plessy's suit to be an affront to them.

For all its obvious callousness, the Supreme Court opinion in *Plessy* represents a shift in the basis for evaluating the segregated institutions being erected in the South. Where the standard had been the commerce clause, as in *Hall* v. *DeCuir* (1878), the new standard would be the constitutional guarantee of equal protection. Building on the ambiguity in the Fourteenth Amendment, the justices gave a reading of constitutional equality in *Plessy* that stands as a clever accommodation with the conventional perception of what equality requires. The racist Jim Crow system was legitimated by a legalistic maneuver designed to separate material and political equality from social equality. Those who held this position saw nothing fundamentally "unequal" about separation and proposed that the values that might make separation offensive were social and beyond the reach of the law. Paradoxically, this position rested on a right to equality in the material realm—an equality presumably in the conditions under which one was transported or schooled. Although it was never fulfilled in the South, the promise of material equality became the basis upon which the doctrine of separate but equal was initially attacked.

Legal Formalism. The majority opinion in *Plessy* acknowledged the importance of protecting political equality, but it distinguished between laws interfering with this kind of equality and those requiring separation of the races in schools, theaters, and other public places. The opinion was written by Justice Henry Brown, the son of an industrialist. Brown had just been appointed from Michigan, a center of laissez faire constitutionalism. He held that legislation mandating social separation had been generally accepted while laws that applied to separation in the political arena had not. He referred to *Strauder* v. *West Virginia* (1880), where a state law limiting jury service to whites was viewed as violating the conditions of political equality, and thus was unconstitutional. This would have to be avoided, as the Constitution would not condone inequality of citizenship. But this was not all. Another level of equality would also have to be protected.

The concession from the majority in *Plessy* to those challenging this ruling was the guarantee of material or physical equality. For whites, the exclusion from railroad cars was a separation, but because the Constitution required that the cars be "equal," the separation was not considered discriminatory. Equal, in this sense, would have to mean materially the same. In addition, the Supreme Court even acknowledged part of Plessy's property and reputation argument. The justices agreed that the reputation of belonging to the dominant race is a property interest, but not one that Homer Plessy could legitimately claim (*Plessy*, 1896:549). The holding reflected legal thought at the time.

Justice Brown's opinion for the majority had affirmed the position of "legal formalism"—restraint based on the limits of the law. He wrote:

> ...the Amendment ... could not have been intended to abolish distinctions based upon color, or to enforce social, as distinguished from political equality, or a commingling of the two races upon terms unsatisfactory to either (*Plessy*, 1896:544).

In the nineteenth century, spokesmen for the state had generally denied a capacity to promote social equality, at least in the redistributive sense of the modern welfare state. Equality before the law or political equality was considered to be different from social equality. Justice Brown's opinion rings with the view, not his own invention, that separation "... doesn't necessarily imply inferiority and has generally been within the competency of the states through the police power." The source was Massachusetts Chief Justice Lemuel Shaw's opinion in *Roberts* v. *Boston* (1849), a case on school segregation that anticipated the focus in the major struggles over constitutional equality. In this Massachusetts case, it was held that legal equality does not mean being treated "the same," but only that the "rights of all" are equally entitled to the paternal consideration and protection of the law.

There were some standards for monitoring this "ideological ploy." Law had to be "reasonable" and enacted not for the "... annoyance or oppression of a particular class." Thus, in *Yick Wo* v. *Hopkins* (1886), the Court held that San Francisco couldn't exclude Chinese laundries from the city. But it was part of the Anglo-American legal tradition for the justices to argue as they did in *Plessy* that the law was impotent when faced with "private" social prejudice. In *Plessy*, the justices claimed that the plaintiff's argument might have seemed more reasonable if they had been convinced that "... the enforced separation of the two races stamps the colored race with a badge of inferiority."

Both *Roberts* and *Plessy* required the equality of all persons "before the law," but they refused to take into account the social meaning of a distinction between people. A distinction, without that social meaning, could satisfy the requirements of constitutional equality. Thus limited, the justices rested more assured that the law had not promised too much and that its promise would be within the competence of the courts to deliver. This distinction between the political and the social sphere has a long tradition and, in a democracy, limits on the reach of judicial power have an honorable foundation. This aspect of Shaw's approach, evident in the *Roberts* decision, is sometimes referred to as "formalism," a style of legality and judicial posturing that was derived from the common law, with its emphasis on judicial neutrality and objectivity. A version of this style has its roots in the anti-slavery jurisprudence of the pre-Civil War South (Nelson, 1974; Scheiber, 1975; Tushnet, 1981). The view that law was at least formally pure and removed from the vagaries of social forces allowed judges who were troubled by the institution of slavery to rationalize their role in a political system that permitted slavery.

Separate but equal, which seems to make so little sense today, was at one time not simply an option but the most likely position for appellate justices to take. The justices who chose this course were more closely associated with the entrepreneurial tradition and commercial interests in the North and the "liberal" jurisprudence that supported it than they were with the South and its emerging segregationist society. In fact, one of only two southerners on the Court, John Marshall Harlan, dissented from the majority opinion in *Plessy*, which was written by Brown, a northern Republican. Brown was joined by corporate lawyers Melville Fuller, George Shiras, and Rufus Peckham, and one of the most skillful legal craftsmen working in the service of laissez faire capitalism, Stephen J. Field, from California. Field, a Lincoln appointee, and his brothers in the majority, represented the industrial North. Because of the familiarity of this refusal to understand law in terms of its social consequences, the majority's position in *Plessy* stuck for 60 years. It was supported by a limited view of legal authority—the view that law is only effective in a narrowly defined sphere and that it cannot be expected to reach into social life.

The one dissenter in *Plessy* was a dramatic exception, not only in this case, but throughout his long tenure on the Supreme Court. John Marshall Harlan, named after Chief Justice John Marshall (but unrelated), was born in Kentucky. His family had been slaveholders, but when the Civil War came he sided with the Union, helping to keep Kentucky out of the Confederacy. By the end of the war, he had set his slaves free voluntarily. Appointed by President Hayes, Harlan served for 34 years and established a reputation for civil libertarian perspicacity that, given where the majority usually stood, won him the title the "great dissenter." In *Plessy*, his most important dissent, Harlan challenged the majority's reading of the limits of the law. He extended the law to the social sphere by holding that separation is a remnant of slavery and a slave society. According to Harlan, equality would not necessarily preclude separation, but in the context of the post-war South, he believed that separation was the cornerstone of a racist society. Interestingly, this former slaveholder treated the promise of political and material equality as a transparent dodge. He naively believed that no one would be fooled by the majority's formulation.

Harlan's position sought to reunite law and society. He viewed their separation in the majority opinion as an attempt to reinstitute a version of slavery. And it was this, the social meaning of segregation, that he attacked. While Harlan mentioned that the Thirteenth Amendment does not permit the imposition "... of any burdens or disabilities that constitute badges of slavery or servitude," he concentrated on the equal protection promise of the Civil War Amendments. His position was sensitive to the law in context and, as a result, he was concerned that statutes not reflect social prejudice. To this end, he employed a concept from Albion Tourgee's brief in *Plessy*. "Our Constitution is color-blind," he said, ". . . and neither knows nor tolerates classes among citizens." To Harlan, colorblindness meant that the Constitution could not countenance a distinction based on a practice of racial discrimination. He knew that the white race was dominant and, in his view, this prejudiced an otherwise neutral distinction (*Plessy*, 1896:559). His position was that the "Jim Crow" legislation was ill conceived and improper. His calculus would have provided for social as well as political and material equality. He failed to acknowledge the ideological authority of the majority position, but he introduced the notion of colorblindness, the concept that would eventually transform constitutional equality.

Colorblindness

The legal politics of equal protection at the constitutional level began to ferment 30 years after the *Plessy* decision. It was then that the Supreme Court first showed concern for the civil rights of black Americans. The stimulus for this attention was the maturation of the Roosevelt appointees, a group that had come to the Court during the New Deal with hopes for a more egalitarian society. Added to this foundation, two decades later, would be an egalitarian, anti-racist consciousness spawned by World War II, especially in Europe, and a new Chief Justice—Earl Warren. But initially, the most important factor was the dynamism on the legal front.

The Margold Strategy. The litigation leading up to *Brown v. Board of Education* (1954) reflects 20 years of struggle, intense suffering for the litigants, and creation of a legal machine that became the NAACP Legal Defense Fund Inc. The successful effort to eliminate legally mandated inequality and the movement for civil rights that followed were the prototype for modern rights movements in America. The focus was on a new reading of equality that would wipe out the doctrine of separate but equal. The struggle involved both individual courage and group support of a financial, psychological, and even physical nature. One of the crucial developments was the founding of the National Association for the Advancement of Colored People (NAACP) in 1900 on the then radical platform of equal rights for Negroes. The founder was W. E. B. Dubois, a black man from the western hills of Massachusetts.

In 1931, the NAACP searched for a strategy to combat segregation in the South. In this effort, the promise of material equality was again employed, this time to make it so costly to maintain segregation that the South would give it up. The plan was known as the "Margold Strategy" after its proponent, Nathan Margold, a lawyer for the NAACP. Margold suggested that the way to overcome segregation was to attack the practice from the perspective of equality. The courts were not particularly progressive at the time, but the Supreme Court was on record as legitimizing segregation by means of the promise of material equality. That was the promise the strategy would try to bring to fruition. The first success attributable to this claim came seven years later, in 1938. Not surprisingly, the justices were most sensitive to the claim of inequality when it arose in law schools. In *Missouri ex rel. Gaines* v. *Canada* (1938), Missouri was ordered to admit a black law student to its law school or to create a new law school. It wouldn't do, according to the Court, to simply pay Lloyd Gaines's tuition at another state's law school, since this would not provide him with an equal education within Missouri.

The attacks on segregation continued to rely on the promise of equality in *Plessy*, even after World War II. Like the concern for toleration that emerged after World War I, the rhetoric of democracy in World War II had convinced many Americans, black and white, that there was something wrong with a democracy where the races were separated and social equality did not exist for 10 percent of the nation's population. Yet, for a short period, the hopes and the success of NAACP litigation were based on the failure of institutions in the South to live up to the promise of equality in *Plessy*, rather than on the evil of separation *per se*. Another legal victory after the war came in *Sweatt* v. *Painter* (1950), when the Supreme Court ordered Texas to admit a black student to its law school. The Court found that no comparable segregated legal education could be provided for blacks in Texas. The ground was still the failure of the state to fulfill its constitutional obligations to provide an equal education, rather than any reassessment of those obligations. The findings in this case, however, gave a sense of the inherent limitations of the "separate but equal" mandate, especially in the area of education. Recognition of those limitations would be the basis for *Brown* v. *Board of Education* (1954), and with recognition of social equality in that case the courts would turn away from the hollow promise of material equality.

The *Brown* opinion was short but monumental. It held segregation unconstitutional in a collection of five cases drawn from Border States, where the commitment to segregation was generally weaker than in the Deep South. It was argued twice, in part because of the personnel change that brought Earl Warren to the Court as Chief Justice and because of an effort to ground the decision in a historical reading of the Fourteenth Amendment. In the end, the Fourteenth Amendment did not provide the ground, and Chief Justice Warren based the attack on separation in new psychological information that linked the law of segregation to the social reality of prejudice. By using the modern tools of the clinical psychologist, Warren's opinion accounted for what Justice Harlan had suggested in his *Plessy* dissent over 50 years before. These tools were provided by Kenneth Clark, whose experiments with dolls showed that black children under segregation had a diminished sense of self-esteem. Separate facilities had to be seen as inherently unequal in that they hurt black students.

The "Pure" Concept. The *Brown* decision eliminated separation from constitutional protection, and its legacy was a new reading of equality. After the decision, attention shifted from the refusal to see separation as a violation at all to a view of separation as *the* violation of constitutional equality. The resulting conceptual apparatus was rooted in the idea of colorblindness and expressed in the constitutional requirement of nondiscrimination. This kind of constitutional right is "pure." It stands outside the struggles that brought it into being and ignores, or leaves behind, the history and implications of those struggles. Because colorblindness becomes the ideological ground for equality, it is useful to look at its roots in *Brown* v. *Board of Education* and the opinion by Chief Justice Warren.

Although it struck down separation, Warren's opinion for the unanimous Court was a response to the earlier doctrine. The focus in the *Brown* decision was on desegregation. This was the direct opposite of the 1896 holding in *Plessy*, which had provided the rationale for segregation. Whereas in 1896, segregation had been justified, Warren's opinion in *Brown* attacked separation of the races. The tradition of legal formalism and distance from social reality that had allowed segregation to exist could not shield that practice from the social reality of segregation in 1954. Recognition that the treatment of blacks by whites in the South was oppressive was responsible for the end of constitutionally sanctioned segregation. The consequence was a view of constitutional equality that disposed of material considerations as part of the false promise that had propped up segregation; this new view put in its place a principle of constitutional equality focused on "de-segregation" or nondiscrimination.

Having withdrawn protection for racism in the law, the doctrinal response provided a basis for ignoring the context by promoting a formal colorblind standard. Its impact was to enshrine Harlan's rhetoric without returning to the issue of equality. The chief justice's majority opinion does not speak about schools in terms of sameness in either size, quantity, or number. It does not establish a right to education of the same value or social importance for everyone. Rather, the injunction against denial of equal protection is like ". . . the historically familiar assertion that all men must stand equal before the law, that justice must be blind to wealth or color, to rank or privilege" (Tussman and tenBroek, 1949:342). In this doctrine, the new formality, although it came from attention to social phenomena, would make it difficult to keep its roots alive during later adjudication. The justices in *Brown* had left a legacy of colorblindness even though they never used the term. They had given birth to a principle that would become dissociated from the oppression of blacks that had brought it about.

Pure concepts, such as colorblindness, are part of a judicial propensity to generalize. There are many similar kinds of concepts that have been identified as the basis for judicial choice. From Herbert Wechsler (1959) came the concept of *neutral principles,* and the key descriptive phrase of "line drawing for all." Wechsler's example of such a principle was the clear and present danger doctrine. He thought the *Brown* decision had fallen short of this ideal. Neutral principles would resolve cases by inclining toward narrowness, and judicial policymaking would exclude the political considerations more characteristic of the other processes. *Universal principles* is a similar concept used by Richard Flathman (1976) for the idea that what is right for one person must be right for every relevantly similar person. This kind of principle would seek sameness across contextual differences. Paul Freund (1964) offered another angle. He was critical of concepts like colorblindness and called them *absolutes* because they ignored practical realities. He held that the law cannot stand apart and ignore the social context and the political realities. Finally, Herbert Marcuse (1968) characterized some legal concepts because they purported to be *pure.* He pointed to the ACLU position on the First Amendment and its claim to tolerate all forms of expression. He suggested that in these concepts there was "no admixture of interests," and thus that to discriminate on the basis of race would be wrong. Missing, in the purity of the concept, was the sensitivity to discrimination against blacks that had produced the concept.

Thus, the legacy of *Brown* was a "pure" concept. The decision came down to the public as standing for colorblindness, and it had a remarkable impact on the popular conception of equality. In the schools of the period, children were taught not to "see" race, and liberal parents encouraged their children to be colorblind. This impact of the ruling was heightened by the separation of the decision on the constitutional issue from any plan of implementation. The first *Brown* decision was about a concept in the Constitution, not its implications. In *Brown II* (1955), however, the Supreme Court held that desegregation should proceed, "with all deliberate speed." Thus began a struggle that is not over yet. Faced with widespread resistance to the judicial order, the response was a kind of color consciousness on the part of the judges charged with implementation. Separation became even more entrenched as the issue in this area. Consequently, it was not restrictions on choice or unequal education, but distinctions that were the focus of equal protection battles. This is the concern we turn to next.

The Pursuit of Equality

The Supreme Court's holding that segregation of the races in public schools could not be "squared" with the constitutional promise of equal protection sparked two decades of political activity. Only six months after the decision in *Brown*, Rosa Parks boarded a bus in Montgomery, Alabama, and refused to sit in the back where blacks had been expected to sit. Instead she sat in the front of the bus. The idea in *Brown* and the action in Montgomery are the vision and the practice that made this the initial struggle in what would turn into the civil rights movement, a decade of struggle to realize the ideals the justices had announced in 1954. All along, however, the idea was somewhat out of synch with the process by which it was implemented. The result would be a number of challenges to efforts taken on behalf of minorities. These challenges would rely on colorblindness.

Colorblindness v. Implementation

The ruling in *Brown* was not just a precedent for the legal sphere, it became, in the words of Martin Luther King, Jr., a dream. The key to the dream was colorblindness. This is a term that has never been used by a majority of the justices of the Supreme Court, but it is one that they have not disavowed, and it exemplifies the popular significance of the 1954 ruling. This standard led to an inconsistency between an elegant promise and a sort of trench warfare employed to implement the policy. The struggle took place largely at the level of the federal district courts whose duty was to enforce the constitutional standard. Interventions by the Supreme Court set the parameters for enforcement and adjusted the methods of implementation to new circumstances.

Colorblind Principles. The promise of constitutional equality was steeped in the struggle of minorities right up to the 1954 decision in *Brown*. After the Civil War, it would include the Irish in 1880 (*Strauder* v. *West Virginia*), the Chinese in 1886 (*Yick Wo* v. *Hopkins*), aliens in 1915 (*Truax* v. *Raich*), Japanese-American citizens in World War II (*Korematsu* v. *U.S.*, 1944), and Chicanos in 1954 (*Hernandez* v. *Texas*). The vision and the hope were that the laws would be made equal so that discrimination would ultimately be eliminated. Even the white majority could hope to benefit since it was composed of ethnic groups, many of which had been discriminated against in the past and might be in the future. The promise was that of a pure or absolute concept that would apply to everybody and under which nobody's race or sex would be taken into account. This was the liberal creed. Justice Lewis Powell characterized it as the inability "to peg the guarantees of the Fourteenth Amendment to the struggle for equality of one racial minority" (*Regents of the University of California* v. *Allan Bakke*, 1978). Colorblindness, like "pure tolerance," had something for everybody.

According to law professor Alan Freeman (1978), the concept of "racial discrimination" that comes from colorblindness can be viewed from the perspective of either its victim or its perpetrator. From the victim's perspective, racial discrimination describes conditions of existence for members of an underclass, including lack of money, lack of jobs, lack of housing. The perpetrator perspective sees discrimination as violations of the constitutional mandate of equal protection. Antidiscrimination law has, at its core, the prohibition of violations—race-conscious actions that disadvantage members of minority groups. Freeman's thesis is that anti-discrimination law has a perpetrator's perspective. The task has been to select actions that violate the principle, outlaw them, and neutralize their effects. It presupposes a world composed of atomistic individuals whose actions are not tied into the social fabric, presupposing that, but for the violation, the system would work. Conditions, or something approaching a victim's perspective, only get taken into account under the banner of a remedy.

According to this scheme, the period from 1954 to 1965 was characterized by a jurisprudence of violation. This was the era that established a focus on violations of a particular sort. The problem of remedies had been relegated to the "equity" category and assigned, by the second *Brown* decision, to the lower federal courts. The major task of the era was to increase the list of perpetrators against whom anti-discrimination law might be directed. This involved discovering new forms of violation, such as restrictive covenants, municipal corporations, and private "conspiracies" (*Guest* v. *U.S.*, 1966). Where the Court did have a chance to elaborate on the basic anti-discrimination principle, as in *Swain* v. *Alabama* (1965), when a black man accused of rape challenged his nearly all white jury, the Supreme Court denied the claim because it failed to find "purposeful discrimination." The most dramatic example of focus on the violation and a rare instance of armed support for a constitutional principle came in 1957 when President Dwight Eisenhower sent troops to Little Rock, Arkansas, to enforce the Supreme Court's ruling desegregating the schools there. The action was upheld by the Supreme Court, affirming the Court's commitment to the principle of *Brown*.

In this period, the distinction between *de jure* and *de facto* discrimination arose. The concepts were used to emphasize that it was *de jure*, or intentional discrimination by means of state law, that *Brown* had made unconstitutional. Thus, *de facto* discrimination (simply a matter of "fact") did not constitute a violation. With regard to the definition of a violation, the story did not differ much in the South from in the North. The concern was with intentional separation of the races. The struggle to remedy past offenses would have two key elements reflecting a very different practice from the popular mythology of colorblindness. Judges operating under the Constitution ended up being race conscious. They justified this by findings of past constitutional violations, or acts of discrimination. In 1964 (*Bell* v. *Gary, Indiana*), however, the Court judged *de facto* segregation not to be unconstitutional.

John F. Kennedy, for all his commitment to racial justice, was able to do little in this area. It was only after he was shot in Dallas that his successor, Lyndon Johnson, pushed through the Civil Rights Act of 1964. Southerners, in an unsuccessful attempt to kill the legislation, inserted sex as one of the protected categories. Ten years later, this was to be a key statutory tool in the women's movement. Section 2 of the act concerned public accommodations, and it was ruled constitutional in *Heart of Atlanta Motel* v. *United States* (1964). The achievements of this period reached their culmination in 1967, when Thurgood Marshall, a former chief counsel to the NAACP who had argued for Linda Brown before the Supreme Court in 1954, became the first black to be appointed to the Supreme Court.

Race-Conscious Remedies. The period from 1965 until 1974 stands out as one in which the Supreme Court focused on remedies implementing the constitutional norm. The law remained within the perpetrator perspective, but the provision of remedies began to create expectations associated with the victim perspective. The Court found plans offering students a choice of schools inadequate in 1968 (*Green* v. *New Kent County School Board*) and ruled that a dual system had to be merged *at once* into a unified system in 1969 (*Alexander* v. *Holmes County Board of Education*). Two years later, in confronting the hostile Charlotte school board, the federal district court appointed an educational consultant who prepared a desegregation plan calling for busing to achieve racial balance. In this case, *Swann* v. *Charlotte-Mecklenburg Board of Education* (1971), the justices said that, all things being equal, children should be assigned to schools near their homes. But since all things were not equal in a system "... deliberately constructed and maintained to enforce racial segregation ... the task is to correct the condition that offends the constitution." Since the state had a history of segregation, the school boards could prescribe measures for desegregation. Thus, the justices were not "colorblind" to obvious violations. Judicial power to supervise where teachers would be assigned and where shools would be built was acknowledged.

Following *Swann*, a number of cases emerged treating the issue of responsibility for a remedy in the South. In *Wright* v. *Emporia* (1972), the trial court had prevented the newly formed city of Emporia from withdrawing its children from the county school system. By a 5-4 majority, Justice Potter Stewart emphasized that a desegregation plan with some disparity in racial balance does not make the plan unacceptable, but he insisted that a town could not withdraw from a district to avoid desegregation. The decision was unanimous in *U.S.* v. *Scotland Neck Board of Education* (1972), where the creation of a new district was substantially motivated by a desire to create a predominantly white system.

Some Northern states tried by their own initiative to eliminate segregation in public schools. The model, however, was again taken from *Brown*, with its emphasis on racial mixing as a key to equality. Massachusetts, for instance, required district wide action whenever a school had more than 50 percent nonwhite students. The leading case for desegregation in the North was *Keyes* v. *School District No. 1* (1973). In this case, dealing with Denver, Justice William Brennan's majority opinion did not question the *de facto-de jure* distinction, but it held that housing patterns were not an excuse where school district policies served to isolate blacks. He set forth criteria to facilitate a finding of *de jure* discrimination where the traditional state-mandated segregation was not obvious. The creation of segregated schools in any part of a district "infected" the whole district with racial bias. Not just statutes, but administrative actions, could also constitute a violation of the Constitution in this period. *Swann, Wright,* and *Keyes* had created an expectation of change akin to the victim perspective in that it looked beyond surface formulations and required race-conscious remedies.

Beyond Separate and Unequal. The story comes full circle by the end of the 1970s, at least, in an optimistic reading of the cases. By 1970, three-quarters of all blacks lived in metropolitan areas. This posed a problem for realizing equality of treatment because, in such instances, the races lived in concentrated areas. In Chicago, the south side, for instance, contained about 2.5 million people, nearly all black. In Detroit, the central city, with almost 1 million people, was largely black. One plan, initially conceived to remedy these situations, which was consistent with the aspiration to equality of treatment, was to bus children from the suburbs to the central cities to equalize the racial composition of the schools.

The plan was put forth in Detroit by a district judge who had considerable vision. His order, in response to a history of state-supported civil rights violations, was on such a dramatic scale that it was described as making "all previous busing programs look like class excursions" (Wilkinson, 1979). In a metropolitan school district of 780,000 pupils, nearly half would be bused for desegregation. By including the suburbs, the judge sought to accomplish an integration of class as well as race, for it was in these suburbs that the more affluent middle classes lived. The judge's idea was to bring those who had fled the city back into the school system. In addition, metropolitan busing actually required fewer buses because the distances were in many cases less, and busing involved less travel time for the students than some inner-city remedies. Judge Roth's remedy reached the Supreme Court for the first time in *Milliken v. Bradley* (1974). The judge had held that the acts of the Detroit Board of Education, as a subordinate entity of the state, were attributable to the state of Michigan, and that the state had a liability to remedy the situation. Roth found that the only way to meet this responsibility was to bus suburban children to the city.

For the Supreme Court, Chief Justice Warren Burger responded that the task is to correct the condition that offends the Constitution, but that the constitutional right of the black respondents residing in Detroit is attendance at a unitary school system in that district. He did not find that the suburbs were implicated. According to Burger, a multi-district remedy to *de jure* segregation required findings that those included in the remedy have failed to operate a unitary school system, that boundaries were established for the purpose of discriminating, that included districts had committed acts that affected segregation within the districts, and that everyone involved had a chance to be heard on the propriety of the remedy or the question of constitutional violation. As Justice Potter Stewart emphasized in his concurrence, the issue was the appropriate exercise of federal equity jurisdiction. The problem, however, was that the constitutional mandate still focused simply on desegregation. Justice William Douglas penned the most articulate and paradoxical lament.

> When we rule against a metropolitan area remedy we take a step that will likely put the problem of the Blacks and our society back to the period that antedated the separate but equal regime of *Plessy* v. *Ferguson*. Today's decision, given *Rodriguez*, means that there is no violation of the equal protection clause though the schools are segregated by race and though the Black schools are not only separate but inferior."

Due to the logic of *Brown*, the country was left without a remedy.

Burger's opinion in *Milliken* is, according to Freeman (1978), a perverse denial of the reality of segregation, where the Court for the first time applied anti-discrimination law to rationalize a segregated result in a case where a constitutional violation had been found. The decision was not inconsistent with the traditional formalism of the constitutional law in this area, however, and the refusal of the Court to step in must be seen in light of the more active forms of social and economic discrimination that created the situations in the first place. The white parents who had fled the older urban areas were participating in the discriminatory social and economic setting that had been left untouched by judicial attention to *de jure* discrimination.

It is possible, however, to read the second *Milliken* case (1977) as transcending the traditional categories. In the first case, the Court had retreated (*Milliken*, 1974). The violation was not inter-district, so the remedy could not be either. In the second case, decided in 1977, the Court faced the situation of a constitutional violation where there was no authority for meaningful remedial action in the traditional form. As part of its equity power, the district court in Detroit had responded to the first case with a "draft on the public purse." Judge Roth had required expansion of various educational programs, such as reading and career guidance, in pursuit of providing a more equal education for the inner-city children. The Court turned from the practice of integration to the provision of equal, or at least more equal, education for the first time since the Margold Strategy leading up to the *Brown* decision. In 1977, by an 8-0 vote, the Supreme Court held that such action by the district court was appropriate. The constitutional principle is one that transcends the limited categories of the desegregation jurisprudence of the period from 1954 to 1974.

The Paradox of Affirmative Action

The ideological view of the law puts the politics of a case in context. The most important thing about a case is not the outcome, but that it has arisen and that the claims make sense. It is often hard to see the implications of this alternative because the outcome is what we so often look for. But a dispute is a product of the ideological tradition out of which it arises. The outcome depends on the fact that we "play the game." That is, cases are chosen and have the significance that they do because of the conceptual system within which they reside.

By the late 1970s, the legal principle of colorblindness and the policy of affirmative action were on a collision course. Each had its own tradition and its own proponents. Colorblindness was the more abstract vision against which legal conduct was measured. Affirmative action was a policy response and a realization that substantial steps had to be taken. The color consciousness that was characteristic of affirmative action was most closely associated with programs of "implementation," that is, strategies for "getting somewhere." Often, this place was a colorblind paradise, but increasingly even that goal took account of race or ethnicity as attractive aspects of a cultural heritage or tradition. That the clash was festering in the society and pressing on the Supreme Court is evident in the cases being brought to the Court in the mid-1970s. In 1974, the justices had heard oral arguments on affirmative action, but they had been able to avoid the issue because the law school whose admission procedures had been challenged admitted the challenger pending the outcome of the litigation. By the time the case got to the Supreme Court, the petitioner was about to graduate, making the case "moot" (*Defunis* v. *Odegaard*, 1974). Thirteen cases were petitioned to the Court in the next two years. Each was denied.

Understanding *Bakke*. The clash of colorblindness with affirmative action surfaced in the 1978 case of the *Regents of the University of California* v. *Allan Bakke*. Although there is important law in later cases such as *Fullilove* v. *Klutznick* (1980), *Bakke* sprang the question and caught the imagination of the public in a way that demonstrates the significance of the ideological dimension of law. The difference between an ideological investigation and an ordinary look at the case are particularly evident here. Like a student applying to medical school, we are conventionally concerned with results. An ideological investigation, however, is attentive to how issues—such as the ones occurring to Allan Bakke and sought by the Court—develop in the way that they do. Bakke's application to medical school was looked at in the context of affirmative action, and his appeal was influenced by the concept of constitutional equality. Consequently, the most interesting thing is that there was a case at all, that a white man could claim that he had been discriminated against, using the decisions that had begun with *Brown* v. *Board of Education* and continued throughout the efforts to end discrimination against black Americans. This is an example of the political significance of legal ideology. With these tools, we can more fully understand the case.

Due to past failures to address the issue, groups on both sides were poised as Bakke's case made its way to the Supreme Court. The proximate cause of the suit was a white male who had generally high ratings in the medical school admissions process, but who was denied admission to the medical school at the University of California in Davis. The university had a program that gave special consideration to disadvantaged groups in an effort to increase their numbers in the school and the medical profession. The university conceded that given his scores, it could not prove that Bakke wouldn't have been admitted if there had not been a special admissions program. The progress of the case was a result of Allan Bakke's challenge and the willingness of those at the University of California to fight it. The brief for the university, by law professor Paul Mishkin, argued that *Brown* should be seen as ". . . impetus for the effort to end barriers to real equality of opportunity for racial and ethnic minorities" and that it "expressed the goal of educational opportunity unimpaired by the effects of racial discrimination." There is an assumption in the brief that Bakke's claim made sense, but that there were extenuating circumstances explaining why the university took his race into account. They attempted to hold that the discrimination standard applies only to minorities that had traditionally been disadvantaged. Thus, the progress of the case was the result of an applicant's challenge and the willingness of those in power to fight it.

Civil rights groups, who were generally willing if not eager to have the constitutionality of affirmative action tested, were unsure of the wisdom of supporting this case. Concern that the decision of California's Supreme Court to overturn the admission process would become national law derived from two problematic elements of this situation. First, the system involved a quota, a nasty word to many like the Anti-Defamation League of B'nai B'rith who could have been counted on, traditionally, to support the civil rights position. To gain the support of such groups, those who favored affirmative action would have preferred a less rigid system. Second, since the school had only been open for 10 years and was situated in a state known for its excessive tolerance, it would be hard to establish the traditional basis for affirmative action as a remedy. Nevertheless, the university pressed, and the Supreme Court went forward with the case.

In the fall of 1977, this case became the focus of widespread political action. Few cases in this half-century have generated as much public debate. This was most clearly a situation where there was a need to have the paradoxical existence of affirmative action under a colorblind Constitution resolved. The liberal press loved the issue, or appeared to, by the large amount of attention it gave to the case. There were background stories on Bakke, the medical school to which he was applying, and even the trauma of the admissions process. More puzzling were the radical groups who used the case as a forum to focus attention that had waned since the 1960s on the issue of civil rights. Bakke's claim was a vivid symbol of what many felt had happened and others feared would soon happen to the dream of a nonracist society. Consequently, the Supreme Court and the debating forums on college campuses were deluged with those who were concerned about the case. Part of the political struggle came to the Supreme Court, as it often does, in the form of *amicus curiae*, or "friend of the court," briefs. The Justice Department, under the administration of Jimmy Carter, submitted that the justices distinguish between quotas and less rigid forms of affirmative action and counseled them to narrow the scope of their ruling. This was one of 58 briefs filed in the case, establishing, some suspected, a record for briefs filed and certainly serving as a sign of the attention generated by the case. There was the perception, perhaps, that in such a situation the Court might even be looking to outsiders for help in resolving the paradox. While civil rights and generally liberal groups joined in support of the university, Bakke had the United States Chamber of Commerce and, surprisingly, the Anti-Defamation League of B'nai B'rith on his side. The organized legal lobbyists of the Jewish community had enlisted on the side against quotas.

The medical school at Davis, the former agricultural college of the California system situated in the heart of the Sacramento Valley, had been opened in 1968 as part of a general expansion of the university system to meet the needs of the state and the baby boom generation. Its enrollment had increased to 100 and stabilized there by 1971. The ordinary admissions process, which Bakke went through twice, involved the collection of the overall grade point average, the average in the sciences, a score on the Medical College Aptitude Test (MCAT), letters of recommendation, and an interview. There was also a special committee that considered disadvantaged and minority groups and made recommendations for seats set aside for members of these groups. Bakke had applied late in 1973 and was denied. He tried again in 1974, and he was again turned down. His suit against the university reached the Supreme Court two years later. There are three opinions from the Court: one that reflects the colorblindness doctrine, another in support of affirmative action, and a compromise position that unites a floating majority, which held that Allan Bakke should be admitted to medical school and race could be taken into account some of the time.

The colorblind opinion was written by Justice John Paul Stevens and also included Justices Burger, Rehnquist, and Stewart. They asked whether Bakke had been discriminated against, rather than the broader policy questions on the constitutionality of affirmative action or whether race could be taken into account in admissions processes. This narrowing of the issues was well within the grand tradition of legal formality and these justices—who are generally on the conservative end of the political spectrum—here narrowed the discussion further by refusing to explore a constitutional basis. They found the answer to their question in the 1964 Civil Rights Act, Title VI, Sec. 601, and they held that the meaning of the section is clear: when it says "No person . . . shall, on the ground of race, color, or national origin, be excluded from participation in, be denied the benefits of . . . any program receiving federal financial assistance," that is what the Congress means, and Bakke must have been discriminated against. The justices held that the university's claim that there was no racial stigma behind the classification is not relevant because, in the legislative history, there is no such provision. In the legislative history, they found that opponents of the Civil Rights Act feared that discrimination might mean racial quotas. They were assured that the act meant "colorblind" administration, and at least a few bought the argument that the principle of colorblindness is one where there might be some hope of a common purpose. The conservative justices in looking to the statute rather than the Constitution for support found it in the speeches of the most vocal liberals—Senators Hubert Horatio Humphrey and John Pastore. Humphrey is quoted as arguing on the floor of the Senate:

> The word discrimination has been used in many a court case. What it really means in the bill is a distinction in treatment. . . . If we started to treat Americans as Americans, not as fat ones, tall ones, brown ones, . . . but as Americans . . . we would not need to worry about discrimination.

His sentiments were echoed by Pastore, who used the word so dear to liberals of that period:

> Title VI will guarantee that the money collected by colorblind tax collectors will be distributed by Federal and state administrators who are equally colorblind.

It was a powerful argument, and it revealed the impact of constitutional interpretation on federal legislation. The colorblind reading, which had originated as a gloss on the equal protection clause of the Fourteenth Amendment, had become the conventional wisdom.

The Court's liberals, Justices Brennan and Marshall, who were most closely associated with colorblindness, disagreed with the interpretation being given to it by their more conservative colleagues. The opinion they put forth was joined by Justices White and Blackmun and proposed the strongest support yet advanced for the policy of affirmative action. Their argument was that "we cannot let colorblindness become myopia which masks the reality of inferior treatment." Yet, in *Bakke* they were boxed in by the constitutional tradition since the arguments used in *Brown* had reached out to whites and provided them with a promise that they would not be simply placed into a category because of their race. These justices went beyond the Civil Rights Act of 1964 and turned to the Constitution in a move that was a classic response to the legislative history presented by Justice Stevens. They were able to make an argument that was much more their own without relying on the words of the 1960s liberals who had written whites into the protections of the Fourteenth Amendment. The effort was much like that of Justice John Marshall Harlan, who, years before in *Plessy*, had called attention to purposes and refused to be bound by the formalism of the law. This was their greatest strength. They argued that colorblindness had never been part of the Constitution. Although it was a statutory strategy, they pointed out that it was never adopted by a majority of the justices. It was not, they argued forcefully, to be found anywhere in the *Brown* decision. They were concerned that the authority of the government not be used to support race hate but rather argued that where classifications serve important government purposes and are benign or remedial they should be allowed to stand.

These justices went a step further and argued for the relevance of past *societal* discrimination as a justification for a racially conscious admissions program. They held that, although court-ordered remedial action requires a finding of discrimination, voluntary remedial action should not. Such voluntary efforts, they believed, should be allowed because they offset past discrimination. This opinion came remarkably close to acknowledging a "group rights" claim, a kind of right that had generally been absent from the legal setting. The absence of group rights claims has epitomized the limits of policy formation in the judiciary (O'Neill, 1981), as opposed to the legislative sphere. The view that individuals and not group rights are involved when racial discrimination is challenged distinguishes the tradition of equal protection in the Constitution from a conventional view. Constitutional rights have been tied to individuals, and there has been a reluctance to acknowledge group claims (Fiss, 1977). Implementation strategies, statutory affirmative action, and pluralist ideology are antithetical to this position.

Powell's Synthesis. More characteristic as a legal response is the synthesis and compromise represented in Justice Lewis Powell's opinion in Allan Bakke's case. The opinion builds on the university's initial concessions that it had made decisions based on race and that they are reviewable under the Fourteenth Amendment to the United States Constitution. The issue, as Powell framed it, became the level of suspicion to use when race is taken into account and what considerations are legitimate to override that suspicion. Powell discussed the statutory claim, but he ultimately turned to the constitutional meaning. He did discount, however, the "colorblind" rhetoric of the legislators in 1964 by emphasizing that they were looking at white racism in their call for equal treatment. He suggested that their statements on colorblindness not be taken out of context. The constitutional issue of classification captured most of Powell's attention. He minimized the quota issue in stating that a line drawn on the basis of race, whether a program like the one at Davis or a more flexible, goal-oriented method, demanded exacting judicial scrutiny. He rejected the benign classification approach and indicated that individuals must not be asked to bear burdens they are not responsible for. Part of his discussion took up the troubling reality of past instances where race had been taken into account. In every instance he emphasized the difference—the remedial nature of school desegregation, the sex discrimination cases that were not subject to the same level of scrutiny, and the employment cases where those who were being helped had suffered. Thus, he approached the question with the traditional suspicion, but like a lawyer he still approached it with the hope that a resolution could be found.

In assessing the justifications presented by the University of California and developing some of his own, Powell looked for the requisite permissible interest to be served that would make the use of the classification necessary. The first was the desire to increase the number of minorities in medical school. This he considered circular in its attempt to justify the end by simply restating its premise. The second was societal discrimination. Although this was a worthy goal, the problem of innocent victims who would be required to pay was, in the context of the legal process, too much to consider. Third, there was the proposal to increase the number of physicians for minority communities. Powell seemed more interested here, yet a proposal had not been worked out in conjunction with the medical school to carry this through. Finally, and ultimately successful, was the desire to obtain the educational benefits that come from a diverse student body.

Thus, Powell felt that it would be reasonable for an admissions program to take race into account to the extent that this characteristic *among others* was a relevant consideration in pursuit of a diverse student body. There were caveats, however. The method used had to be the least threatening to the individuals who were to bear the burden of any affirmative efforts on the part of minority groups. In the case of the Davis program, the failure to treat applicants as individuals was ultimately fatal to their system. It was on these grounds that the applicant and petitioner in the Supreme Court would be admitted to the Davis program.

In this case, the synthesis achieved by Justice Powell was more than a political compromise. Although it failed to uphold the group rights claim implicit in the university program, it did present the collective interest in bringing diversity to an educational institution. In this context, race would be taken into account for the benefit of the society and presumably for the majority, rather than the other way around, whatever the justice of the claim.

The aftermath of this case, like any involving the Constitution, is difficult to discern. One can point to Bakke's admission to medical school just a few months after the decision was rendered. There is also the possibility that the decision kept minorities away from Davis medical school. Prior to the decision, the school had enrolled about eight blacks per year. The year Bakke's case was decided, four entered the school. In subsequent years, the number stayed near zero, leading the school to hire a consultant—paid for by a federal grant—to attract blacks to an institution that had come to symbolize the affirmative action controversy. In general, although the decision condoned implicit consideration of race, it also provided a basis for resisting affirmative action where that was the predisposition. The result was a flurry of activity aimed at influencing the way the decision would be read. The most important context was bureaucratic.* In the government, agencies from the old Department of Health, Education, and Welfare (HEW) to the Civil Rights Commission offered interpretations that gave a very optimistic reading of the future of affirmative action programs run by the government. The effort in individual institutions, however, probably depends on how much pressure is put on them locally. The government still presses, although the election of Ronald Reagan reduced the pressure to some degree. Educational administrators are still sensitive to that pressure where the local environment reinforces the law on affirmative action. The consequence of all this is that the paradox was settled by compromise, with some lasting value for the struggle to reach social justice, but with an inevitable confusion remaining.

Classification and Equality

This section portrays how equal protection has expanded beyond race with attention to the constitutional logic that has been applied to statutory classifications. The logic for evaluating classifications of all kinds stems from treatment of race issues. We first turn to the nature of that logic. This is a key to constitutional discourse and an example of the unique reason that makes up the constitutional tradition. More extensive treatment is given to two enduring, troubling, and fascinating classifications, those based on wealth and those about sex. Here, the implications of the logic are given a degree of analytic attention to match popular interest in the issues.

The Logic of Equal Protection

Equal protection is about classification, or the distinctions we make between people. Making distinctions is one of the tricks for getting through life, or at least life is predicated on recognition of differences. We distinguish between people who are in our family or who are not, who are at our university or some other, or between those who are faculty and those who are students. Politics and social life begin with distinctions. Our tradition has also said that sometimes we make distinctions that turn out to be questionable, given some change in sensibility or some deeper understanding of how we want to live. That was the situation with regard to race in this country. The result was a logic, the emergence of a mechanism for looking at classifications, and dynamic attention to a variety of classifications. The logic actually lays out how classifications should be assessed. It refers to the kinds of

---

* In non-affirmative action contexts as well, the continuing significance of anti-discrimination law has been closely associated with the administrative and regulatory process; see *Bob Jones University* v. *United States* (1983) for a ruling that racially discriminatory private schools are not eligible for federal tax-exempt status.

scrutiny discussed in preceding sections. There are three parts to the logic: the A, B, C's of equal protection.

Suspect Classifications. The first aspect of the logic of equal protection is that there has to be a *classification* that is suspicious—one that has been troublesome, that has a history of abuse, like racial classifications, as opposed to one that distinguishes members of a family from those who are outside it. Classification by family membership certainly can cause problems; it determines who inherits wealth and who does not, for instance. There is no avoiding its significance and potential for controversy, but we have not indicated in this society that we are bothered by this sort of thing. We have said, however, that to distinguish simply on the basis of race is usually a very bad idea. This differential suspicion is one aspect of the logic of equal protection.

There are a number of classifications to which the logic of equal protection has been applied. One of the first was illegitimacy. Children born outside of marriage would not seem to be the kind of group that would have ready access to the appellate courts, but in fact they have received quite a bit of attention from the courts (*In re Baby Girl*, 1982). Treatment of "resident aliens" has also been looked on with suspicion. This derives from the fact that the Fourteenth Amendment stipulates that it is "persons" rather than citizens who are entitled to the protection of the Constitution. Other classifications that have been regarded with suspicion are those based on age or physical handicap. In this sense, it is obvious that civil liberties reflect wider political concerns. Those concerns get translated into constitutional discourse and constitutional formulations, and they are evaluated in terms of the logic of equal protection.

Affected Interests. Another aspect of the logic is the understanding that a *fundamental interest* has to be affected. Such an interest is a concern of constitutional lawyers. Thus, in addition to classifications that are historically suspect, justices want to know what someone claiming discrimination stands to lose. Although sexual distinctions may be suspicious, a claim to use a particular bathroom designated for the opposite sex would not traditionally make constitutional sense. In this instance, the fundamental interest affected by the classification would be lacking. Traditionally, this means a deep loss, like the right to vote, the right to get married; that is, the loss of something substantial.

Levels of Scrutiny. The third aspect of this logic is the *level of scrutiny.* If a classification is suspicious and something fundamental is being lost, then a strict degree of "scrutiny" is required. This means that unlike most legislation, such a classification would have to be justified. This was the move Justice Powell made in the *Bakke* case to suggest what was adequate justification for a racial classification. There are diluted

235

levels of scrutiny when some of the interests that are affected are not fundamental or when the classification is not meant to be entirely suspicious, like sex. One response in cases like this has been a "heightened" level of scrutiny, heightened, that is, from no scrutiny at all. This means that when the justices come upon such a situation, they will not look at it as carefully as they would race.

In his interpretation of constitutional law, Laurence Tribe has offered a subtle analysis of the strict scrutiny approach to equal protection questions. Most constitutional theorizing about strict scrutiny has focused on the "judicial review aspect" (Tribe, 1978:1001), that is, the question of judicial oversight and judicial competence. This has led to justification of strict scrutiny with reference to reasons for not being deferential to the legislative process or reasons why the traditional deference need not be operative. Tribe suggests that this is the wrong question. He believes that we should instead be asking about the proper approach to equality and discrimination, and how that approach can be articulated to provide a standard worthy of a fundamental right. The discussion of classifications that follows is informed by these questions.

The Problem of Wealth

An area of fundamental importance, which the justices have treated marginally, is wealth. American society, it is easy to see, would not function the way it does without distinctions based on wealth. In spite of the prevalence of this distinction, constitutional decisions on the matter have been relatively rare. Yet, wealth as a classification has been considered by the Court on various occasions. The justices have been most sensitive to people who are deprived of basic rights because they do not have enough money, and many of these developments have been associated with criminal due process. The result has been holdings to the effect that the Constitution will not allow a person to be absolutely deprived of a fundamental interest on the basis of wealth. In this area, fundamental interests are defined narrowly. For instance, the fact that people were being deprived of the right to vote on the basis of wealth led to the abolition of the poll tax, first by the Twenty-fourth Amendment at the national level and then in *Harper* v. *Virginia State Board* (1966) in the states. Some of the important activity in this area has involved the legal process, where some things are considered fundamental and others are not.

Legal Process. It has only been since the 1960s that governments throughout the United States have provided indigent persons with a lawyer. The obvious reason for the provision was the belief that people were being deprived of a fundamental interest in a fair trial when they could not obtain a lawyer. Since the 1930s, avoiding capital punishment

Equality

has been sufficient interest to merit provision of counsel. But it was not until the 1960s that the government provided a lawyer to people in instances where the punishment was less severe. This was the situation that for Anthony Lewis (1964) characterized the best of the Court's work during the 1960s. With regard to interests that are this fundamental and this closely tied to the claim of legitimacy, wealth discrimination has been moderated by the Constitution.

Another aspect of the criminal process, the appeal, is both more costly and more discretionary than the trial. Consequently, the courts have not been so clear about what sort of appellate rights are to be available for those without the ability to pay. At the very least, appellants have the right to be provided with a transcript from their trial (*Griffin* v. *Illinois*, 1956), and after that, what is available depends in part on how compelling a claim can be made.

Punishment of indigents has always been problematic when the issues of social justice and equality are raised. Indigents are more likely to find themselves in court. And once there, they face a process conditioned by ability to pay. This is true most obviously with fines, but it is also a function of punishment more generally. Penalties are related to the amount of loss, whether in terms of stature or actual material wealth, although the Constitution does set limits and cases still do arise that refine the operative constitutional norm. For example, Danny Bearden took the state of Georgia to the Supreme Court in 1983 when they sent him to prison after he had failed to pay a fine. Justice Sandra O'Connor's opinion made it clear that a defendant cannot be sent to jail for lack of funds. She wrote that when the trial court automatically revoked Bearden's probation, it did not exercise adequate care and violated Bearden's constitutional rights (*Bearden* v. *Georgia*, 1983).

In the area of civil procedure, there have been fewer instances where the Court has seen something fundamental as being in jeopardy. In one case that received attention, the state of Connecticut up until 1971 required a fairly substantial fee to file for divorce. People without adequate funds contested this infringement on the right to end a marriage (*Boddie* v. *Connecticut*, 1971), and the state had to abolish the practice. Moreover, the burden on the poor of a Wisconsin remarriage statute was considered in *Zablocki* v. *Redhail* (1978), and the statute was held to be unconstitutional.

Education. One of the most important cases in the area of wealth discrimination, *San Antonio School District* v. *Rodriguez* (1973), involved access to education. The issue was whether children were being deprived because the public school system was funded by the property tax, which is a reflection of the wealth of the community. Most education, through high school, is supported this way, at least in part. Although the state of Texas now tries to "equalize" the disparities between districts by spreading part of its support according to need, wealthy communities still can provide a better education than can poor communities. The claimants in San Antonio, Texas, argued that the barrio they lived in was unable to provide the same level of education as the wealthier Anglo suburbs. Perhaps the most extraordinary thing about this dispute over wealth as a classification is that the Supreme Court took the case, indicating a willingness to at least consider the possibility that people were being deprived of an education because they were poor. What they ended up saying in their decision was not as important as the potential for concern in this area relative to discrimination on the basis of wealth. While the majority of the Court decided that nobody was being absolutely deprived of an education, there was recognition of the effect on the quality of education available to the Chicano claimants. This is consistent with the tradition that a deprivation in this area must be substantial, as with the inability to conduct a legal defense or bring an appeal without a lawyer. In *Rodriguez*, the Court took particular note of the state's efforts to equalize the differential in the quality of education between rich and poor communities. Because the classification based on wealth had been mitigated by the state, however, it was considered more acceptable.

A decade after *Rodriguez*, there is still little sensitivity on the Supreme Court to wealth discrimination affecting schooling, but the cases do get heard in lower courts. This was the situation in January 1983, when, without comment, the Supreme Court refused to hear a constitutional challenge to New York's system for financing public education. This was true even though two lower courts in New York had agreed with the plaintiffs that reliance on the local property tax to finance schools was unconstitutional on the ground that resulting inequities in the abilities of rich and poor districts to pay for education violated the equal protection guarantees of the state and the federal constitutions. The Supreme Court, however, let stand the decision of the New York Court of Appeals, the state's highest court, which had found the prevailing school finance system to be constitutional (*Board of Education* v. *Nyquist*, 1983).

An area very close to education and bearing heavily on it is that of housing and residence. As in education, the economic makeup of a community is an important determinant of the level of deprivation. As one moves from the fundamental and relatively precise state-provided guarantees of education to the realm of housing and residency, however, the sensitivity of the Constitution to discrimination on the basis of wealth weakens still further. This was evident in *Warth* v. *Seldin* (1975), and it continues to be evident.

Health. The abortion controversy has raised some compelling challenges to discrimination or deprivation of fundamental interests because of financial status. The discussion of constitutional privacy showed that the Supreme Court's decision in the abortion cases did more to stimulate controversy than to settle the issues. In the 10 years that followed *Roe* v. *Wade* (1973), over 100 cases were appealed to the Supreme Court. Almost all involved limitations on the breadth of the decision. In *Maher* v. *Roe* (1977), the Court held that a state's decision not to pay for abortions, even though it paid for childbirth, did not violate the Constitution. In *Maher*, the district court had ruled that the presence of a fundamental right to an abortion required strict scrutiny of the distinction between abortion and childbirth and, by implication, a similar level of scrutiny over the distinction between those able to pay and those not able to pay. This scrutiny led them to invalidate the legislation. But Justice Lewis Powell, writing for the Supreme Court, held that the lower court had "misconceived the nature and scope of the fundamental right recognized in *Roe* . . . [in that] the right protects the woman from unduly burdensome interference with her freedom to decide whether to terminate her pregnancy." Holding that past decisions do not indicate "that financial need alone identifies a suspect class for purposes of equal protection analysis," the Court found that "the state has imposed no restriction on access to abortions that was not already there." This insensitivity to the plight of impoverished pregnant women, pointed out by the dissenters, is striking because it reveals the limitations of constitutional equal protection, given the strict logic of fundamental interests. The decision was extended in *Harris* v. *McRae* (1980), a major abortion decision, where the justices held that the liberty in *Roe* includes the freedom of a woman to decide whether to terminate a pregnancy but not a public obligation to make that choice a reality.

Much of the rest of the litigation on wealth involves such things as utility overcharges (*Memphis Light, Gas and Water Division* v. *Craft,* 1978) and repossession of furniture (*Flagg Brothers, Inc.* v. *Brooks,* 1978). In some instances, the wealth discrimination area shows how civil liberties reflect wider social concerns and controversies, as in the case of abortion. In other instances, the Constitution in this area seems simply to be serving as an occasional check in the most desperate of situations. In any case, the translation into constitutional discourse means the issue will be looked at in terms of the logic of equal protection.

Sex Discrimination

Sex has always been an intriguing classification. As with many other classifications, we make distinctions based on sex all of the time. Yet, since the early 1970s sex has appeared suspect, and there has been a great deal of controversy surrounding protections the Constitution holds for distinctions made on this basis. Sensitivity to these distinctions is linked to the women's movement itself and, like that movement, the application of equal protection in the Constitution to sex discrimination owes a great deal to earlier struggles for racial justice. Racial discrimination, as defined by the Constitution, has been the model in this setting. Treatment of the race issue focused attention on classifications that had been abused, and it is from that issue that the standard for evaluating such abuse evolved. The link is a matter of constitutional history, and consequently it has conceptual significance.

Despite its similarity to racial classifications, there have been some aspects of the constitutional politics of sex discrimination that distinguish these classifications. With sexual politics, highly charged movement activities preceded constitutional development, rather than coming later as had been the case with the civil rights movement following the NAACP's litigation efforts. The statutory arena has included legitimate protective measures for women, such as alimony, as well as those which discriminated against women. This has been a different legacy from race. Consequently, there have been a wider range of statutory interpretations, some of which are simply old paternalism, while others are true public policy puzzles. In addition, less litigation in the area has been based on the Constitution. This is, in part, because during much of the time that decisions were being handed down, the nation was considering a constitutional amendment (the Equal Rights Amendment, or ERA). The result has been a rare and, for all its democratic significance, not altogether uplifting experience of popular instruction regarding the meaning of the Constitution. While the proposed Amendment was being considered, the justices were deferring to the political arena and, given the outcome, that judicial abstention is likely to be one of the more important consequences of the ERA's demise.

Since there have always been legitimate grounds for distinctions on the basis of sex, the constitutional classification issue has been to determine which are acceptable and which are not. It might be said, at least in constitutional law, that discrimination on the basis of sex has been absolute only in the political area. As far as social and material equality, there has been less clarity. Since the governments never legislated such gross distinctions by sex as they had for race, the constitutional response has been more moderate. The most enduring standard has been a "heightened" amount of scrutiny and a requirement that legislatures have good reasons for their schemes. In the process of working in this area, however, they have had to be rather more suspicious of benign classifications than they have been in the other areas.

The Early Years. One of the earliest modern sex discrimination cases came before the Supreme Court in 1948 and involved a challenge to a Michigan law restricting barmaid licenses to wives and daughters of bar owners. This was during a period of deference to legislative judgments, especially in the area of business regulation, and it preceded modern sensitivity to classification that emerged from racial struggles. The standard used in this case (*Goesaert* v. *Cleary*, 1948) was that the legislation should bear a "rational relation" to legitimate state objectives. In this case, those objectives included preserving the family and the morality of women. On this standard, the law was upheld. A little over 20 years later, the constitutional order in the field of equal protection had been transformed. In 1971, the California Supreme Court would invalidate similar bartender restrictions (*Sailor Inn* v. *Kirby*) by employing the higher standard requiring the state to show a compelling interest and by bringing a different view of family and morality to the case. In 1971, there was no longer an interest in preserving the morals of women by keeping them from mixing drinks.

Although the Warren Court has been known for its liberalism, this inclination did not extend to sex discrimination. The one case the justices did consider on this issue, *Hoyt* v. *Florida* (1961), involved the constitutionality of a state law granting women an absolute exemption from jury duty because their place was assumed to be in the home. The plaintiff, a woman convicted of murdering her husband with a baseball bat, argued that the all-male jury she had faced violated her constitutional right to impartiality. The Warren Court, in 1961, stated that "Despite the enlightened emancipation of women from the restrictions and protections of bygone years . . . woman is still regarded as the center of home and family life." This quite liberal bench deferred to Florida's legislative judgment and allowed women a choice in what, for men, was considered a duty. This stance is sometimes called paternalism or pedestalism since it put women in a special place. But the special place Ms. Hoyt found herself in was not to her liking. It was not, on the other hand, the same sort of discrimination that the courts had faced in dealing with racial discrimination, since it gave women an opportunity that they were not forced to take. In 1975, the Burger Court overturned a similar statute (*Taylor* v. *Louisiana*, 1975), setting right this blemish on the progressive record of the Warren Court justices.

Arbitrary Preferences. The first contemporary Supreme Court case in this area was *Reed* v. *Reed*, decided in 1971. Ms. Reed challenged an Idaho statute that gave preference to her former husband when they both applied for control over their son's belongings after he died. The Court did not employ strict scrutiny or a high level of suspicion in its official logic, but it relied on a requirement of minimal rationality to hold that *arbitrary* preferences in favor of males violated the equal protection of the laws. The opinion held that a classification must bear a rational relationship to a legitimate state objective. Here, the state's objective was to lower the workload of the probate court. The justices ruled that the method of preferring men was unacceptable because, essentially, it was not minimally rational. In practice, it may well have been that the justices were becoming just a bit more sensitive to the historic propensity to abuse this classification by using indefensible stereotypes. Over the next decade, nearly 60 percent of the 20 or so cases that challenged legislation as being in violation of the equal protection clause would succeed.

The high point of the Burger Court's consideration of sexual discrimination came in *Frontiero* v. *Richardson*. This 1973 case concerned the right of a female member of the Air Force to claim her spouse as a dependent for the purpose of obtaining increased quarters allowances on an equal footing with male Air Force personnel. According to Air Force policy, a serviceman could claim his wife as a dependent without regard to whether she was in fact dependent upon him. A service woman, on the other hand, could not claim her husband as a dependent under these programs unless she could show that he was dependent upon her for over half of his support. The decision, written by Justice William Brennan and agreed to by three other justices, held that the history of sex discrimination made classifications on this basis "suspect." Consequently, the Court required the Air Force to show a compelling interest behind the classification. The Court held that "... any statutory scheme which draws a sharp line between the sexes, solely for ... administrative convenience ... involves an arbitrary choice" and is thus unconstitutional. This was the most sympathetic holding for the position that sex was a suspect classification. It came at the peak of liberal fascination with the women's movement and in the same year that the Supreme Court made abortion legal in *Roe* v. *Wade* (1973).

Heightened Scrutiny. The following year (1974), the justices returned to the level of rationality that they usually associate with sex classifications—a sort of middle range or heightened scrutiny. In a case involving California's disability insurance coverage, a challenge was presented to the exclusion of pregnancy and childbirth from coverage. The justices held that this was not a discrimination based on sex as such. Although only women can become pregnant, they said, it does not follow that every legislative classification concerning pregnancy is a sex-based classification (*Geduldig* v. *Aiello*, 1974). The program was viewed as dividing potential recipients into two groups, pregnant women and non-pregnant persons. The justices argued that while the first group is exclusively female, the second includes members of both sexes. The decision suggested that this type of classification was not "invidious," that is, it was not meant to harm or be unfair since there was no risk from which men were protected and women were not. This sort of tortured logic following a year of surprising victories received a great deal of criticism. The effort was necessary, however, because the requirement was that some justification be provided for sex classifications. Using the same standard for review, the justices did overturn an Oklahoma statute prohibiting the sale of 3.2 beer to males under the age of 21 and to females under age 18 (*Craig v. Boren*, 1976). The holding that the statute denied equal protection to men was based on the opinion that it did not "serve important government objectives and was not substantially related to their achievement." This would be the predominant mode of analysis for sex discrimination. While the justices deferred to the financial burden on the state in the California case, the Oklahoma claim about protection of the public health was rejected.

Although not as strict as suspect classification standards requiring a compelling state interest, the heightened scrutiny standard has proven effective in quite a few cases since the mid-1970s. In June of 1977, the Court ruled that height and weight requirements for prison guards discriminated against women because employers had failed to demonstrate that the tests had a real relationship with ability to handle the job. The case involved an Alabama law requiring state guards to be at least five feet two inches tall and to weigh at least 120 pounds. The requirements excluded 41 percent of the female population of the country from such jobs as opposed to less than 1 percent of the male population. The Court majority held this to be a significantly discriminatory pattern "on its face." The state officials, the justices held, had failed to offer any evidence to justify the statutory standards. The justices did, however, believe that women could be excluded from jobs in male prisons per se due to a demonstrable threat to the security of the institution, but that argument was not behind the statute. In *Personnel Administrator of Massachusetts* v. *Feeney* (1979), the Court set aside a lower court ruling that had invalidated a veterans preference provision in the state civil service law. Women competing for advancement in the state bureaucracy had contended that the Massachusetts statute discriminated against them because few had been able to serve in the armed forces in the past. The justices reminded the lower court that a state law with disproportionate impact was not necessarily unconstitutional for that fact alone. Throughout nearly this whole period, the Court had a running battle with Utah over its having set a different age of majority for men and women (*Stanton* v. *Stanton*, 1975). Utah authorities argued that the "biological facts of life" allowed that women reached maturity before men, but this was not enough to satisfy the Supreme Court's test for rationality.

Benign Classifications. So-called benign classifications, in which those who have been traditionally discriminated against stand to gain from the classification, have had a little greater success in withstanding review by the Supreme Court. In *Kahn* v. *Shevin* (1974), a widower was unsuccessful in his attack on a Florida law granting only widows a $500 property tax exemption. The justices believed that "... the differing treatment rests on some ground having a fair and substantial relation to the object of the legislation." It was distinguished from Sharron Frontiero's claim (*Frontiero* v. *Richardson*, 1973) because of the benign nature of the classification and given support by a traditional deference to tax classifications. Justice Douglas wrote for the majority in this case against a dissent by Justices Brennan and Marshall who called for closer judicial scrutiny. Although benign classification was accepted in *Kahn*, subsequent cases indicated that the Court would allow this justification only if it were clearly supported by the legislative record (Gunther, 1980). Nonetheless, three-quarters of the constitutional distinctions between men and women during this period were in statutes that "preferred" women over men. In one of the many cases challenging Social Security regulations, women were allowed slightly higher retirement benefits (*Califano* v. *Webster*, 1977). The Court approved this classification because it did not penalize women and justified it on the basis of compensation for women who had been discriminated against in the past. Even when men prevailed, as in *Califano* v. *Goldfarb* (1977), where a widower claimed discrimination based on a standard of identical treatment because he had to prove a dependency on his wife for public benefits, the benefits could be said to have been earned by his wife posthumously, making her the winner as a result of the litigation.

There have been a number of cases which, like *Bakke* in the preceding section, reveal a use of the classification standard in a way that is just a little surprising. Sex blindness and colorblindness have affinities but some important differences as well. The most significant cases are *Rostker* v. *Goldberg* (1981), which concerned the drafting of women, *Michael M.* v. *Superior Court of Sonoma County* (1981), about statutory rape, and *Mississippi University for Women* v. *Joe Hogan* (1982), which dealt with admission to an all-female nursing program. All involved men who argued that they were being discriminated against by not receiving identical treatment with women. In *Rostker*, the claim was given a boost during the summer of 1980. When registration for the draft was reinstituted, a district judge in Washington, D.C., declared the all-male registration to be unconstitutional. That summer, Justice Brennan, acting for the Supreme Court while it was in recess, allowed the registration to go on, pending a ruling by the whole Court. The following year, in an opinion by Justice Rehnquist, the Court allowed the statute to stand. Their basis can only be described as an unusually minimal rationality that relied on the undocumented claim that the military would have administrative difficulties dealing with women, who were not allowed to engage in combat.* In *Michael M.*, a California statutory rape law was challenged over its inequitable impact. It defined unlawful sexual intercourse as ". . . an act of sexual intercourse accomplished with a female not the wife of the perpetrator where the female is under the age of 18 years." The male petitioner, who appears to have been particularly aggressive, was nevertheless only 17½, just a year older than his partner. Although Rehnquist purported to use a scale of "minimum rationality with a sharper focus," his willingness to accept the state's argument that it was trying to cut down on teenage pregnancy revealed a remarkable tolerance. In his dissent, however, Justice Stevens wondered whether a law would affect the amount of teenage pregnancy and expressed concern about only holding half the participants culpable. For Stevens, the only acceptable justification for disparate treatment of two participants in an act must be a judgment that one is more guilty than the other. Sexual class, he felt, is an unwise substitute for a factual determination. The nursing school case (*Hogan*, 1982) contained Justice Sandra Day O'Connor's first majority opinion. In addressing the challenge from a male student who wished to enter a women's nursing program, O'Connor took a traditional nondiscrimination position, even though the state had other nursing programs that admitted men. Justice O'Connor dismissed the argument that a single-sex admissions policy could legitimately compensate for past discrimination. Her opinion expressed concern about perpetuating a sterotypical view of nursing. This led to a standard of review which called for "exceedingly persuasive justification," unmitigated by the fact that the discrimination was against a man. The result was that the school would have to allow men.

The sexual preferences challenged in these cases had been around for a long time, and there was clearly a new sensitivity to inherent problems of classification. But perhaps equally important was the impact of the constitutional sensitivity to distinctions. The similarity between these cases and *Bakke* is that they used a pure concept that had lost the original meaning it had as an object of political struggle.

Sex is not a classification that society is readily going to dispose of. Not only does it have obvious romantic and procreative dimensions,

---

* In cases related to the draft issue and raising discrimination questions of their own, the federal courts in 1983 upheld the prosecution of draft resisters who refused to register, even though there was evidence that the prosecutions were selective (Taylor, 1982).

but it is highly correlated with a number of social phenomena. Women outlive men; whites live longer than blacks; and Mormons grow older than non-Mormons generally. Yet, sex is the only one of these indicators that is used widely. Women often pay more for retirement systems but less for car insurance. Past treatment of these issues has been largely in the statutory context. But recently, the Court found that the truth of a generalization does not justify different treatment of individuals based on sex. In *Manhart* v. *City of Los Angeles Department of Water and Power* (1978), a city pension plan required female employees to make larger contributions than male workers because the women lived longer. The basis for review was Title VII of the 1964 Civil Rights Act, but the rhetoric in the opinion was more sweeping. It described such practices as based on "...traditional assumptions about groups rather than thoughtful scrutiny of individuals." Because of the constitutional standard, with its abhorrence of distinctions, there is increasing pressure to stop such practices. In the case of *Arizona* v. *Norris* (1983), the justices split 5-4 against retirement plans that distinguish between men and women. The insurance industry has been fighting back against the threat to their way of estimating risk, but suspicion of sex classifications has become part of the constitutional tradition.

Casualties of Pure Equality

The ideological view proposes that ideas, rather than rules and precedents, explain the compulsion of constitutional rights. The pervasive idea emerging from equal protection has been a "pure" response directed at an offending classification, whether it is race, sex, or other invidious distinctions. This is a form of "blindness" to the history of an offense, and it is often taken for granted. When an idea achieves that status it no longer operates as a rule, but instead our view of what is possible becomes constrained and limited.

The view of equal protection in the Constitution as simply a protection from classifications is a legacy of *Plessy* v. *Ferguson* (1896), where a classification was allowed to stand because the justices refused to take account of the harm it was doing. The reaction to that harm, in *Brown* v. *Board of Education* (1954), was a dramatic reversal, which was preoccupied with the prior decision and thus dominated by its framework. As in *Plessy*, the decision in *Brown* dealt with separation, and it became the foundation for an integrationist interpretation of the Constitution. A major casualty was the promise of material equality. Other casualties have been due to the propensity to deal with discrimination through pure concepts, without regard to the historical situation that produced the constitutional standard in the first place.

These failures have been numerous. In the case of race, pure equality has threatened affirmative action programs and undercut efforts to provide materially equal education to all citizens, whether they live in the inner city or in the country. In the case of sex, some of those same threats in the name of equal protection have begun to eliminate historical bastions of diversity, such as public degree programs for women. This reading of the Constitution, however, failed to become part of the document. A form of pure equality was the conceptual frame in the Equal Rights Amendment (ERA), the most significant part of which reads:

> Equality of rights under the law shall not be denied or abridged by the United States or by any State on account of sex.

The tradition of "pure equality" with its emphasis on generalization backfired against proponents of the ERA and threatened the interests for which feminists have traditionally fought.

In the case of the ERA, the failure was not just due to the level of political resistance. That resistance can at least partially be attributed to fear that the phrasing of the amendment generated in the minds of those who had become attached to some traditional sexual distinctions. When the defeat came in June of 1982, the post-mortems were intense, but because of the focus on the political, they were not very searching. Although the organizers of the ratification campaign were not prepared for the level of resistance they got, there is even more to be learned from the fact that the resistance was grounded in the propensity of the organizers to uncritically accept the constitutional form of sex blindness. The fear of unisex bathrooms, homosexual marriages, and women on the front lines during wartime might have been diffused if those fears had not been grounded in the very wording of the amendment. Had the amendment simply protected women from discrimination, the issues would not have arisen. But, it was worded to protect everyone. Oddly, the fear of male domination was more characteristic of opponents of the amendment than of its supporters. The opponents argued that men would use the provision to eliminate some of the advantages women traditionally had in alimony payments, custody battles, and military service. Thus, constitutional equality seems to have had implications for struggles over discrimination against women that have not been widely recognized.

The ideological view gives a familiar story some new dimensions and suggests that we look at constitutional equality, without the usual orientation of the political view. This chapter brings to a close the elaboration of the five fundamental constitutional concepts that comprise civil liberties. In discussing each one, the effort has been to explore their implications for American democracy. In the final chapter, more explicit attention is paid to the challenges and prospects surrounding the coexistence of individual rights with democracy.

Democracy 7

Democracy is the standard by which governments are evaluated throughout the world today. We do not expect to hear someone say, even in translation, "This is a totalitarian dictatorship—I love it." Occasionally, there are expressions of affection for monarchs. But this is more often due to a kind of nationalism than out of fondness for that system of government. Not every government is actually a democracy, nonetheless most would prefer to be described in this way. Although there are other things we might expect of a government, such as providing for the public welfare or treating its citizens well, a government is supposed to be democratic.

The standard looks to people for legitimacy. This sometimes seems to be a nearly undifferentiated mass of people and the appeal of this referent is not universal. The idea of the mass is not very appealing to American ears, but in many respects these are "metaphoric" people. They are a barometer against which the principles and the performance of institutions can be measured. In contrast to this standard, there is another side in America that looks to the individual. This also can be unattractive. Rights are a vehicle by which the mass is differentiated and individual interests are placed in a social context. Rights are rooted in a mercantile society, and thus they appear linked to the commercial interests from which they emerged. There sometimes seems to be a tension between individual rights and democracy, reflecting that of individual interests versus the whole. This inquiry has sought to transcend that tension.

We have not emphasized one side or the other, but concentrated on the ideology of constitutional rights. The significance of ideas has been the starting point and an issue to which we have returned often. We have shown how the ideological view differs from both the mechanical view of formal jurisprudence, and the political view of how law works. Today, few take the mechanical view seriously, rather political jurisprudence is more often the norm. But the destruction of the ideal in law—

that arose as a backlash against the mechanical view—has gone deeper than its proponents could have anticipated. The absence of the ideal has resulted in a view that law is simply the result of political interests. The ideological view offered here has been an attempt to take account of both Higher Order ideals and political interests. On this foundation, the present treatment has remained attentive to democracy throughout by considering the popular basis of rights. We have asked whether rights derived from bourgeois individual interests can serve democratic ends. The answer to this question has been implicit in the way rights have been presented. From an ideological point of view, rights are part of American democracy. In this, the last chapter, we turn more explicitly to the relationship between constitutional rights and democracy.

A Constitutional Polity

All political systems rely on ideas. In a constitutional polity, or political system, the government gets its authority from the ideas in the constitutional tradition. This section examines two facets of that tradition. The first is the role of judges in a democracy. In this part we apply an ideological perspective to the work of the courts. In the second part, we focus on the social foundations of rights. We consider the extent to which rights can stand apart from the interests of those with wealth and power, as well as the concept of "relative autonomy." Finally, since civil liberties is an area where the worlds of law and those of ordinary action seem separate, we attempt to establish the link between legal rights and popular understandings.

Judging and Democracy

Judging in America is widely recognized as policy making, at least in part. Judges do not just mechanically respond to the questions that arise, however. The human and political element generally influences their responses. Although the element of human insight is looking more attractive as the claims made for artificial intelligence increase, there is concern about how the policy contribution of judges can be justified. A portion of this section is addressed to the question of how best to approach and examine the policy activity of judges.

Constitutional Interpretation. In looking at ideas, we have considered some of the different traditions and developments in legal thought. Most modern critics of judicial "activism"—that is, of justices becoming too obviously political—have looked to legal forms as a check on judicial politics. Law professors such as Herbert Wechsler, Alexander Bickel, and

John Hart Ely have advocated that the judiciary be above the political fray, that judges deal in principles and processes without political content (Wechsler, 1959; Bickel, 1970; Ely, 1980). They have held up political justices to critical scrutiny, saying that justices—who represent the voice of principled reason—must not fall prey to political concerns. But Bickel and others of his generation made the classic mistake of that period by suggesting that the rightness or wrongness of a decision would ever be determined by something other than some standards of reasonableness.

Ultimately, history's evaluation of judicial activism will be conditioned by the social insight present in constitutional interpretation. Justifications for various judgments are all around us. But success in interpreting the Constitution will depend on integrating an interpretation into the set of possible meanings in a society. Thus, the power of the Warren Court's "idea of progress" was its capacity to identify, articulate, and become linked with the dominant conceptions of its time. The doctrines did not only capture a segment of popular opinion, but the Court actually gave to the culture the definitions over which it struggled. Although falling short by Wechsler's measure of neutral principles, the justices provided ideas that succeeded to the extent that they become associated with the struggles for civil rights, freedom of expression, and due process.

The search for a justification of judicial review continues to be a vital activity in our democratic society. This search is not likely to be abandoned as long as the tension between democratic sovereignty and legal professionalism exists. A much discussed work, *Democracy and Distrust* (1980), by John Hart Ely, a law professor at Harvard, is a recent example of that continuing search. In this work, Ely sets out to find fundamental values capable of justifying judicial review. Ely adheres to the traditional process-based arguments—that it is the responsibility of the Supreme Court to police the efforts of elected representatives and thereby to keep open the political system—and finds judicial interpretation of process to be the best justification for judicial review. Ely goes back to *U.S. v. Carolene Products Co.* (1938) and to Justice Harlan Fiske Stone's famous footnote, four in this case, where Stone declared it the responsibility of the Supreme Court to "police the process of representation." Laurence Tribe (1980), on the other hand, believes that such process-based arguments are a futile effort to avoid substantive judgments. Tribe argues that process is linked to substantive promises, from the "compensation" clause to the First Amendment and that there are substantive choices behind even the most basic of the procedural promises, such as the right to vote. Thus, Tribe believes that process-based theories "impoverish the relevance of the Constitution" to all but those who would monitor the process—the lawyers and the judges. The process-based arguments are professionally centered and elite oriented. They are inevitably in contradiction to the democratic processes they purport to serve. Although Ely's focus and his title address the concern put forth in this chapter, the tension between judicial review and democracy cannot be resolved in this way. As Tribe has cautioned, the resolution inevitably will depend on the substance of rights.

Beyond Winners and Losers. The view of the judiciary represented by scholars as diverse as the behavioralists and the Legal Realists has been preoccupied with identifying "winners and losers," thereby focusing on politics to the exclusion of law (Casper, 1976). This political position has been critical of the judicial myth of impartiality, and it can be understood as an effort to demystify the robe. Consequently, law is relegated to the "non-policy" or nonpolitical realm, and politics on the bench to the nonlegal sphere. This book has suggested an understanding of judging (and litigating) in a democracy that reaches beyond "winners and losers."

By attention to concepts from an ideological perspective, we can show how developments in the law itself are policy outputs. Thus, the concepts themselves constitute the "objects" of political struggles. For example, as we have seen, privacy was introduced into the constitutional setting by Justice Brandeis whose earlier work had launched statutory protection of privacy. After the claim for constitutional protection of privacy was attached to the Fourth and Fifth Amendments, it became available as a tool of policy formation. Ultimately, it served as the foundation for Justice Douglas's *Griswold* decision (see Chapter 4) and the focus, from 1965 to 1975, of a veritable privacy industry. Thus, before 1965, it would not have made sense to speak of a constitutional right of privacy. Now, however, it does.

It is necessary for a concept to be available in this way, as a basis for justification, if a claim is to be made. It does not mean that a particular claim will successfully be argued before a court. That depends on the makeup of the court and the peculiarities of a case. Ideology is simply a sort of conceptual gatekeeper (Goldman and Jahnige, 1976). If a situation cannot be described in the terms available for appellate review, it will not be considered. This is not due to the mechanical limits of logic or rules but to limits in perception and the ideas with which reason proceeds. Since the terms of legal discourse are limited, so are the types of conflict that can be considered.

Today, ideological approaches are penetrating the study of law. Some of the work is very powerful and suggestive, such as that by Colin Sumner (1979). However, other work, while claiming to be "critical," is simply a fashionable construction of political jurisprudence (Unger, 1976). The present effort has focused on the nature and significance of institutional creations in an effort to go beyond the Realist critique.

Of course, there must be some connection of these ideas to the decision itself (Brigham, 1978). Although the ideological perspective has yet to be fully integrated into the material on the decision process, the best biographies provide one approach. This was true of Carl Brent Swisher's monumental biography, *Stephen J. Field: Craftsman of the Law* (1930). There, man, conditions, and doctrine are woven together. Another approach involves attention to the strategies and interplay of judges (Murphy, 1964). And, a more recent and less theoretical work, *The Brethren* (Woodward and Armstrong, 1979), although it is the ultimate exercise in political jurisprudence, also considers the ideological implications of court decisions.

It is necessary to go beyond the event and transcend the politics if one wants to understand the tradition of rights. The prospect of finding something "beyond winners and losers" has motivated our inquiry. We have resisted the compelling desire to focus on the present, to predict or influence outcomes. This is difficult, however, and any treatment of a tradition of discourse is bound to include some commentary to the effect that something was said or some position was taken "because...." The challenge is to keep these urges under control. The concepts of law are not lenses through which to observe a process that is independent of them. Rather, the ideas of constitutional law constitute the political arena (Klare, 1979).

Rights in Society

The issue motivating this final chapter is the place of constitutional rights in a democracy. Although democracy is used primarily in the political sense to describe a form of government "by the people," democracy also implies government "for the people." Implicit in the use of democracy to evaluate rights, in fact, are social rights. We must ask whether there can be due process or property rights in a society that contains race prejudice or gross material deprivation. Some of these questions have already been answered and others will be taken up in the final section, which deals with the conditions necessary for a constitutional democracy. In this section, two points need to be made as a foundation for subsequent discussion. Both amplify the nature of a political system organized under a constitution.

Relative Autonomy. There is a relationship between the legal apparatus, which includes constitutional rights and civil liberties, and the society. Law is inevitably linked to social conditions. It is a crude caricature that treats law and society as separate spheres, especially when it presents one as ideal and the other as real. The more accurate portrayal is that these spheres, in a complex relation to one another, constitute a political totality. Their history and logic are intertwined; the reality of each can be distinguished but never totally separated from the other.

The relationship between law and society is the subject of exciting debates in some law schools and among many social scientists over the degree to which law is autonomous from the interests of the wealthy and powerful (Sumner, 1979; Kairys, 1982). The truth is that law in the United States, including constitutional rights and civil liberties, has been relatively autonomous or somewhat insulated from the demands of the social environment. The powerful have determined to some degree the nature of rights in America; in turn, the perenially powerless have been able to use those rights to gain a more equal share of wealth and power. The constitutional tradition contains high ideals compared with everyday life. There is little in American society that offers as much protection from arbitrary judgment as do constitutional concepts like due process and property rights. Although ideals can be an opiate, they can also be a banner for change (Scheingold, 1974). The principles of civil liberties in constitutional law can be employed in the second sense. These principles are capable of acting as a lever for change while preserving basic rights.

Legal ideas are not completely autonomous; they do not stand entirely apart from interests that exist in society. Ideas are resources and can be made to serve interests. Business interests influenced the idea of property in the late nineteenth century by transforming the settled expectations of persons into new rights for corporations (Paul, 1969). Civil rights helped to develop the conception of equality that is now part of the Fourteenth Amendment. The litigation strategies of the NAACP employed the promise of material equality in the doctrine of separate but equal to eliminate the barrier of separation. Later, that promise was lost. The result, as we have shown, was a notion of equality that has little of the meaning that is associated with democratic movements (Kluger, 1976). The service of interest is limited by the nature of the instrument—by the grammar of the concept itself (O'Neill, 1981)—and the context in which it is used. Thus, ideas serve some interests and not others.

Practical Significance. In describing the ideas of constitutional rights and civil liberties, we have shown that they matter in each of the areas discussed in this book. Equal protection, for instance, was presented as being the source of the conventional view of equality, the basis for the expectation of blindness toward race and sex that is the source of some forms of progressive political action in the United States. Free expression doctrines have contributed to the widespread perception that there are no limits to freedom of speech. A consequence is that those from the women's movement who have attacked violent pornography have assiduously avoided turning to legal means to restrict such pornography, for fear that their movement will be viewed as antithetical to the First Amendment. Due process is both a promise and an institutional reality through which government is made legitimate. This is an idea Felix Frankfurter fought for before he became a justice, and it is a commitment that explains his activities in support of the anarchists Sacco and Vanzetti—whose trial for a political bombing failed to meet traditional due process requirements. The same things can be said about liberty and property. Ideas are the terrain on which interests array themselves as liberal or conservative, progressive or reactionary. As rights, ideas have been objects of struggle.

This investigation has given particular attention to how contemporary political questions have been affected by the ideological traditions of civil liberties. We have looked for the relationship between constitutional concepts and political concerns. We have shown how some current movements have sought to extend traditions such as property or due process to political issues such as protection of entitlements in statutory benefits or protection against sexual harassment. At other times, we have seen traditions change, as was the case with interpretation of the First Amendment following the First World War and interpretation of the Fourteenth Amendment after the Second World War—in this instance, in equal protection cases. In each of these cases, the constitutional meanings have had significance for the larger political arena, where we struggle over what we believe to be right or wrong. In all the instances covered, popular struggles have been characterized by interests emerging into a political universe already constituted by concepts like equal protection and due process.

The ideological perspective has taken the work of legal thinkers and judges as its starting point. The link with popular ideas has been alluded to throughout. At this point, the purpose is to emphasize the fact that constitutional formulations, largely generated by an elite, get disseminated throughout a democracy. This is not meant to disregard studies that found surprisingly little impact in upper court decisions. Nor is it meant to be disrespectful to the earlier legal historians, who found principles of law in the actions of people who had less abstract and more tangible concerns (Hurst, 1956). Rather, this perspective is meant to counter the belief that scholarly debate like that over the meaning of free expression in the 1920s or constitutional equality fifty years later is just window dressing with little practical significance. Such discussion should not be dismissed so easily, for the ideas in the Constitution do matter in American politics.

The Democratic Prospect

Having examined how rights are put forth by judges and operate in society, we turn to an evaluation of rights by standards derived from a democratic vision. Traditional treatments of civil liberties have often linked civil liberties closely to the ideal of individual freedom from government (Abraham, 1982). The preceding discussion has sought to correct that imbalance, changing this erroneous portrayal of the basis for American liberties and addressing the challenges for the future suggested by a democratic standard. We assess the threats and the conditions for a constitutional democracy as the concluding portion of the book.

The Rule of Law

Civil liberties have their roots in the struggle for political and economic power of a middle class emerging from a feudal straitjacket in the last part of the seventeenth century. But they depend on the existence of rights in a modern sense: rights being attached to individuals not as a result of their status but as a result of their common citizenship (Macpherson, 1962). Reliance on rights is seldom challenged in the American context. This is because of the predominance of the liberal tradition and a fundamental agreement on the principles of government. It may also be because middle-class ascendancy has become a characteristic of American life, taking on broad significance for American democracy.

Rights are as likely to be the basis for criticism of the status quo as they are to lend support to the status quo. Yet, the fact that in many instances the ideas that constitute Western civilization emerged from the struggles of an ascending middle class is not an adequate basis for dismissing them. To the contrary, the vulnerability of rights to disruptive social forces at any time dramatizes the need to consider what they offer rather than simply where they came from. This was the conclusion reached by E. P. Thompson in his seminal discussion of the rule of law. In *Whigs and Hunters*, Thompson looked at the "Black Act" of the eighteenth century. He described his work as ". . . the study of a political oligarchy inventing callous and oppressive laws to serve its own interests." He wrote that in a social context of gross inequality, the law will always be ". . . in some part sham." At the same time, however, he felt that it is also possible to see that law is a "... true and important cultural achievement" (Thompson, 1975:265-266). It is necessary to account for these seeming contradictions in order to understand how law functions as a check on the exercise of power. This proposition has informed the present work and sets the tone for the following discussion.

Threats to Constitutional Democracy

In trying to anticipate the future of civil liberties, it is useful to try and identify the interests that might arise and that might disrupt democratic institutions. Pressures on democracy may come from international movements, as well as from technical and professional sources. All these pressures would threaten ordinary people's claims to sovereignty. Although it is not possible to know exactly how the threats will arise or how they will make themselves felt, educated speculation is possible. The most likely threats to constitutional democracy in America appear to be from three sectors—the elites, the people, and the experts.

From Elites. The suggestion that there could be a threat to democracy from the top is unusual in mainstream social research.* We do not hear much about the dangers to our liberties from those who hold the balance of economic and military power. In fact, the liberties sometimes appear as gifts given by this sector to the people. Yet, the development of these liberties often has been in response to governmental actions that had been taken in the interests of elites. Consequently, it is prudent to consider the case of regimes where the mechanisms of the liberal exercise of power are not so fully inculcated, where the military and the private elites are consistently vying for power, and government is more obviously subject to their will.

That these eventualities are not without precedent in the United States is evident in our experience with military government on the West Coast during the Second World War and the affronts to liberty that have been justified in the name of emergency, such as curfews during power failures and natural disasters. We need to be aware of the implications of martial law for our constitutional system. They are revealed as the system cracks in times of panic and crisis, times that produce shame when they pass and the panic subsides.

The constitutional cases that followed exclusion of the Japanese

---

* C. Wright Mills's *The Power Elite* (1956) is of course an exception, but it is not generally considered mainstream social research. Mills's perspective demonstrates in a highly visible, if somewhat one-dimensional way, the significance of elite structures of power as challenges to the meaningful existence of constitutional rights.

from California during the Second World War deal primarily with race, but they also tell a great deal about martial law. In *Korematsu* v. *United States* (1944), the Supreme Court, at the hands of its more liberal members, sanctioned forceable removal of over one hundred thousand American citizens and resident aliens of Japanese descent from their homes. They were shipped to camps in the remote interior of the country without even a nod to due process (Irons, 1983). This was under the authority of the military and of the Governor of California, Earl Warren, whose civil libertarian sensibilities appear to have succumbed to the exigencies of war. There have been other cases in wartime. During the panic of the early Cold War, for example, the moratorium on civil liberties for alleged subversives amounted to something like martial law. More generally, however, the clear and present danger test is an ever-present justification for dilution of civil liberties in the face of a threat to the established order. Thus, it is clear that we should always be alert to unconstitutional usurpation of state power, whether it is by unaccountable private interests or under the justification of military emergency.

From the People. It is peculiar that the threat to constitutional democracy from below has been presented more vividly in America than the threat from the top. It seems peculiar in a democracy at least. Rather than the Founders' concern about abuse of power by those who hold it, we more often hear of a threat to the established order from those who do not have a share in it.

Governments should, of course, respond to those with little stake in the system, at least in part because these people may not be overly concerned about the niceties of middle-class rights when they confront the dislocations of the modern economy and its cavalier disregard for their well-being. Some scholarship has amplified this concern. Samuel Stouffer's (1954) survey of the population's commitment to civil liberties, for instance, evaluated popular support for traditional liberties by presenting situations where people would have to demonstrate a commitment to the principles in practice, such as whether they would allow a Communist to speak to elementary school children. Stouffer determined that most Americans in the 1950s did not support the Bill of Rights, and that there was declining support for those rights as one moves down the economic pyramid. Recent studies have re-examined these findings and raise some questions about them (Sullivan, 1982), but there is still reason to believe that these precious liberties are not lodged firmly in the hearts of average Americans and that those who suffer most from inequities in the economic system have little commitment to these liberties at all.

This threat from the bottom ought to be taken seriously by anyone committed to constitutional democracy. The alienation from civil liberties is real, both in the relative sense of popular disorientation from the professionally fashioned tenets of the American Civil Liberties Union as they were used in the Skokie protests (discussed in Chapter 2) and in the deeper sense of widespread alienation and cynicism about the capacity of the government to provide for the welfare of all, inevitably leading to a disregard for middle-class promises. Civil liberties are propositions that require a modicum of fundamental economic well-being in order to work. The surprise in Stouffer's study was that even those individuals who had some stake in the system did not know its basic tenets and revealed little intuitive commitment to them (although the greater the stake the more commitment there is). It would be ludicrous to think of a study being conducted, for instance, about the commitment to civil liberties among the 50,000 homeless men and women who inhabit the doorways and live under the steam vents in a city like New York or even among those unemployed who have discovered that their jobs are the price politicians are willing to pay for reducing inflation. Thus, there is a threat from those who do not have a stake in the system.

From the Experts. Ultimately, the most sinister threat to constitutional democracy is the domination of civil liberties by legal experts, the professionalization of the capacity to deal with fundamental rights. Civil liberties, as presented here, are a part of constitutional law, law that is the expression of popular sovereignty. This claim meant something in the early years of the republic, when ordinary people—albeit of a predominantly white, male, property holding caste—would debate the meaning of the Constitution or the nature of the governmental powers that were expressed in a compact to which they were a party. Although first asserted in the early 1800s, deference to the justices of the Supreme Court in matters of constitutional law was not widespread until the end of that century. And it was not until halfway through the twentieth century that the Court could assert a right to review acts of the legislature without fear of contradiction. It is only since that time that judges have been able to claim the role of final arbiters of constitutional rights without even having to share that power with other members of the government. This power of judicial review—the idea that the ultimate reading of the Constitution should be left to a legal elite—has transformed constitutional law into a form of judge-made, and hence professionally crafted, legal discourse. This development has had an impact that goes beyond law and the Constitution. Its significance for American democracy is in relation to the general movement to policymaking by experts. Expert claims in the realm of constitutional interpretation are simply the most important politically.

Judges are not the only experts who are likely to claim an expertise affecting the realization of constitutional rights. On occasion, the government defines new technologies like atomic energy as special and not subject to traditional values. Information and facilities are guarded; discussion is truncated. This affects the content as well as the form of civil liberties (Morland, 1979; Warnock, 1979). We also hear claims that the society is more complex and that the old rights are inadequate for that reason. This is seldom a legitimate claim, however, since the government claiming to be more complex and to have superior needs is constituted by those very liberties it seeks to balance. But it is a threat nonetheless.

These changes and the shift just discussed substitute familiarity with one's rights and participation in the democracy for deference to experts. For example, in the case of universities (considered in Chapter 3), the substitution of legally defined rights for commitment to those rights in the institution changes the nature of the institution. The result is often administrators who are afraid to act because of what the courts might say or, what is sometimes worse, who act simply with concern for lawyers' definitions of what due process means and with little regard for what the academy might develop as a process consistent with its mission and with the constitutional standard. In the case of the criminal process, the shift to professional legal domination has only recently been acknowledgd in the legitimization of plea bargaining by the Supreme Court. Ignored for generations, this widespread practice has come under the supervision of the justices in order to legitimize it. The consequence of this development is that deals rather than rights have come to characterize the criminal process. Where the tradition of due process promised the citizenry that they could respect the institutions of government because of the high level of respect they would receive themselves, in the context of deference to legal professionals, the basis for legitimacy has shifted to claims of legal expertise. The implication is that civil liberties like due process no longer reside in the minds of most Americans.

The Conditions for Constitutional Democracy

Democracies cannot survive any of these threats. Each would, in its own way, destroy the tradition of popular government. The seizure of political authority from the top, and its use in the interests of elites, would destroy the autonomy of the state. It would be very hard to return to the balance that is the hallmark of liberal democratic regimes if such a description occurred. Seizure from the bottom also would be brutal and disruptive. In its rage, such a seizure would probably lack the commitment to niceties of citizenship like due process and constitutional liberty. Finally, seizure by the experts (which appears to be well underway) would destroy the capacity of other members of the community to respond intelligently and rationally to fundamental political questions. For on the one hand, those at the top would be transformed into clients with little ability to communicate their needs and interests. And on the other hand, those at the bottom would be deprived of the avenues and values by which the polity resists becoming a mass. To prevent the realization of any of these threats, it is necesary to guarantee the conditions for constitutional democracy.

Knowledge: The Political Resource. Constitutional democracy relies on an informed citizenry. The promises and prospects that have been handed down since before colonization and that have been viewed as constitutional rights for almost 200 years are the terrain of American politics. These are the substantive rights and constitutive principles around which political struggles have been waged. Institutions provide the bond holding together a constitutional democracy, and in the United States, civil liberties are a part of that institutional setup, not simply appendages. As with all aspects of the Constitution, ideas are the shared practices guaranteeing that battles will not get out of hand and promising that political outcomes will be grounded in conventions, whether the issue is economic expectations or cultural autonomy.

Traditionally, the individual has been pictured as the base for civil libertarian values, and rights have been seen as the "... loaded gun that the right holder may shoot at will in his corner of town" (Unger, 1983:597). That picture is of relatively recent origin, going back not much further than the late nineteenth century. This is not the original reading of constitutional rights, however, nor is it the best reading for our time. Civil liberties antedate capitalism, and although they share some of its roots, they are part of an organized social life with links to feudal as well as technocratic modes of production. Yet, it is ultimately not the social but the political order to which civil liberties are tied. They are a protection against the state by virtue of their origins in the late eighteenth century and the subsequent actions that constituted the government in the first place. The base for civil liberties is not the individual, however, but the citizen as person who was the source of a new kind of power (Vining, 1976).

Rights have been the traditional alternative in society to the political expression of majority preferences. Hence, we have balanced the first chapter, with its presentation of the meaning of rights and how they function, with the present treatment of the claims on rights that arise in democratic systems. Rights have some autonomy beyond individual or mass interests. When they capture the ideas of a progressive humanism, they become an attractive leavening for a modern democracy. The basis of rights must be popular and to constrain action rights must operate from within. Civil liberties are presumed by liberal democracy, but they remain a promise that will be more threatened than threatening unless they are widely understood. This the most attractive prospect for democracy. As Roberto Unger has argued before the Conference for Critical Legal Studies and in the *Harvard Law Review*, the hope is of ". . . a social order all of whose basic features are directly or indirectly chosen by equal citizens and rightholders rather than imposed by irresponsible privilege or blind tradition (Unger, 1983:591)." These rights must reside, as Judge Learned Hand said in a much quoted passage, ". . . in the hearts of men and women" (Hand, 1944). It would also help if the rights were in their minds as well.

Equality: The Democratic Right. Equality is basic to the democratic claim. It is the key to the response from the bottom, and to the prevention of disruptions in a democracy. Only with equality as the underpinning of a democratic existence can the liberal rights be held up as ideals (otherwise they are simply a fraud). Equality is the right that links liberal democracies with economic democracies in the global ideological contests of the present century. The link between this special right in the array of civil liberties and the others will partially determine how the great challenges of the next decades are handled.

Although equality is part of the conception of liberalism, it is not always emphasized (Dworkin, 1983). This is in part because it is also capable of cutting through the promises of liberalism. It is the right most likely to bring forth attention to social conditions and penetrate the very foundations of government. Although its meaning has been limited by recent courts with their focus on liberal integrationist strategies, the power of the equality of condition has not been absent from the constitutional tradition. This promise of equality of condition is the most basic right of all. Without making good on that promise, all the conditioning in the world toward a rights-conscious citizenship will be wasted. Without it, we cannot address the destitute and excluded in such civilized terms as would be desirable. The language of civil liberties requires reasonable access to the necessities of life before it is likely to be comprehensible.

Courts cannot take the promise of equality as far as it might go. Equality as a democratic promise, stems from the political equality of all citizens. But, it is not only the linchpin of bourgeois liberties in a democracy, it is also a vehicle for bringing these liberties out of the courtrooms and law schools before they end up in the streets. Courts cannot bring the promise of constitutional democracy to Detroit or the south side of Chicago; only people can.

Fairness: The Legitimate Expectation. Fairness is a condition behind the administration of rights in a democracy. The perception of interests in this claim have not always been as they are now. In the early part of this century, Max Weber, a modern student of the forces operating in Western society, found that the propertied classes were demanding rational administration of the state, that is, formal adherence to law. By comparison, he observed that the poorer classes preferred charity, what he called "Kahdi justice," a primitive although compassionate form of rule (Weber, 1969). As an observation for his time, this may have been at least partially accurate, and it was a widespread perception of how the needs of the society should be understood. The government was doing less for the poor, and they were the recipients of "charity" or generosity if they received any aid at all. Those with property were receiving licenses and grants to aid their commerce and defending their property with claims of rationality and the rule of law.

Now we have come to see that these grants and licenses also are a form of charity; they are the generosity of the government to those in positions to make their demands heard. Grants like those to Lockheed or Chrysler are the most obvious, but the tax write-offs of corporate expense accounts are another of the many forms of charity doled out to the propertied classes. On the other hand, today those of the poor who are on welfare and relying on the entitlements of Social Security and the other grants that have been made to them in the last 40 years have begun calling for rational administration. The promise of the law has more meaning now than it did when it so generously allowed both the poor and the rich to sleep in the public parks. Thus, the claim for rights is more compelling where there is fairness to all in their implementation.

Knowledge, fairness, and equality are the conditions for constitutional democracy in a meaningful sense. In the context of civil liberties, the conditions may legitimately become aspirations. The promise is contained in the rights we have described. The democratic prospect will depend on considerations just discussed.

While many have hoped for much more, and some would dismiss legal ordering because it will not produce radical transformations, it is necessary to recognize that any tradition in law will inhibit such change. There can be no doubt that constitutional rights preserve tradition. That is their appeal. The business of a legal system, said Harold Laski, ". . . is to make the postulates of a society work." As he went on to point out, it would be remarkable if the traditions could be so worked as ". . . to secure their fundamental transformation" (Laski, 1935). That would be too much. It is enough to nurture the humanism and advance the democratic prospect to be found in civil liberties.

Rights and Liberties
in the Constitution of the
United States of America

We the People of the United States, in Order to form a more perfect Union, establish Justice, insure domestic Tranquility, provide for the common Defence, promote the general Welfare, and secure the Blessings of Liberty to ourselves and our Posterity, do ordain and establish this Constitution for the United States of America.

ARTICLE I

Section 9.

[2] The Privilege of the Writ of Habeas Corpus shall not be suspended, unless when in Cases of Rebellion or Invasion the public Safety may require it.

[3] No Bill of Attainder or ex post facto Law shall be passed.

ARTICLE III

Section 2.

[3] The trial of all Crimes, except in Cases of Impeachment, shall be by Jury; and such Trial shall be held in the State where the said Crimes shall have been committed; but when not committed within any State, the Trial shall be at such Place or Places as the Congress may by Law have directed.

Section 3.

[1] Treason against the United States shall consist only in levying War against them, or, in adhering to their Enemies, giving them Aid and Comfort. No Person shall be convicted of Treason unless on the Testimony of two Witnesses to the same overt Act, or on Confession in open Court.

[2] The Congress shall have Power to declare the Punishment of Treason, but no Attainder of Treason shall work Corruption of Blood, or Forfeiture except during the Life of the Person attainted.

ARTICLE IV

Section 1.

Full Faith and Credit shall be given in each State to the public Acts, Records, and judicial Proceedings of every other State. And the Congress may by general Laws prescribe the Manner in which such Acts, Records and Proceedings shall be proved, and the Effect thereof.

Section 2.

[1] The Citizens of each State shall be entitled to all Privileges and Immunities of Citizens in the several States.

[2] A Person charged in any State with Treason, Felony, or other Crime, who shall flee from Justice, and be found in another State, shall on demand of the executive Authority of the State from which he fled, be delivered up, to be removed to the State having Jurisdiction of the Crime.

[3] No Person held to Service or Labour in one State, under the Laws thereof, escaping into another, shall, in Consequence of any Law or Regulation therein, be discharged from such Service or Labour, but shall be delivered up on Claim of the Party to whom such Service or Labour may be due.

ARTICLE V

The Congress, whenever two-thirds of both Houses shall deem it necessary, shall propose Amendments to this Constitution, or, on the Application of the Legislatures of two-thirds of the several States, shall call a Convention for proposing Amendments, which, in either Case, shall be valid to all Intents and Purposes, as Part of this Constitution, when ratified by the Legislatures of three-fourths of the several States, or by Conventions in three-fourths thereof, as the one or the other Mode of Ratification may be proposed by the Congress; Provided that no Amendment which may be made prior to the Year One thousand eight hundred and eight shall in any Manner affect the first and fourth Clauses in the Ninth Section of the first Article; and that no State, without its Consent, shall be deprived of its equal Suffrage in the Senate.

ARTICLE VI

[2] This Constitution, and the laws of the United States which shall be made in Pursuance thereof; and all Treaties made, or which shall be made, under the Authority of the United States, shall be the supreme Law of the Land; and the Judges in every State shall be bound thereby,

any Thing in the Constitution or Laws of any State to the Contrary notwithstanding.

[3] The Senators and Representatives before mentioned, and the Members of the several State Legislatures, and all executive and judicial Officers, both of the United States and of the several States, shall be bound by Oath or Affirmation, to support this Constitution; but no religious Test shall ever be required as a Qualification to any Office or public Trust under the United States.

AMENDMENT I [1791]

Congress shall make no law respecting an establishment of religion, or prohibiting the free exercise thereof; or abridging the freedom of speech, or of the press; or the right of the people peaceably to assemble, and to petition the Government for a redress of grievances.

AMENDMENT II [1791]

A well regulated Militia, being necessary to the security of a free State, the right of the people to keep and bear Arms shall not be infringed.

AMENDMENT III [1791]

No Soldier shall, in time of peace be quartered in any house, without the consent of the Owner, nor in time of war, but in a manner to be prescribed by law.

AMENDMENT IV [1791]

The right of the people to be secure in their persons, houses, papers, and effects, against unreasonable searches and seizures, shall not be violated, and no Warrants shall issue, but upon probable cause, supported by Oath or affirmation, and particularly describing the place to be searched, and the persons or things to be seized.

AMENDMENT V [1791]

No person shall be held to answer for a capital, or otherwise infamous crime, unless on a presentment or indictment of a Grand Jury, except in cases arising in the land or naval forces, or in the Militia, when in actual service in time of War or public danger; nor shall any person be subject for the same offence to be twice put in jeopardy of life or limb; nor shall be compelled in any criminal case to be a witness against himself, nor be deprived of life, liberty, or property, without due process of law; nor shall private property be taken for public use, without just compensation.

AMENDMENT VI [1791]

In all criminal prosecutions, the accused shall enjoy the right to a speedy and public trial, by an impartial jury of the State and district wherein the crime shall have been committed, which district shall have been previously ascertained by law, and to be informed of the nature and cause of the accusation; to be confronted with the witnesses against him; to have compulsory process for obtaining witnesses in his favor, and to have the Assistance of Counsel for his defence.

AMENDMENT VII [1791]

In Suits at common law, where the value in controversy shall exceed twenty dollars, the right of trial by jury shall be preserved, and no fact tried by jury, shall be otherwise re-examined in any Court of the United States, than according to the rules of the common law.

AMENDMENT VIII [1791]

Excessive bail shall not be required, nor excessive fines imposed, nor cruel and unusual punishments inflicted.

AMENDMENT IX [1791]

The enumeration in the Constitution, of certain rights, shall not be construed to deny or disparage others retained by the people.

AMENDMENT X [1791]

The powers not delegated to the United States by the Constitution, nor prohibited by it to the States, are reserved to the States respectively, or to the people.

AMENDMENT XIII [1865]

Section 1.
Neither slavery nor involuntary servitude, except as a punishment for crime whereof the party shall have been duly convicted, shall exist within the United States, or any place subject to their jurisdiction.

AMENDMENT XIV [1868]

Section 1.

All persons born or naturalized in the United States, and subject to the jurisdiction thereof, are citizens of the United States and of the State wherein they reside. No State shall make or enforce any law which shall abridge the privileges or immunities of citizens of the United States; nor shall any State deprive any person of life, liberty, or property, without due process of law; nor deny to any person within its jurisdiction the equal protection of the laws.

AMENDMENT XV [1870]

Section 1.

The right of citizens of the United States to vote shall not be denied or abridged by the United States or by any State on account of race, color, or previous condition of servitude.

AMENDMENT XVI [1913]

The Congress shall have power to lay and collect taxes on incomes, from whatever source derived, without apportionment among the several States, and without regard to any census or enumeration.

AMENDMENT XIX [1920]

[1] The right of citizens of the United States to vote shall not be denied or abridged by the United States or by any State on account of sex.

AMENDMENT XXIV [1964]

Section 1.

The right of citizens of the United States to vote in any primary or other election for President or Vice President, for electors for President or Vice President, or for Senator or Representative in Congress, shall not be denied or abridged by the United States or any State by reason of failure to pay any poll tax or other tax.

AMENDMENT XXVI [1971]

Section 1.

The right of citizens of the United States, who are eighteen years of age or older, to vote shall not be denied or abridged by the United States or by any State on account of age.

Bibliography

Abernathy, M. Glenn. 1981. *The Right of Assembly and Association.* Columbia, South Carolina: University of South Carolina Press.

Abraham, Henry. 1982. *Freedom and the Court: Civil Rights and Liberties in the United States.* 4th ed. Oxford: Oxford University Press.

Ackerman, Bruce A. 1977. *Private Property and the Constitution.* New Haven: Yale University Press.

Anastaplo, George. 1971. *The Constitutionalist.* Dallas: SMU Press.

Arendt, Hannah. 1963. *On Revolution.* New York: Viking Press.

Arons, Stephen. 1983. *Compelling Belief: The Culture of American Schooling.* New York: McGraw-Hill.

Auerbach, Jerald. 1969. "The Patrician as Libertarian: Zechariah Chafee, Jr. and Freedom of Speech." *New England Quarterly* 42:5.

Austin, John. 1861. *Lectures on Jurisprudence.* 5th ed. London: Murray, 1885.

Balbus, Isaac. 1973. *The Dialectic of Legal Repression.* New York: Russell Sage.

Barker, Ernest. 1930. *Church, State and Study.* London: Methuen.

Beard, Charles. 1913. *An Economic Interpretation of the Constitution.* New York: Macmillan.

Becker, Lawrence. 1977. *Property Rights: Philosophic Foundations.* London: Routledge and Kegan Paul.

Berlin, Isaiah. 1959. "Two Concepts of Liberty." In *Four Essays on Liberty.* Oxford: Oxford University Press.

Beth, Loren P. 1971. *The Development of the American Constitution, 1877-1917.* New York: Harper and Row.

Bickel, Alexander. 1962. *The Least Dangerous Bench.* Indianapolis: Bobbs-Merrill.

———. 1970. *The Supreme Court and the Idea of Progress.* New York: Harper Torchbooks.

Black, Charles. 1969. *Structure and Relationship in Constitutional Law.* Baton Rouge: Louisiana State University Press.

Blackstone, William. 1859. *Commentaries on the Laws of England.* Reprint. Philadelphia: J. B. Lippincott, 1900.

Blumberg, Abraham. 1967. "The Practice of Law as a Confidence Game: Organizational Cooptation of a Profession." *Law and Society Review* 1:15.

Bobbitt, Philip. 1982. *Constitutional Fate: Theory of the Constitution.* New York: Oxford University Press.

Bonsignore, John, et al. 1979. *Before the Law.* 2d ed. Boston: Houghton Mifflin.

Bosselman, Fred, et al. 1973. *The Taking Issue.* Washington, D.C.: Government Printing Office.

Brest, Paul. 1975. *The Processes of Constitutional Decisionmaking: Cases and Materials.* Boston: Little, Brown.

Brigham, John. 1978. *Constitutional Language.* Westport, Conn.: Greenwood Press.

——. 1980. *Policy Implementation: Penalties or Incentives?* Beverly Hills, Calif.: Sage Publications.

——. 1984. "Do the Justices Make Sense?" *Polity,* 16.

Brigham, John, and Diane Burns. 1980. "Implementing the Supreme Court's Abortion Decision." Paper presented at the Northeastern Political Science Association meeting, New Haven, Conn., November 12-13.

Casper, Jonathan D. 1972. *The Politics of Civil Liberties.* New York: Harper and Row.

——. 1976. "The Supreme Court and National Policy Making." *American Political Science Review* 70:53.

Chafee, Zechariah. 1956. *Three Human Rights in the Constitution of 1787.* Lawrence and London: University of Kansas Press.

Choper, Jessie H. 1980. *Judicial Review and the National Political Process: A Functional Reconsideration of the Role of the Supreme Court.* Chicago: University of Chicago Press.

Clune, William, 1975. "The Supreme Court's Treatment of Wealth Discriminations Under the Fourteenth Amendment." *Supreme Court Review,* 289.

Cole, George F., Roger A. Hanson, Jonathan E. Silbert. 1981. "The Role of Mediation in Resolving Prisoner Disputes." Paper presented at the Law and Society Association meeting, Amherst, Mass., June 3-5.

Commons, John R. 1924. *The Legal Foundations of Capitalism.* Madison: University of Wisconsin Press.

Conlyn, Ales. 1973. "The Supreme Court's Changed View of the Guilty Plea." *Memphis State University Law Review* 4:49.

Connolly, William. 1974. *The Terms of Political Discourse.* Lexington, Mass.: D. C. Heath.

Cooley, Thomas. 1888. *Treatise on Torts.* 2d ed. Chicago: Callaghan and Co.

Cortner, Richard C. 1981. *The Supreme Court and the Second Bill of Rights: The 14th Amendment and the Nationalization of Civil Liberties.* Madison: University of Wisconsin Press.

Corwin, Edward S. 1928. *The Higher Law Foundations of American Constitutional Law.* Ithaca, N.Y.: Cornell University Press.
——. 1934. *Twilight of the Supreme Court.* New Haven: Yale University Press.
Cox, Archibald. 1981. *Freedom of Expression.* Cambridge, Mass.: Harvard University Press.
Davis, Frederick. 1959. "What Do We Mean By Right to Privacy?" *South Dakota Law Review* 4:1.
Devlin, Patrick. 1965. *The Enforcement of Morals.* Oxford: Oxford University Press.
Dixon, Robert G. 1971. *The Right of Privacy.* New York: DaCapo Press.
Dumbauld, Edward. 1957. *The Bill of Rights and What It Means Today.* Norman: University of Oklahoma Press.
Dunham, Allison. 1962. "*Griggs* v. *Allegheny County* in Perspective: Thirty Years of the Supreme Court Expropriation Law." *Supreme Court Review,* 105.
Dworkin, Ronald. 1975. "Hard Cases." *Harvard Law Review* 88: 1057.
——. 1980. "Is the Press Losing the First Amendment?" *The New York Review of Books* 27:49.
——. 1983. "Why Liberals Should Believe in Equality." *The New York Review of Books* 30:15.
Edelman, Bernard. 1979. *Ownership of the Image: Elements for a Marxist Theory of Law.* London: Routledge and Kegan Paul.
Eichbaum, June A. 1979. "Towards an Autonomy-Based Theory of Constitutional Privacy: Beyond the Ideology of Familial Privacy." *Harvard Civil Liberties Law Review* 14:361.
Ellis, Richard E. 1971. *The Jeffersonian Crisis: Courts and Politics in the Young Republic.* New York: W. W. Norton.
Ely, John Hart. 1973. "The Wages of Crying Wolf: A Comment on *Roe* v. *Wade.*" *Yale Law Journal* 82:920.
——. 1980. *Democracy and Distrust: A Theory of Judicial Review.* Cambridge, Mass.: Harvard University Press.
Emerson, Thomas Irwin. 1970. *The System of Freedom of Expression.* New York: Vintage Books.
——. 1971. "Nine Justices in Search of a Doctrine." In *The Right of Privacy,* ed. R. Dixon. New York: DaCapo Press.
Fair, Daryl R. 1977. "Judging or Legislating? Application and Evaluation of Diverse Formulae." Paper presented at the annual meeting of the American Political Science Association, Washington, D.C., September 3-6.
Farber, Daniel A. 1981. "National Security, the Right to Travel, and the Court." *Supreme Court Review,* 263.
Feeley, Malcolm M. 1979a. "Plea Bargaining Symposium." *Law and*

Society Review 13:2.

———. 1979b. *The Process is the Punishment.* New York: Russell Sage.

Fiss, Owen. 1977. "Groups and the Equal Protection Clause." *Equality and Preferential Treatment,* ed. Marshall Cohen et al. Princeton: Princeton University Press.

Flathman, Richard. 1976. *The Practice of Rights.* New York: Cambridge University Press.

Foucault, Michel. 1972. *Archaeology of Knowledge.* New York: Harper and Row.

———. 1973. *The Order of Things: An Archaeology of the Human Sciences.* New York: Vintage Books.

Frankfurter, Felix. 1947. "Reflections on Reading Statutes." In *The Supreme Court: Views from Inside,* ed. A. Westin. New York: W. W. Norton, 1961.

Freedman, Max, ed. 1967. *Roosevelt and Frankfurter: Their Correspondence, 1928-1945.* Boston: Little, Brown.

Freeman, Alan David. 1978. "Legitimizing Racial Discrimination Through Antidiscrimination Law: A Critical Review of Supreme Court Doctrine." *Minnesota Law Review* 62:1.

Freund, Paul. 1964. "Rationality in Judicial Decisions." In *Rational Decision,* ed. C. J. Friedrich. New York: Atherton Press.

Friedelbaum, Stanley H. 1976. "A New Bill of Rights: Novel Dimensions of Liberty and Property." In *Civil Liberties,* ed. S. Wasby. Lexington, Mass.: D. C. Heath, Lexington Books.

———. 1982. "Independent State Grounds: Contemporary Invitations to Judicial Activism." In *State Supreme Courts: Policy Makers in the Federal System,* eds. Mary C. Porter and G. Alan Tarr. Westport, Conn.: Greenwood Press.

Friedman, Lawrence M. 1973. *A History of American Law.* New York: Simon and Schuster.

Funston, Richard. 1978. *A Vital National Seminar: The Supreme Court in American Political Life.* Palo Alto, Calif.: Mayfield Publishing Co.

Garvey, Gerald. 1971. *Constitutional Bricolage.* Princeton: Princeton University Press.

Geertz, Clifford. 1973. *The Interpretation of Cultures.* New York: Basic Books.

Goldman, Sheldon and Thomas P. Jahnige. 1976. *The Federal Courts as a Political System.* 2d ed. New York: Harper and Row.

———. 1982. *Constitutional Law and Supreme Court Decision-Making.* New York: Harper and Row.

Grais, David. 1977. "Statutory Entitlement and the Concept of Property." *Yale Law Review,* 86:709.

Grey, Thomas C. 1980. "Eros, Civilization and the Burger Court." *Law &*

Contemporary Problems 43:84.

Grossman, Joel, and Richard Wells. 1980. *Constitutional Law and Judicial Policy-Making.* New York: Wiley.

Gunther, Gerald. 1980. *Cases and Materials on Constitutional Law.* 10th ed. Mineola, New York: The Foundation Press.

Habermas, Jurgen. 1975. *Legitimation Crisis.* Boston: Beacon Press.

Hamilton, Alexander, et al. 1788. *The Federalist Papers,* ed. C. Rossiter. New York: New American Library, 1961.

Hamilton, Walton H. 1932. "Property-According to Locke." *Yale Law Journal,* 41:864.

Hand, Learned. 1944. "The Spirit of Liberty." In *The Spirit of Liberty: Papers and Addresses.* New York: Vintage Books.

Haney, Craig, and Michael J. Lowy. 1979. "Bargain Justice in an Unjust World: Good Deals in the Criminal Courts?" In "Plea Bargaining Symposium," ed. M. Feeley. *Law and Society Review* 13:2.

Harrington, Christine B. 1980. "Voluntariness, Consent and Coercion: The Neighborhood Justice Center." *Policy Implementation: Penalties or Incentives?,* eds. J. Brigham and D. Brown. Beverly Hills, Calif.: Sage Publications.

Harris, William, 1982. "Binding Words and Polity." *American Political Science Review* 76:34.

Hart, H. L. A. 1961. *The Concept of Law.* Oxford: Clarendon Press.

Hartz, Louis. 1955. *The Liberal Tradition in America.* New York: Harcourt Brace Jovanovich.

Harvard Civil Rights and Civil Liberties Law Review. 1981. "Comment: Substantive Due Process Limits on the Duration of Civil Commitment for the Treatment of Mental Illness." *Harvard Civil Rights and Civil Liberties Law Review* 16:1.

Harvard Law Review. 1977. "The Supreme Court, 1976 Term." *Harvard Law Review* 92:57.

Heumann, Milton. 1978. *Plea Bargaining: The Experiences of Prosecutors, Judges and Defense Attorneys.* Chicago: University of Chicago Press.

Hirschkop, Phillip J., and Michael A. Millerman. 1969. "The Unconstitutionality of Prison Life." *Virginia Law Review* 55:832.

Hohfeld, W. W. 1919. *Fundamental Legal Conceptions.* New Haven: Yale University Press.

Holmes, Oliver Wendell, Jr. 1881. *The Common Law.* Boston: Little, Brown.

Horowitz, Donald. 1977. *The Courts and Social Policy.* Washington: The Brookings Institution.

Horwitz, Morton. 1973. "The Transformation in the Concept of Property in American Law, 1780-1860." *University of Chicago Law Review* 40:248.

——. 1978. *The Transformation of American Law, 1780-1860.* Cambridge, Mass.: Harvard University Press.

Houseman, Gerald L. 1979. *The Right of Mobility.* Port Washington, N.Y.: Kennikat Press.

Howard, J. Woodford. 1981. *Courts of Appeals in the Federal Judicial System.* Princeton: Princeton University Press.

Hufstedler, Shirley M. 1979. "Invisible Searches for Intangible Things: Regulation of Government Information Gathering." *University of Pennsylvania Law Review* 127:1483.

Hurst, James Willard. 1956. *Law and the Conditions of Freedom in the Nineteenth Century United States.* Madison: University of Wisconsin Press.

——. 1960. *The Growth of American Law: The Law-Makers.* Boston: Little, Brown.

Irons, Peter. 1981. "Fighting Fair, Zechariah Chafee, Jr., The Department of Justice, and the Trial at the Harvard Club." *Harvard Law Review* 94:1205.

——. 1983. *Justice at War.* New York: Oxford University Press.

Jaworski, Leon. 1974. "Oral Arguments in *U.S. v. Nixon.*" *New York Times* (July 9):24.

Kairys, David. 1982. *The Politics of Law: A Progressive Critique.* New York: Pantheon.

Kalven, Harry. 1960. "The Metaphysics of the Law of Obscenity." *Supreme Court Review,* 1.

Kalven, Harry, and Hans Zeisel. 1966. *The American Jury.* Chicago: University of Chicago Press.

Kaminer, Wendy. 1980. "A Woman's Guide to Pornography and the Law." *The Nation* (June 21):754.

Karst, Kenneth L. 1980. "The Freedom of Intimate Association." *The Yale Law Journal* 89:624.

Kelly, A., W. Harbison, and H. Belz. 1983. *The American Constitution: Its Origins and Development.* 6th ed. New York: W. W. Norton.

Kircheimer, Otto. 1961. *Political Justice.* Princeton, N.J.: Princeton University Press.

Klare, Karl. 1979. "Law-Making as Praxis." *Telos* 40:122.

Kluger, Richard. 1976. *Simple Justice.* New York: Random House.

Lader, Lawrence. 1974. *Abortion II.* Boston: Beacon Press.

Laski, Harold J. 1935. *The State in Theory and Practice.* New York: Viking Press.

Lawrence, D. H. 1930. *Pornography and Obscenity.* New York: Knopf.

Leclaire, John R. 1981. "Public Health, Privatization, and the Constitution: The Alaska Example." *Boston University Law Review* 61:969.

Lempert, Richard. 1975. "Uncovering 'Nondiscernable' Differences: Empirical Research and the Jury-Size Cases." *Michigan Law Review* 73:643.

Lerner, Max. 1933. "The Supreme Court and American Capitalism." In *Essays in Constitutional Law*, ed. R. G. McCloskey. New York: Vintage Books, 1957.

Levi, Edward H. 1949. *An Introduction to Legal Reasoning*. Chicago: University of Chicago Press.

Levy, Leonard. 1957. *The Law of the Commonwealth and Chief Justice Shaw*. Cambridge, Mass.: Harvard University Press.

——. 1960. *Legacy of Suppression: Freedom of Speech and in Early American History*. Cambridge, Mass.: Harvard University, Belknap Press.

Lewis, Anthony. 1964. *Gideon's Trumpet*. New York: Random House.

Lewis, Felice. 1975. *Literature, Obscenity and the Law*. Carbondale: Southern Illinois University Press.

Lindblom, Charles. 1979. *Politics and Markets*. New York: Basic Books.

Lockhart, William B., et al. 1981. *Constitutional Rights and Liberties*. 5th ed. St. Paul, Minn.: West Publishing Co.

Ludes, Francis J., and Harold J. Gilbert, eds. 1965. *Corpus Juris Secundum*. Brooklyn, N.Y.: The American Law Book Co.

McCann, Michael W. 1983. "Abdication or Transformation? The Changing Status of 'Property' in the American Constitutional Tradition." Paper presented at the annual meeting of the American Political Science Association, Chicago, Ill., September 1-4.

McCloskey, Robert. 1962. "Economic Due Process and the Supreme Court: An Exhumation and Reburial." *Supreme Court Review*, 34.

McIlwain, Charles H. 1940. *Constitutionalism: Ancient and Modern*. Ithaca, N.Y.: Cornell University Press.

MacKinnon, Catherine. 1979. *Sexual Harassment of Working Women: A Case of Sex Discrimination*. New Haven: Yale University Press.

Macpherson, C. B. 1962. *The Political Theory of Possessive Individualism*. Oxford: Oxford University Press.

——. 1973. *Democratic Theory: Essays in Retrieval*. Oxford: Oxford University Press.

——. 1978. *Property: Mainstream and Critical Positions*. Toronto: University of Toronto Press.

Magrath, C. Peter. 1967. *Yazoo*. New York: W. W. Norton.

Maine, Henry. 1886. *Popular Government*. New York: Holt.

Marcuse, Herbert. 1968. "Repressive Tolerance." In *A Critique of Pure Tolerance*, ed. R. P. Wolff. Boston: Beacon Press.

Mather, Lynn, and Yngvesson, Barbara. 1980-1981. "Language, Audience, and the Transformation of Disputes." *Law and Society Review* 15:775.

Meikeljohn, Alexander. 1948. *Free Speech and Its Relation to Self-Govern-*

ment. New York: Harper and Row.

Michelman, Frank. 1967. "Property, Utility, and Fairness: Comments on the Ethical Foundations of 'Just Compensation' Law." *Harvard Law Review* 80:1165.

——. 1969. "The Supreme Court 1968 Terms." *Harvard Law Review* 83:181.

——. 1979. "Welfare Rights in a Constitutional Democracy." *Washington University Law Quarterly,* 659.

Michigan Law Review. 1980. "Foreign Intelligence Surveillance Act." *Michigan Law Review* 78:116.

Mill, John Stuart. 1859. *On Liberty.* New York: W. W. Norton, 1975.

Miller, Charles A. 1977. "Due Process." In *Due Process: Nomos XVIII,* ed. J. R. Pennoch. New York: New York University Press.

Miller, Perry. 1953. *Roger Williams: His Contribution to the American Tradition.* Indianapolis: Bobbs-Merrill.

Milton, John. 1644. *The Areopagitica.* London: Dent, 1927.

Morland, Howard. 1979. "H-Bomb Secret." *The Progressive* (November):14-17.

Mott, Kenneth F., and Lovette Mott. 1981. "Property and Personal Privacy: Interrelationship, Abandonment and Confusion in the Path of Judicial Review." Paper presented at the Northeast Political Science Association meeting, Newark, N.J., November 9-11.

Murphy, Paul L. 1972. *The Meaning of Freedom of Speech: First Amendment Freedoms from Wilson to FDR.* Westport, Conn.: Greenwood Publishing Co.

——. 1979. *World War I and the Origin of Civil Liberties in the United States.* New York: W. W. Norton.

Murphy, Walter F. 1964. *Elements of Judicial Strategy.* Chicago: University of Chicago Press.

——. 1978. "Constitutional Interpretation: The Art of the Historian, Magician or Statesman?" *Yale Law Journal* 87:1752.

Nelson, William E. 1974. "The Impact of the Antislavery Movement Upon Styles of Judicial Reasoning in Nineteenth Century America." *Harvard Law Review* 87:517.

Oakes, James L. 1981. "Property Rights in Constitutional Analysis Today." *Washington Law Review* 56:583.

Oberst, Paul. 1973. "The Strange Case of *Plessy* v. *Ferguson.*" *Arizona Law Review* 15:2.

O'Brien, David M. 1979. *Privacy, Law, and Public Policy.* New York: Praeger.

——. 1980. "The Seduction of the Judiciary: Social Science and the Courts." *Judicature* 64:8.

O'Neill, Timothy J. 1981. "The Language of Equality in a Constitutional Order." *American Political Science Review* 75:626.

Packer, Herbert, 1964. "Two Models of the Criminal Process." *University of Pennsyvlania Law Review* 113:1.

Paul, Arnold. 1969. *Conservative Crisis and the Rule of Law: 1887-1895*. Ithaca, N.Y.: Cornell University Press.

Paulson, Monrad G., ed. 1959. *Legal Institutions Today and Tomorrow*. New York: Columbia University Press.

Pennock, J. Roland. 1981. "Rights and Citizenship." *News: For Teachers of Political Science*. Washington, D.C.: American Political Science Association.

Perry, Michael J. 1982. *The Constitution, the Courts, and Human Rights*. New Haven: Yale University Press.

Pound, Roscoe. 1959. *Jurisprudence*. St. Paul, Minn.: West Publishing Co.

Prest, W. R. 1972. *The Inns of the Court: 1590-1640*. Totowa, N.J.: Rowman and Littlefield.

Preston, W. 1963. *Aliens and Dissenter: Federal Suppression of Radicals, 1909-1933*. Cambridge, Mass.: Harvard University Press.

Pritchett, C. Herman. 1948. *The Roosevelt Court: A Study in Judicial Politics and Values*. Chicago: University of Chicago Press.

———. 1977. *The American Constitution*. New York: McGraw-Hill.

———. 1984. *Constitutional Civil Liberties*. Englewood Cliffs, N.J.: Prentice-Hall.

Prosser, W. 1960. "Privacy." *California Law Review* 48:383.

Ragan, Fred D. 1971. "Justice Oliver Wendell Holmes, Jr., Zechariah Chafee, Jr., and the Clear and Present Danger Test for Free Speech: The First Year, 1919." *Journal of American History* 58:37.

Read, Conyers. 1938. *The Constitution Reconsidered*. New York: Columbia University Press.

Reich, Charles. 1964. "The New Property." *Yale Law Journal* 73:733.

———. 1965. "Individual Rights and Social Welfare: The Emerging Legal Issues." *Yale Law Journal* 74:1245.

Renner, Karl. 1949. "The Institutions of Private Law." In *Sociology of Law*, ed. V. Aubert. London: Penguin Books.

Roche, John P. 1961a. *Courts and Rights: The American Judiciary in Action*. 2d ed. New York: Random House.

———. 1961b. "The Founding Fathers: A Reform Caucus in Action." *American Political Science Review* 55:799.

Roth, Philip. 1983. Review of *The Anatomy Lesson* by R. Kiely. *New York Times Book Review* (October 30):1.

Rubin, Edward L. 1982. "Generalizing the Trial Model of Procedural Due Process: A New Basis for the Right to Treatment." *Harvard Civil Rights and Civil Liberties Law Review* 17:61.

Sandoz, Ellis. 1978. *Conceived in Liberty: American Individual Rights Today*. North Scituate, Mass.: Duxbury Press.

Sax, Joseph. 1971. "Takings, Private Property and Public Rights." *Yale Law Journal* 81:149.

Schauer, Frederich. 1979. "Speech and 'Speech'-Obscenity and 'Obscenity': An Exercise in the Interpretation of Constitutional Language." *Georgetown Law Journal* 67:899.

Scheiber, Harry N. 1975. "Instrumentalism and Property Rights: A Reconsideration of American 'Styles of Judicial Reasoning' in the 19th Century." *Wisconsin Law Review* 1:1.

———. 1982. "Law and the Imperatives of Progress: Private Rights and Public Values in American Legal History." In *NOMOS XXIV: Ethics, Economics and Law*, eds. J. Roland Pennock and John Chapman. New York: New York University Press.

Scheingold, Stuart. 1974. *The Politics of Rights*. New Haven: Yale University Press.

Schwartz, Richard D. 1969a. "A Proposed Focus for Research on Judicial Behavior." In *The Frontiers of Judicial Research*, eds. J. Grossman and J. Tanenhaus. New York: Wiley.

———. 1969b. "Comments." In *The Frontiers of Judicial Research*, eds. J. Grossman and J. Tanenhaus. New York: Wiley.

Shapiro, Martin. 1964. *Law and Politics in the Supreme Court*. New York: The Free Press.

———. 1968. *Supreme Court and Administrative Agencies*. New York: The Free Press.

———. 1978. "The Constitution and Economic Rights." In *Essays on the Constitution*, ed. M. J. Harmon. Port Washington, N.Y.: Kennikat Press.

———. 1981. *Courts: A Comparative and Political Analysis*. Chicago: University of Chicago Press.

Shklar, Judith. 1964. *Legalism*. Cambridge, Mass.: Harvard University Press.

Siegan, Bernard H. 1981. *Economic Liberties and the Constitution*. Chicago: University of Chicago Press.

Simpson, A. W. B. 1979. "The Horwitz Thesis and the History of Contract." *University of Chicago Law Review* 46:533.

Skinner, Quentin. 1974. "Some Problems in the Analysis of Political Thought." *Political Theory* 2:277.

———. 1977. "Political Language and the Explanation of Political Action." Paper presented at the annual meeting of the American Political Science Association, Washington, D.C., September 3-6.

Spaeth, Harold J. 1977. *O'Connor v. Donaldson*. San Francisco: W. H. Freeman.

Steinem, Gloria. 1978. "Erotica and Pornography." *Ms.* (November):53.

Stone, Julius. 1968. *Legal System and Lawyer's Reasoning*. Stanford, Calif.:

Stanford University Press.

Stouffer, Samuel A. 1954. *Communism, Conformity and Civil Liberties.* Garden City, N.Y.: Doubleday.

Sullivan, John L., et al. 1982. *Political Tolerance and American Democracy.* Chicago: University of Chicago Press.

Sumner, Colin. 1979. *Reading Ideologies: An Investigation into the Marxist Theory of Ideology and Law.* London: Academic Press.

Swisher, Carl Brent. 1930. *Stephen J. Field: Craftsman of the Law.* Washington, D.C.: The Brookings Institution.

Taylor, Charles. 1971. "Interpretation and the Sciences of Man." *Review of Metaphysics* 25:3.

Taylor, Stuart. 1982. "Draft Registration: Snags Emerge in Prosecutions." *The New York Times* (December 8):II:8.

Teachont, Peter R. 1978. "Chains of Tradition, Instruments of Freedom: Contours of the Emerging Right to Community in Obscenity Law." *Capital University Law Review* 7:683.

Thompson, E. P. 1975. *Whigs and Hunters.* New York: Vintage Books.

Tribe, Laurence. 1978. *American Constitutional Law.* Mineola, N.Y.: Foundation Press.

——. 1980. "The Puzzling Persistence of Process-Based Constitutional Theories." *Yale Law Journal* 89:1063.

Tushnet, Mark. 1981. *The American Law of Slavery, 1810-1860.* Princeton: Princeton University Press.

Tussman, Joseph, and Jacobus ten Broek. 1949. "The Equal Protection of the Laws." *California Law Review* 37:341.

Ulmer, S. S., et al. 1972. "The Decision to Grant or Deny Certiorari: Further Considerations of Cue Theory." *Law and Society Review* 6:640.

Unger, Roberto M. 1976. *Law in Modern Society: Toward a Criticism of Social Theory.* New York: The Free Press.

——. 1983. "The Critical Legal Studies Movement." *Harvard Law Review* 96:561.

Van Alstyne, William. 1977. "Cracks in 'The New Property': Adjudicative Due Process in the Administrative State." *Cornell Law Review* 62:445.

——. 1980a. "Due Process and College Students." In *The Sociology of Law: A Social-Structural Perspective*, ed. W. Evans. New York: The Free Press.

——. 1980b. "The Recrudescence of Property Rights as the Foremost Principle of Civil Liberties: The First Decade of the Burger Court." *Law and Contemporary Problems* 43:66.

Vining, Joseph. 1976. *Legal Identity.* New Haven: Yale University Press.

Warnock, Donna, ed. 1979. *Nuclear Power and Civil Liberties—Can We Have Both?* Washington, D.C.: Citizen's Energy Project.

Warren, Charles. 1922. *The Supreme Court in U.S. History.* Cambridge, Mass.: Harvard University Press.

Warren, Samuel D., and Louis Brandeis. 1890. "The Right to Privacy." *Harvard Law Review* 41:193.

Wasby, Stephen L. 1976. *Continuity and Change: From the Warren Court to the Burger Court.* Pacific Palisades, Calif.: Goodyear.

Way, H. Frank, Jr. 1976. *Liberty in the Balance: Current Issues in Civil Liberties.* New York: McGraw-Hill.

Weber, Max. 1958. *The Protestant Ethic and the Spirit of Capitalism.* New York: Scribner's.

——. 1969. "Kahdi Justice." In *Sociology of Law,* ed. V. Aubert. Baltimore: Penguin Books.

Wechsler, H. 1959. "Toward Neutral Principles of Constitutional Law." *Harvard Law Review* 73:1.

Westin, Alan F. 1961. *The Supreme Court: Views from Inside.* New York: W. W. Norton.

——. 1967. *Privacy and Freedom.* New York: Atheneum.

Wilkinson, J. Harvie. 1979. *From Brown to Bakke: The Supreme Court and School Integration.* New York: Oxford University Press.

Wolff, R. P., ed. 1968. *A Critique of Pure Tolerance.* Boston: Beacon Press.

Wolin, Sheldon S. 1960. *Politics and Vision.* Boston: Little, Brown.

Woodward, Bob, and Scott Armstrong. 1979. *The Brethren.* New York: Simon and Schuster.

Wright, Benjamin F., Jr. 1938. *The Contract Clause of the Constitution.* Cambridge, Mass.: Harvard University Press.

Yale Law Journal. 1963. "Charity v. Social Insurance in Unemployment Compensation." *Yale Law Journal* 73:357.

Case Index

Subject Index